RARE BOOKS
AND RARER PEOPLE

Also by O. F. Snelling

DOUBLE O SEVEN
James Bond: a Report

A BEDSIDE BOOK OF BOXING

Some Personal Reminiscences of 'The Trade'

O. F. SNELLING

WERNER SHAW

© O. F. SNELLING, 1982

ISBN 0 907961 01 0

Printed in Great Britain for the publishers, Werner Shaw Limited,
12/13 Henrietta Street, Covent Garden, London WC2E 8LH,
England, from typesetting by Alacrity Phototypesetters, Banwell
Castle, Weston-super-Mare, Avon BS24 6NX

This book is for my wife
MOLLY

Contents

Acknowledgements

Some of the chapters in this book have already appeared, in a modified form, within the pages of a periodical. Had they not done so I think it unlikely that the present volume would have appeared at this time. I therefore take pleasure in thanking the publisher of the *Antiquarian Book Monthly Review*, and its former editor, Julian Bingley, for printing my pieces and for granting permission to incorporate them here.

I should also like to thank Helene Hanff, David Low, John Pashby, Barry Phelps, and Alan G. Thomas for allowing me to reproduce snippets of their writings.

I am obliged to Louis W. Bondy, Harold Edwards, John G. Garratt, Selwyn H. Goodacre, P. A. Jaggard, Eric Norris, and Justin G. Schiller. I have benefited both directly and indirectly from the correspondence of these gentlemen. They will immediately recognise why, should they chance to read these pages.

Finally, a thank you to my former colleagues, Rene Matthews and Elizabeth Tait, who were quite unremitting whenever administrative or secretarial spade-work was necessary during our association.

Of all the branches of the sport connected with book collecting, that of attending book auctions is the greatest, the most stirring ... The book auction is an adventure. Other adventures may lose their glamour if you repeat them, but each experience at a sale of books brings a delightful thrill never to be duplicated.

A. W. S. Rosenbach, *Books and Bidders*

The rare book business has its battlefield: the auction room. No combatants ever faced each other with more determination, or more fight-to-the-death spirit, than bidders competing to buy the same book. The fever of the auction room is contagious and paying record prices can become an obsession.

H. P. Kraus, *A Rare Book Saga*

'It is naught, it is naught', saith the buyer:
But when he is gone his way, then he boasteth.

The Proverbs of Solomon

... The established auction houses remain the best bet for the private vendor — you may have to endure occasional high-handed ill-manners, bloody-mindedness and ignorance, but with luck you will get courtesy, scholarship and understanding — and perhaps even the right price.

Brian Sewell, 'Of Busts and Boobs', *Evening Standard*

How these curiosities would be quite forgott, did not such idle fellowes as I am putt them downe.

John Aubrey, *Brief Lives*

Introduction

This book is by no means an autobiography. Such works, in my opinion, should be limited to those people who have attained some eminence or celebrity — at the very least to persons who have led unusually varied or interesting lives, preferably adventurous or amorous. Unfortunately, I am disqualified on all counts.

And yet this book is written in the first person, I figure prominently in its pages, and I am never very far from the scene of action — what action there is — and it might be thought that I am blowing my own trumpet.

Not so. This is a chronicle about *other* people, most of whom I have known. My observations are extremely personal ones, and if I appear to come into the act all too often it is only in order to shed some further light upon the people I happen to be writing about.

The idea of these reminiscences germinated after an Annual General Meeting of the Society of Booksellers' Employees, back in the nineteen-seventies. This was a group popularly known in the book trade as the Bibliomites. At our gatherings, we had all listened to some very interesting talks by such people as Sam Joseph, of Charing Cross Road, Bill Fletcher, of Cecil Court, and John Watson, of — where? Shall we just say the West End? In his time he worked for three of the most famous book-selling businesses in London, Britain or, indeed, the world. These talks, given in the nineteen-seventies, had been about the business back in the 'twenties and the 'thirties. They were listened to, for the most part, by youngsters who had not been born until the 'forties or the 'fifties. And when it came down to it, there proved to be the minimum of actual *bookselling* about these impromptu chats, but the maximum of anecdotes about booksellers, their sometimes eccentric assistants and clients, and what they had all got up to in those old days.

But the talks were no less interesting, for all that. The talkers had been recruited primarily because each had, many a time, engaged listeners with extempore reminiscences over a pint or two of bitter in a pub after working hours, or in some hotel room while waiting for a country sale.

Dennis Burgess, who was in the chair at that particular Bibliomites' meeting, remarked what a pity it was that more of our little clan didn't give us such chats, or try to get something down on to paper. Inevitably, the old 'uns retired, or died, and with them went much of the history of our trade, never to be recalled. Dennis suggested that the Bibliomites should

11

try to compile a sort of Who's Who of Bookmen, with potted biographies of some of the characters we had known and worked with, or had served. Plenty were mentioned.

The idea was received enthusiastically, of course. But everyone waited for somebody else to do the job.

One of the curses of our age is apathy. Even the very idea of the Bibliomites, first conceived nearly thirty years earlier by a few friendly young exuberants as a social club and benevolent society, faded as its founding members retired or passed on. And, after all, a night out with the lads may have been a big deal when you were young, impoverished, and dwelling in lonely digs, but a comfortable armchair, the television set, and the conjugal blessings of your own home hold greater charms in middle age.

Still, it has always seemed to me rather strange that the greatest talkers of this world, those people who appear to want to communicate with others so desperately, and who often tend to monopolise the conversation, also have the greatest reluctance to take pen in hand and put their thoughts down on to paper.

Comparatively few people in the book business seem to have exercised themselves in print. Frank Swinnerton, of course, first as a publisher's office-boy, then as a publisher's reader, later a novelist and reviewer, garnered much. He was prolific when writing of the old days at Dent's and Chatto's, and telling of Booksellers' Row. And there is a now half-forgotten maverick named Lionel Britton, who documented something of the life of the bookseller's drudge-employee in the early nineteen hundreds. That was in a strange novel called *Hunger and Love*, published over half a century ago. George Orwell treated us to *his* experiences working in a bookshop as an assistant, only a few years later. There exist too, of course, noble tomes of the histories of all the great publishing houses, their pages spattered with the names of most of the great figures in our literature. Many of these books are turgid, and constipatedly compiled by 'official' and designated biographer-historians, but one or two do actually get written by human beings closely connected with the firms they are dealing with, and then they become readable and entertaining.

When we come to the antiquarian, or 'second-hand' bookmen's written offerings, things still seem to me to be pretty lean. Dear old Andrew Block was a busy writer in his younger days. So was Gilbert Fabes. But both of these primarily confined their writings to bibliography — or near-bibliography. This is no bad thing in itself, of course. John Carter, too, while always seeming readier to write books than to sell them, inclined towards things like *The ABC of Book-Collecting*, and *Taste and Technique in Book-Collecting* — to say nothing of the famous and monumental *Enquiry*.

But what anecdotes and entertaining stories they all could have told us in print! I have listened to yarns related verbally by two of that trio. How I wish that the cassette tape-recorder had been available then.

Percy Muir was a little more forthcoming; his bibliographical offerings were interesting and valuable enough, but the best thing he ever wrote, I think, was the entertaining history of his firm, Elkin Mathews, and which he called *Minding my Own Business*. Walter T. Spencer published his *Forty Years in my Bookshop*, but I have been told that it was "ghosted" by somebody else. I don't doubt that at all. Much of what he knew has certainly gone into limbo. Most definitely, some of the best tales I ever heard about Spencer's dealings never got into his book. Much more recently, David Low gave us *with all faults*, pertinently titled in lower case. (I, for one, see a far better reason for this idiosyncracy than e.e. cummings or *in our time*.) My one criticism of this work is that it is far too short. I found it fascinating, and so did others. We wanted lots more of the same thing. I'm sure David Low has it to give.

Many other people have it, too. But, as I say, they talk it, but they will never write it. The major part gets forgotten, and lost forever.

The Americans, of course, have pipped us in this direction, with their enthusiasm and exuberance, as they often do in many other directions. Wilmarth Lewis and A. Edward Newton wrote the best books that I have read from the point of view of the avid collector, and the great Dr. A. W. S. Rosenbach was responsible for the most entertaining effort from a dealer, his famous *Books and Bidders*. John Fleming, his former assistant, shares the credit of having produced a most readable biography of this illustrious if buccaneering bookseller. But I wonder how many people know that Rosenbach actually produced a work of fiction, no less, *circa* 1925? You seldom come across it, and you don't often hear it mentioned. It is called *The Unpublishable Memoirs*. How on earth this busiest of men ever found time to write fiction, with his other multifarious activities, is quite beyond me, but he did. While his short stories of "the trade" will never gain a lasting place in the annals of great literature, he did at least have a go, and they make interesting reading.

Heir to the throne occupied for so long among dealers by Rosenbach was Hans P. Kraus. He called his memoirs *A Rare Book Saga*. If you would like to read of famous bookselling coups and auction room dramas involving record prices of many thousands of pounds then that book is certainly the one for you. On the other hand, should you lean towards and identify more closely with some of the humbler and less exalted members of the book business I can do no better than to mention that minor classic by Helene Hanff, *84 Charing Cross Road*.

* * *

The pages which follow are a series of reminiscences and anecdotes about some of those people among book-lovers with whom I have come into close contact personally. You might argue that they are nothing but a gallery of grotesques and eccentrics, and that I have applied the trowel of exaggeration over-plentifully. I would reply that this is not so, and that everything I have written is the truth. There are plenty of quite normal people in the book, of course, but if some of the characters seem larger than life I can only say that I remember them, and chose to write about them, for the very oddities they bore. I have met a lot of dull people as well, but I have either forgotten them or I do not consider them worth telling you about.

Naturally, *I* have found it all interesting; I hope others will do so as well. Unhappily, the complete text of my jottings can never be published, and those sufficiently intrigued to read it would probably be obliged to examine a typescript — if they could ever get their hands on it, which would be difficult. Slander is one thing — we have all indulged in it to some extent, one way or another. You can say scurrilous things about people over a pint and get away with it. Libel is quite another thing: the awful nakedness of print is irretrievable, and strictly for my own amusement, in the past, I have written what could be considered some unflattering things about people who are still very much alive. It is a truism to say that the best stories are those you daren't relate. But should any acquaintances of mine reading this book think to themselves: 'Why didn't he write about me?', the answer just *could* be that I probably did and then later edited it out in order to avoid a red face on the one hand and a punch in the nose on the other. But as 'Sportin' Life' said so lyrically, 'it ain't necessarily so.'

Some of the pieces included here have already appeared, in a modified fashion, in periodical form. For the most part they were appreciated, but you can't please all of the people all of the time. One or two rather sensitive readers from the United States have accused me of anti-semitism, racial intolerance and bigotry. I never cease to be amazed at some people's discovery of prejudice where none was intended and — as far as I am aware — never even inferred. I will admit that some of the characters I have written about happened to be Jewish. But couldn't that possibly be because a goodly proportion of book-lovers also happen to be Jewish, with quite a few of those bearing amusing eccentricities? I have laughed gently at an Indian who was a hypocrite, a Dane who was miserly and anti-social, and a Bible-thumping Protestant Puritan who was also a very pleasant man. No Indians or Danes have charged me with casting ethnic aspersions, and no nonconformists have taken offence to my knowledge. I went to the trouble of sounding out more than one or two of my Jewish friends to see how they felt about the matter. They thought the criticisms ludicrous. I am afraid that those touchy people who see me as intolerant are blood-brothers to the ones who look upon Shakespeare as an anti-semite for Shylock and Dickens as a Jew-baiter for Fagin.

Strictly speaking, perhaps I shouldn't have called these reminiscences *Rare Books and Rarer People*. For one thing, there is much less in the following pages about the volumes themselves than about those who bought, sold, read and collected them, and so possibly the books ought to take second place. For another thing, it has been brought to my notice that many years ago there was a book with a similar title. But after all, books and people have been the most important interests in my life, albeit in reverse order. I have made a concession to euphony. And anyway, there is no copyright in titles, so I will let it stand.

It may be noticed that when I write of Hodgson's, my first firm, and in whose premises I worked for so long, I refer to the Sale Room, particularly, with capital letters, but that when I am speaking of the sale room or the auction room generally, I use the lower case. You will also see that I often refer to the Front Room, the Counting House, and the Pound. I make no excuse for this: whenever I use capital letters it is simply because when these words were used at Hodgson's they were *spoken* in capitals! I am sure that the same sort of thing applies in many other old family firms.

Finally, please forgive my style. Telling of one thing, more often than not I am reminded of another. One of my greatest weaknesses is a tendency to digress. But I plead that one discursive rambling has a bearing upon another, and I wanted to get as much in as I could, after all. Inevitably, I shall remember a lot more when it is too late.

The Hodgsons

In late 1949 I answered an advertisement in the Situations Vacant column of the *Daily Telegraph*. As far as I can remember, it read as follows:

Sale Clerk wanted for firm of Book Auctioneers. State salary required. Hodgson & Co., 115 Chancery Lane, WC2.

I had no idea what a Sale Clerk was, I had never attended an auction in my life, and I had never consciously heard of Hodgson's. But I naively thought I knew quite a lot about books, and that this job would be ideal for me.

I should say that at this stage in my life I was in my early thirties. I was unmarried, and I was earning about six pounds a week in the stores of a firm of motor part engineers in North London. I had been doing this sort of work for a year or two, merely as a means of subsistence. At that time I had literary or — more accurately — journalistic ambitions, and the going was none too smooth.

By the good grace of a friend of mine who had a three-roomed flat at thirty-six shillings a week, I had occupied one room of it for the sum of twelve shillings each week since my demobilisation from the army in 1946. For a time, at first, I had sat in this room knocking out articles, reviews, indexes, and whatever came my way, on a 'captured' German typewriter bought for £25 on a fifty-fifty basis with another friend. My share had come from my War Gratuity of £70, the largest sum of money I had ever had in my life when I returned to a civilian existence in the austerity period of rationing and coupons in the years immediately after the war.

I made a few pounds from my writings, but hardly enough to live on. Much of my time, just then, was also utilised in the writing of whole books — no less — one of which ran to a quarter of a million words! While some of my articles sold, the books did not. So twice a week I journeyed to Walthamstow Stadium with a capital of £12 and the object of making £3 profit by backing favourites in the greyhound races. I had no gambling instinct or inclination: I simply bet to win £3 in order to buy food and to pay rent. Once that was accomplished I walked out until the next time.

Sometimes I made my money in the first race. Sometimes I was obliged to carry on well into a meeting before a favourite came up, and now and again I only made about £2 profit, or just covered my losses and then got cold feet and a dry throat. But I managed to live in this way for a year, doing the sort of work I wanted to do without having to go into the employ of someone else.

Eventually, of course, the inevitable happened. I went to the dogs, both literally and metaphorically. It was a double meeting, I recall: Bank Holiday Monday, with twice the number of races as usual — afternoon and then evening. Not a single favourite won. At least, if a favourite *did* win, it was well after my meagre capital had gone. I walked out — completely cleaned out. I suppose that I was lucky to have had such a run for my money.

It is rather ironical. I, the most industrious of men, one who toiled for far more hours each day than many others, now actually had to *go to work* for a living.

I deliberately got myself a night job, in order that I might be free during part of the day to meet editors who called me, and other persons of influence who kept normal working hours. I was paid six pounds a week in the factory, plus a small bonus for night work. But eventually that night work stopped, and I was transferred to days. I didn't like this for two reasons: one was that my daytime freedom now became limited, and the other was that having become used to living on six pounds plus I resented going back to six pounds. It wasn't that I couldn't live on the money I was earning, for I could — quite comfortably. I told myself it was the principle of the thing. I was quite aware that the manager of my particular department in the factory had come to rely on me considerably, and I felt that I rated an increase in wages, rather than a cut. I started looking round for something else.

I suppose it is *just* possible that had this particular disruption not occurred I might still be working in that factory's stores today. And yet I doubt it. I think that sooner or later I would have had to make some sort of change. But one thing is certain: had I not made the effort at the precise moment I did, I would have missed an opportunity that was unique. I think that the majority of people go through life doing the sort of work they don't particularly like, but just make the best of it. I answered that advertisement hopefully because it appealed to me, and I fell into a wonderful job and became that very unusual thing: a square peg in a square hole. I haven't loved every minute of it, of course, but had a fortune dropped into my lap I would never have given it up voluntarily. I liked it that much.

My first interview at Hodgson's took place just after Christmas, in 1949. When I first stepped into that historic building in Chancery Lane I little realised how well I would get to know the place in the following years, what with its mustiness and dustiness, and its almost wholly Dickensian atmosphere. There was the dim and inadequate lighting, which cast the place in gloom, except on exceptionally sunny days, when the Sale Room became quite a blaze of light, with its high glass roofing. There was the old-fashioned, open-fire heating in one corner, again quite inadequate for a place of its size. I was to get to know the primitive telephone switchboard, the perpetually leaking hand-operated hydraulic goods lifts 'worn but servicable', as the maintenance man always entered on his report — and the single noisily-clattering old typewriter, vintage 1928. You stepped out of the twentieth century right back into the nineteenth, with one or two new-fangled concessions like that typewriter, when you walked into Hodgson's Rooms in those days. If you didn't like it you just had to lump it.

I was interviewed at first by Sidney Hodgson and his son Wilfrid. At that time Sidney was already elderly: a well-preserved and vigorous man in his early seventies. I was to know him for almost another quarter of a century, before he died at the age of ninety-six. Wilfrid was a man of roughly the same age as myself. We were to work together for well over thirty years.

I got the job, provisionally, but I was asked to come back again in a day or two and see the senior member of the firm, John Hodgson, who was several years older than his brother and partner, Sidney. In due course I was interviewed by John in his upstairs sanctum, reached by worn, plain-board stairs. The room had barred windows: a deterrent to burglars, and row upon row of open bookshelves bearing loose-cased volumes of *The Library*, and endless catalogues. At one end of the room was an old-fashioned roll-topped desk, and a swivel chair.

John was well into his seventies. He had an enormous bald dome fringed with white curls above his ears, and a huge white walrus moustache. I recall very little about that interview now, yet two things do stick in my mind.

'You're familiar with books?' he probed. 'What have you read?'

'Oh — everything,' I told him nervously, and extremely rashly and inaccurately. I meant that I had touched upon most of the great classics briefly, and was fairly familiar with much of current literature.

'Have you ever read Dr. Johnson? Or Boswell's *Life*?'

'Well —,' I said, 'some of it. I haven't ploughed right through.' This was true. I had a copy, and had dipped.

'A great man — Samuel Johnson,' he informed me. 'You should persevere.' I was soon to learn that this writer was one of John Hodgson's passions. He had a magnificent collection of the author.

Finally, he looked at me rather strangely and said: 'And you'd come to work for us here for six pounds a week?'

I really think that this must have been the clincher. I have no idea how many, if any, other people applied for the situation. But I believe that my modest wage demands, as a single man, were instrumental in getting me the job.

I started work at Hodgson's Book Auction Rooms in early January, 1950. I think I should say something about this remarkable firm in detail.

It was founded in 1807 by one Robert Saunders, who was joined by Edmund Hodgson a few years later. The business was then in Fleet Street, on the site where Hoare's Bank now stands, almost directly opposite St. Dunstan's Church. I think that one of the very earliest references to this firm is in *The Second Tour of Dr. Syntax*, by William Combe, published in 1812. Although Hodgson's is not actually mentioned by name, there is no mistaking it. I think, too, that there in *Dr. Syntax* might be found one of the first allusions to that hoary old cliché of the auction room, where somebody present happens to nod or wink inadvertently and finds that a lot has been knocked down to him. The section is well worth quoting in its entirety.

— Nothing, indeed, escap'd his view,
He saw St. Dunstan's men strike two,
And walking on he look'd around
To see what more was to be found;
When a door was fix'd a book,
In which he felt dipos'd to look,
And saw, amidst the noisy din,
There was a sale of books within.
This he presum'd would form a treat,
So in he went and took a seat.
As far as he could judge or see,
There was a curious company;
Authors, booksellers, and what not
Had in the place together got;
Though, here and there, he seem'd to ken
A little lot of gentlemen,
Who sometimes gave a book a run
As it appear'd from vexing fun,
And raised a work above its price,
To tease a tradesman's avarice,
While those same worthies of the Row,
Would pay the gents a quid pro quo.
The sale went on, and books knock'd down
From fifty pounds to half a crown.

Syntax in musing silence thought
On what was sold and what was bought;

And let his keen reflecting trace
How solid learning chang'd its place.
—Some Authors by the hammer's fiat,
Were sent away to sleep in quiet,
While others, who with leaves unclos'd,
Had for full half a century doz'd,
Were doom'd to pass their dog's ear'd lives,
As ever-moving fugitives.
Thus from their titles, looks and dates,
He doom'd them to their sev'ral fates;
Though, as he sat with watchful eye,
He sometimes even long'd to buy;
But sage discretion held his hand,
And did his longing tongue command.

    At length the solemn auctioneer
Did in his hand a tome uprear,
All gilt, and in morocco green,
Fit for the boudoir of a queen;
I know not why so very fine;
Thought Syntax, for the work is mine:
But now, I shall most surely know
What to fair truth the work doth owe;
And public fancy may bestow;
For here its value I shall see,
Without a spice of flattery.
Its value was most warmly stated,
Its Author's talents celebrated,
Its humour, verse and moral powers,
Suited to grave and laughing hours,
And deck'd by nature and by fun,
With the gay skill of ROWLANDSON.
Syntax, delighted beyond measure
Nodded to express his pleasure,
But started when the auctioneer,
Told him he was the purchaser.

AUCTIONEER

'The book's knocked down at two pounds two,
The money to be paid by you'.

SYNTAX

'This sure is reas'ning most absurd,
Why, Sir, I never spoke a word.
I might have nodded twice or thrice
To see the book fetch such a price;

With secret pride I was complying,
But that had nought to do with buying'.

AUCTIONEER

'Nodding is bidding, Sir, well known
In ev'ry auction-room in town,
And now the book, Sir, is your own'.

SYNTAX

'I know 'tis mine because I wrote it,
But you will never say I bought it.
Nay, that would be a scurvy trick,
Enough to make the Author sick.
If my nods bought it, as you say,
Why nods should be the coin to pay.
For this same I could not bid,
A fool I must be if I did.
Besides I safely may express,
That he who doth the work possess,
Were I at any time to try
His honest liberality,
Would give me copies half a score,
Did I demand them, aye and more'.

The doctor now engross'd the eye
Of the surrounding company,
Nor was his person sooner known
Than ev'ry mark'd respect was shown:
Nay, as he did the case explain,
The Volume was put up again;
While on its page 'twas made a claim,
That he would just inscribe his name,
When this same autograph was found
To raise the price another pound,
And Syntax felt an added glee
When 'twas knocked down for three pounds three.

Nowadays, *Syntax* and similar works sell primarily for the Rowlandson illustrations, hand-coloured. William Combe was a very long way from being the best poet in the world, but I think he was an excellent reporter. I am amused to notice some of the things he mentioned that still prevailed after well over a century and a half. 'St Dunstan's men', those figures high above Lord Northcliffe's bust in Fleet Street, continue to strike the bell each hour. Auctions were still in progress at two in the afternoon until 1981. 'When on a door was fix'd a book' almost certainly refers to the catalogue of the current sale within, and ever since those days a copy

MR. HODGSON'S
NEW AUCTION ROOMS,

No. 115, CHANCERY LANE, W.C. (NEAR FLEET STREET.)

ESTABLISHED in **FLEET STREET** and **CHANCERY LANE** upwards of **FIFTY-FOUR YEARS.**

[PLEASE TURN OVER.

Mr. HODGSON'S NOTICE OF REMOVAL

OF HIS

AUCTION ROOMS,

FOR

THE SALE OF BOOKS,

AND

LITERARY PROPERTY OF EVERY DESCRIPTION,

ENGRAVINGS, PAINTINGS,

LIBRARY AND OFFICE FURNITURE,

STOCKS OF PAPER, PRINTING MATERIALS, &c. &c.,

To No. 115, CHANCERY LANE, near FLEET STREET.

HAVING REMOVED TO HIS NEW PREMISES AT No. 115, CHANCERY LANE, W.C.,

Mr. Hodgson takes this opportunity of addressing Gentlemen, as Executors or having Libraries of their own for disposal, as well as the public in general, who desire to find the most satisfactory mode of Sale, and he assures them that *Public Sale by Auction in London* is, without exception, the best means of realising such property.

The experience which Mr. Hodgson has had for the last thirty-five years in arranging, cataloguing and selling Libraries, Stocks of Books, Copyrights, and other Literary Property; the central position of his New Auction Rooms, and the fact of his present Premises being entirely new, and built by him expressly for the purpose of carrying on his various professional pursuits with increased facility, induce him to solicit a continuance of favours from those Gentlemen who have so kindly patronized him, and to assure others who have not tried his plan of disposing of Books, or other Literary property, that every attention is paid in its arrangement, to the best mode of introducing the property to the public, as well as of securing a full realisation of the same.

The Bookselling Trade of London attend the Sales regularly. Mr. Hodgson has also a very extensive private connexion of Gentlemen, Book Collectors, and others, whose presence in the Auction Room is very frequent; to all of whom, as well as most of the leading Country Booksellers, Catalogues are regularly sent.

Small parcels of Books are received at any time and inserted in suitable Catalogues, are sold within a fortnight from the time of receiving them, and the accounts settled a short time after the Sale.

The terms on which Sales are conducted are, a moderate commission on the amount sold, including all expenses of cataloguing, printing, and arranging for Sale,—the only extra charge being for removal, and when the Property is required to be packed by Mr. Hodgson's own servants. The Carriage by Railway from any part of the Kingdom is now moderate as well as expeditious. Packing Cases will be forwarded, when required for the purposes of Packing, on the shortest notice.

Valuations for Probate or other purposes, and Arbitrations promptly adjusted.

Cash to any amount advanced on Property for Immediate Sale.

usually hung outside the doors whenever books were on view or were being sold—although in recent years they were not infrequently pinched, and two copies became available for perusal on stands just within the portals. Those 'worthies of the Row', of course, are long since dead, and so is the old 'Booksellers' Row' from whence they came, but their equally worthy successors of Cecil Court, Great Russell Street, and points west will still 'pay the gents a quid pro quo' if they are not careful. I am particularly interested in Combe's lines: 'Nay, as he did the case explain, / The Volume was put up again;' for right to the end a Hodgson's Rooms auctioneer would always adhere strictly to the Conditions of Sale printed at the front of the catalogue. 'In the event of a dispute the lot shall be immediately put up again for sale.' This was done in the interests of fairness and strict impartiality. Many are the 'tradesmen' who don't like this rule, and never did. They are hardened professionals, sitting below and close to the rostrum, they concentrate keenly, and they seldom make mistakes. They don't nod to each other when that nod might be misconstrued by an auctioneer, and since his eye is usually upon these clients their bids are rarely missed. Other bids in the body of the room sometimes are—more often than not when the gesture is hidden by somebody immediately in front of the bidder—and the gavel will come down with a crack, to be followed by a howl from somebody at the back that *he* was bidding. The gentleman presiding will usually apologise and carry on selling the lot. Those of the trade usually used to argue 'too late' or 'hammer down', particularly if one of their number might otherwise have been the buyer at a lower price. The present generation just looks discontented.

The Hodgson business was eventually removed from opposite St. Dunstan's to the corner of Chancery Lane, subsequently the premises of Partridge and Cooper, then the Solicitors' Law Stationery Society: the later Oyez. The firm flourished here for a number of years before Edmund and his son, Henry Hill Hodgson, built new premises in about 1863 just a stone's throw up Chancery Lane.

Edmund Hodgson was remarkably prudent when he erected this new building. Chancery Lane is a narrow street, but only in my own time there did it become 'one way' for traffic; double-decker buses and coaches had the devil of a job passing each other. Old Edmund, with remarkable foresight, must have visualised a day when Chancery Lane might be widened. He built his place well back. Indeed, you will find that there is almost what amounts to a lay-by as far as the kerb and gutter are concerned. This, in a way, was to the firm's perpetual detriment: drivers just loved to park their cars there, particularly when we were anticipating a van or a pantechnicon to disgorge a load of several thousand volumes, loose, or a hundred or so tea-chests, full.

But when old Hodgson built those premises he made sure that the actual auction room was well back. You approached through a long hall, or passage. *If* Chancery Lane is ever widened, those famous premises will suffer little. But I think it is going to be a very long time before such a disaster occurs. A few yards from the Hodgson building stands the Law Society edifice: a most impressive and inviolable pile. Directly opposite is the Public Records Office. *Is* it actually an office? It looks more like a castle, and just as impregnable. Property developers: eat your hearts out.

From all accounts, it was Henry Hill Hodgson who really made the firm. Its heyday was certainly during his lifetime. Queen Victoria was on the throne, it was a prosperous and booming era, he was a good business-man, and he was an autocratic employer and auctioneer. While his father had come to work in Fleet Street on horseback, I have been told that he was in the habit of catching the same train late every afternoon to his South London home before the rush hour began. He let nothing interfere with this routine — not even the auctions, upon which his livelihood depended. Sales at Hodgson's, I should mention, always took place in the afternoon, in order not to clash with other similar functions elsewhere in London. If the sale began to lag, or if the bidding was not too brisk, old Henry Hill would glance up at the clock high on the wall which faced the rostrum, and would suddenly put on the equivalent of a final spurt. He intended to catch his usual train home, come what might, and I believe the regular bidders came to recognise what was happening. They had to be on their toes, so to speak, or down came that hammer like lightning. Any vendor who happened to be in the room watching the sale of his books would often see them knocked down for a fraction of their true value, and many a bookseller or collector must have cursed as that inexorable gavel cracked down before he had a chance to open his mouth or raise his catalogue.

I am perfectly aware that the contents of the above paragraph would appear to contradict what I had to say previously about the fairness of Hodgson's auctioneers. But they don't, really. Henry Hill only started 'sprinting' when he got into the final straight, and then only if he was making bad time. And in any case, I was speaking primarily of the family auctioneers in my own time. 'One hundred and twenty lots an hour: two per minute.' If this dictum wasn't actually Holy Writ, it could be taken more or less as gospel, so to speak. Great effort was made to keep to it. Things often went a bit awry, of course, particularly if a vendor suddenly withdrew fifty or so lots — which he was quite entitled to do — but generally speaking that was the speed.

I don't think old man Hodgson's final spurts could be accomplished today so easily. The levelling process has seen to that. Many a bookseller is far more important, and wields much more influence, than an auctioneer. But in the old days the man on the rostrum was a 'gentleman', as omnipotent as God, and the groundlings sitting below him were merely 'trade', and it would appear that they knew their place. Henry Hill Hodgson made decisions like a High Court judge dispensing justice, and unless he admitted an error there was no appeal.

The business flourished: as I have said, they were prosperous times. And here was a freehold building, already mounting in value. It was the only auction house in London *solely* devoted to the sale of books and literary property. Firms like Christie's and Sotheby's, farther west, were older and perhaps more famous, but their activities were much more diverse than Hodgson's, and lots of people had fingers in their pie. This business in Chancery Lane was strictly a family concern, and it looked like continuing to be so.

Henry Hill Hodgson had two sons who came into this business *fin de siècle* — speaking quite literally. Nothing at all about them, accepting that term in its usual sense: advanced, modern, or decadent, applied. First was John Edmund, a tall and handsome man of noble presence. Second was his younger brother by a few years, Sidney, who was shorter, gentler, and not so formidable. Both were educated at the public school of Tonbridge.

When the time came for them to enter this family concern, their father more or less apprenticed them to London bookselling firms to learn the basics of the trade. John went to Bickers', and Sidney worked for David Nutt. This sort of thing appears to have been common practice at that time. But I can imagine what might well happen were one or two prominent London booksellers of my present acquaintance approached to teach a fledgling the tricks of the trade, with the certainty that the trainee would, in only a year or two, be leaving to enter 'the enemy camp', so to speak, with his freshly-acquired knowledge and closely-guarded secrets like code and clientele. You go and get stuffed! This would, perhaps, be the politest reaction.

However, both John and Sidney did their stints. They took their knocks and had their corners rubbed off a little, and eventually both settled down at Chancery Lane. They became book cataloguers and, in due course, auctioneers, like their father and grandfather before them.

I worked with them both. They were good men on the rostrum. You couldn't faze John — either on or off it. Sidney, who was a mild-mannered man who did not appear, in everyday life, to have the strength of personality to command an auction sale, became an entirely different man once he had climbed to his seat and had taken up the gavel. I can only guess at the agonies it must have caused him in his younger days. But I have known many other auctioneers of a similar disposition. I believe there are actors like it too : a bundle of nerves before they walk on to the boards — and then complete command.

John, the older brother and senior partner after his father died, lived as a bachelor until fairly late in life. He was both a scholar and a sportsman. When I knew him he had been based for some time in Tunbridge Wells. One of his primary interests, as I have mentioned earlier, was Dr. Samuel Johnson. but there is not the slightest doubt that it was aeronautics which occupied most of his leisure time, and for which he will be remembered.

But do not imagine that he was just an armchair aeronaut. John had been an intrepid balloonist and pioneer, long, long before 'those young men in their flying machines'. He was also the author of the definitive work on his subject, *The History of Aeronautics in Great Britain*, a magnificently illustrated book published by the Oxford University Press in the early 'twenties.

He was an old man, stooped and riddled with rheumatism and arthritis, when he first took me on. He was aided at the time, first, by his wife, Norma, a woman many years his junior, and second, by a ferruled stick. His boots were cut open at the front to give access and relief to his tortured toes. It required two people to get him up on to the rostrum to take a sale. Once there, he was the master.

I recognised the man's qualities, but I must confess that I never particularly liked him. First, he was a terrible old snob. Second, while he was pleasant enough to his clients, he often treated the humbler members of his staff badly, which, perhaps, is much the same thing. He could also be a rotten bully, even to his partner and brother, the mild-natured Sidney. I always kept out of John's way as much as possible, but I couldn't avoid him on sale days, when I had to work in close co-operation with him at the desk beside the rostrum. One of his most annoying habits was to knock a lot down to somebody in the room whom he did not know and then nod in the general direction of about forty people.

'That man,' he would say, if I hadn't noticed the bidder.

'Which one?' I would ask. 'The gentleman just over there?'

On one occasion I was rash enough to extend my finger towards the client I meant.

'Don't point — it's rude!' he snapped, and he immediately went on to the next lot, without finalising the previous one.

In my very early days at the job I did not know the clients as I was to come to know them later on, of course, and one of the very first sales I ever clerked with John had my book gaping with blank spaces where the names of the buyers should have been. Hodgson's never ran to the luxury of a number two clerk, or 'runner' — that is, a youngster employed to keep a double check and to pass out cards for the names and addresses of successful bidders unknown to us. I was up and down at that desk all afternoon, frantically trotting out into the room to check a name and hurrying back to book the price of the next lot. John never paused or slowed down in an effort to help me. He was completely self-centred and self-absorbed. When the sale was over I could quite cheerfully have killed him. It was weeks before I finally got my records straight, with all prices and buyers right.

One story I heard about the man always amused me. The event took place long before my time — during the heyday of the famous Dr. A. W. S. Rosenbach, in fact. An obscure but very important book was listed in a Hodgson catalogue, and few people had recognised its importance. When the volume came up for sale one or two of the dealers gave it a half-hearted run, but old Heinrich Eisemann was after it, and he bid very strongly against them all. Eventually the figure reached £1,200, and John Hodgson raised the gavel after a short pause.

'Thirteen hundred,' called someone from the back.

Eisemann shot a venomous glance in that direction. 'Fourteen hundred,' he snapped.

'Fifteen.'

Eisemann was no fool. He knew that he was now beaten, and he shook his head.

'Fifteen hundred pounds I am bid,' called John with great pleasure. Down came his hammer. 'Name, sir?'

'Rosenbach.'

In those days, within the book trade, no more respect would have been shown had the bidder called: 'Jesus Christ.'

John Hodgson's eyebrows shot up: he wasn't used to such illustrious clients in his domain. He bowed from the rostrum. 'A pleasure to do business with you, sir,' he said.

The successful purchaser nodded his acknowledgement. It was actually Sam Patch, the humble sale clerk from Sotheby's. Rosenbach had asked him to go down to Chancery Lane during his lunch hour and buy the book!

John was also a chronic 'hisser'. Wishing to engage a visitor or client in conversation he would, of course, approach and address the person by name. But desiring to attract the attention of one of his employees who was intend upon some job or other, he would 'Zzzzzzz' at him through his teeth. Fortunately, I was warned about this unpleasant and irritating habit as soon as I joined the firm, by one who particularly disliked being hissed at, and so I was on my guard. Now all John had to do, if he wanted to speak to me, was simply to call my name, which he knew well enough. But I would hear him clump down a couple of stairs heavily, even half see him from the corner of my eye as I worked at my desk, and then listen to him hiss at me. I rather bravely just let him carry on until he grew tired of it, and called me. He soon gave up this trick.

Sidney was a totally different man. He was kind, considerate, and gentle. For most of his life he was overawed and subjugated by his big brother, and there were times when I don't think he was particularly happy in his work. But in all the years I knew him I never remember seeing him lose his temper, and I rarely heard him utter an angry word. I admired him greatly for this, for he was often sorely tried. I stress this matter, since I fly off the handle quickly myself, and tend to lash out in all directions, only to be contrite and apologetic minutes later.

Sidney's ruling passions were his family, his garden, and the Stationers' Company. During the whole period of our acquaintance he lived at Bickley, near Bromley, in Kent, in very pleasant surroundings. His wife was a most delightful lady, a motherly soul devoted to her husband and children. I knew her only in the last decade or so of her life, when she grew almost blind, and suffered from diabetes.

I understand that she and Sidney met when they were both Sunday School teachers, before the first World War, and I have been told that they were actually on their honeymoon in Switzerland in the summer of 1914 when that war broke out, and were obliged to make a somewhat hasty and tortuous return to England — a sort of 'last train from Zurich' situation. Their eldest child, Wilfrid, was born the following year, to be followed by two daughters.

Sidney, as I have said, was a great family man and home-body, but he took time off from domesticity as a Liveryman at Stationers' Hall. His father had been a Master of the Stationers' Company, as had *his* father before him. The day would come when Sidney himself would don the robes and chain of office, and the day would arrive, too, when I would see his son Wilfrid occupy this apparently coveted position. I have had considerable to do with both friends and acquaintances who have been connected with the Stationers, but nobody has ever yet been able to explain to me — satisfactorily — the true function and use of these many City Companies. But there is no doubt that Sidney Hodgson knew what he was up to. His brother John, however, had no interest in the Stationers at all, but there is one amusing story I have heard concerning them both.

It appears that an important dinner was to be held at Stationers' Hall, at which Bernard Shaw was to be the guest of honour. Now, John was a bit of a lion-hunter, as well as a snob. He wanted to meet this great man, and he hinted to his brother that he was prepared to donate a couple of hundred pounds to the Company if *he* were invited and if it could be arranged that he sat next to Shaw at the coming dinner This was in the days when two hundred pounds was a substantial sum. The story goes that it was so arranged, but that the whole affair proved a fiasco. Shaw hardly spoke a word to John the whole evening, and devoted almost his entire conversation to the guest on his other side. As may be imagined, John, now two hundred quid lighter, never had much more than a grunt at mention of the Stationers' Company.

Sidney was also very interested in his old school, Tonbridge. One morning, walking up Chancery Lane during the 1914-1918 war, he stopped a young man who was wearing an Old Tonbridgian tie. They got into conversation, and Sidney elicited from the youth the fact that he was at present unemployed. On the strength of the Tonbridge association, and the young man's admitted interest in books and literature, he got a temporary job at Hodgson's as a cataloguer. I first heard this story from old Sidney himself, more or less as I have related. He was rather proud of it, for the youngster was John Langdon-Davies, who was to become famous as a writer, a foreign correspondent, and a book-collector. I heard another story some forty years after the event occurred, from the man who had got the job.

'He gave me the job, all right,' I learned, 'and I was glad to get it at the time. But Sidney thought I was just a Tonbridge man out of work and marking time until I was called up for the army. Actually, I was a conscientious objector, waiting to go to prison — probably.'

Langdon-Davies was a strongly-principled man utterly opposed to the ideals of those advocates of that particular holocaust, and it needed courage of an unusual kind to stick out for one's principles in those jingoist days. Sidney was a highly-patriotic and conformable man. Had he imagined John Langdon-Davies' attitude at that time I am sure he would never have taken him on. You couldn't let the old school down by being a conchie.

My old friend, David Low, an erudite bookseller whom I had known had worked for Hodgson's many years previously in his young manhood, never actually told me the circumstances of his joining. I had to wait until his entertaining book, *with all faults*, (1973), came out. He had this to say:

> I went to Hodgson's in 1926, replying to their advertisement in the *Times Literary Supplement*. In those days, applications were in handwriting, and the Hodgson brothers seeing the script which they had learned at Tonbridge in 1889-90, and I, during the First World War, looked no further. The old boy network may be deplorable, but it does have its charm. Mr. John, the senior partner, had written, and the Oxford University Press just published (1924), *The History of Aeronautics in Great Britain to the Latter Half of the Nineteenth Century*. In

Chancery Lane he looked after important books and clients, while
Mr. Sidney saw that the three cataloguers got ready the catalogues for
the fortnightly sales. His hobby and love was for the Stationers'
Company of London. Two years ago, having to wait for a train at
Charing Cross Station, I went into the tea-room. The table I made for
had Mr. Sidney at it, correcting catalogue proofs. He was then 92, and
too busy to notice me sitting down beside him, and in reply to my 'Still
these catalogue proofs, Mr. Sidney?' came his old familiar 'Bless my
soul! Well I never!'

That's Sidney Hodgson all right. I may be entirely mistaken, of course,
but it is my guess that David had to remind the old chap of his identity.
Sidney grew very forgetful of people in his last years. Many a time I
watched a man approach him in the Sale Room during a viewing and hold a
ten- or twenty-minute conversation with him during his declining days,
and then walk away pleased to be remembered. Invariably, Sidney would
sidle up to me afterwards with his usual apologetic cough and say: 'Who
was that I was speaking to just now, Snelling?' When I would remind him
he would nod and laugh, admitting his forgetfulness, and say, in much the
same way that David Low had captured: 'Bless my soul! Yes — of course.
What a frost!'

Old George Jeffery, *père*, one of the last of the famous Farringdon Road
bookstall-keepers, once summed up my two senior employers for me very
early on in my career with the firm.

'John and Sidney Hodgson,' he informed me, 'are the two meanest men
in London.'

Perhaps I may be forgiven for doubting this most sweeping statement at
the time, and for giving old Jeffery a bit of an argument, since I didn't
know either of the gentlemen very well just then, and he was taking in a
great deal of territory. (*The Publishing Unwins*, by Philip of that ilk, had
not yet been written or even thought about, but it would be difficult to
find a tighter-fisted bookman than Sir Stanley Unwin, from the tales his
nephew tells about him.) But over the years I came to recognise that if
Jeffery's pronouncement was more than something of an exaggeration,
perhaps the generalisation behind it was true.

As far as I know, the Hodgson family had always been pretty well off.
They had certainly never known the pinch of near-poverty, or of wondering where the next week's rent might come from. Although the business
wasn't doing any too well in the nineteen-fifties, for the up-and-coming
Sotheby's had grabbed the lion's share after 1945, the two brothers did
own the freehold of the fine building in Chancery Lane, and it was worth a
lot of money. At that time, an expert in such matters volunteered to me the
information that the property was then worth something in the region of

between a quarter and half a million pounds. Until he told me this I had never even thought about it. Afterwards, I did — once or twice. It occurred to me then that if it were true that the Hodgsons were mean about their own money, then they were equally mean, in a different manner, about other people's money, too. They rented a portion of the building off to a firm, adjoining and partly above our Sale Room. I happened to handle all the incoming cheques and monies, and entered them all into a cash book. Regularly every quarter came the rent from the firm next door. Considering the space these people were occupying, with its number of floors and rooms, and its desirable position just within the City of London, they were getting it for a mere pittance. I myself, a humble clerk with no enormous income, had just moved my abode, and I was paying almost as much for a couple of furnished rooms in Earl's Court, and just managing, although it was a struggle. Many a business would have been glad to have paid the Hodgsons four, five, or six times the amount they were asking for those offices.

Certainly, the brothers were never over-generous in their scale of wages, but this was not unique. At first I used to think that almost every employee of other book firms I met must be making a lot more than I was, but I have since discovered that this was not so. Very, very few booksellers' assistants made a great deal of money. Some of the cleverer and more adventurous ones struck out on their own after a time and did pretty well, of course, but *they* grew rather tight-fisted when it came to taking on assistants of their own.

But none of us at Hodgson's were compelled to work for the money we were paid. I joined the firm at a time when there was something like full employment throughout the country, and with a bit of effort I could have earned more money elsewhere, although perhaps not in such congenial circumstances. No, I stuck to this particular job because I very soon found that I liked what I was doing, and this has always meant more to me than how much money I made.

Although the Hodgson wages had apparently always been notoriously modest, there was one thing that could be relied upon. Every Christmas, every national holiday, every summer fortnight's vacation — when, of course, we all picked up three weeks' wages in one go, and felt opulent — there was *always* a handsome bonus tucked into the pay envelope. This never failed. The higher-paid employees got the most, and the lower-paid got the least, naturally. That was in the nature of things: that the weekend joint of beef cost much the same whether you wore a tie or a choker, and that the train fare to and from genteel Chelsea or not-so-genteel Fulham differed little whether or not you dropped your aitches, was not even considered.

In my later years with this firm we also got a bonus based on the year's takings, and I would be the first to say that some of those bonuses were very generous indeed. Further, for some time we received a gross amount, until the accountants pointed out to our benefactors that income tax should have been deducted.

To sum things up, I would say that the principals of the firm of Hodgson and Co. could be most generous at times in big things, but incredibly mean and petty in small matters. Yarns about them were told from year to year — in a few cases stories passed from generation to generation.

For instance, on one occasion a customer had been in to collect his purchases, and he had tipped Old Jim, the tiny porter, a sixpence in the Sale Room. Jim dutifully touched his forelock and pocketed the tanner. But he always wore hand-me-downs and other cast-off clothing. The particular pair of trousers he was wearing at that time had a hole in the pocket, and the coin fell through to the floor. It didn't have very far to fall, and it made no sound. A few minutes later, John Hodgson came out into the Sale Room, on his way out to lunch.

'Hullo,' he said, looking down, 'there's a sixpence here.'

Lew Atkinson, the packer, took in the situation immediately. 'Oh, yes,' he said. 'That must be Jim's. He was standing just there.'

Jim was duly brought forward, he searched in all his pockets, and he confirmed that indeed his tanner was missing. But the finder was reluctant to surrender his unexpected windfall too easily.

'Well, I'll tell you what we'll do,' said the sporting John. 'We'll toss for it!'

A rather glum Jim agreed to this arrangement — he could do little else. He called Heads. It came down Tails. John Hodgson pocketed the sixpence and went out in a very good mood. He probably enjoyed a lunch a little more expensive than usual.

There was another tale about John which was not allowed to be forgotten. It was not exactly told at the drop of a hat — old Tom Wheaton was inclined to relate it if anyone as much as made a move towards his headgear. Tom was a morose and embittered misanthrope who spent some sixty years in Hodgson's basement. He had a civil word for nobody, not even his bosses, and he spoke only to snarl a grievance. I often wondered why he was tolerated, in my very early days, but I was informed that he was extremely useful. I suppose he must have been: quite literally, a lifetime spent mooching about this basement locating, numbering, and transporting innumerable literary properties made him invaluable. He could put his hand on any book at a moment's notice.

But back in the distant past, well before any of us listening had been born, he had accompanied John out into the country to inspect, pack up, and transport a library of books to London for sale at Chancery Lane. During his chores he came upon a very rare book which his experience told him was worth a great deal of money. He drew his employer's attention to it. John had missed it entirely. As for the owner — he didn't even know he had it! In due course the library was sold, and this book realised a very handsome sum. The delighted vendor showed his appreciation in the best possible manner, and he sent ten pounds for the man who had found the book. Unfortunately, he sent the money to John, with a covering letter.

Downstairs went the honest and beneficent John to Tom, in whom he was well pleased. 'Here you are, Tom,' he said graciously, 'five pounds for you, and five pounds for me!'

It rankled with Tom for the rest of his life. During the short time I knew him he was barely approachable. The guv'nors avoided him as much as they possibly could, but he did his job faithfully and pocketed the wage envelope thrust to him every Friday without a word of thanks or acknowledgement. In his old age he had a painful throat ailment — probably cancer — which eventually killed him. I shall forever remember Tom slinking about and muttering curses round that basement, hawking and spitting on the floor, and raising the pitch of his obscene soliloquy whenever one of the principals happened to be near: ''Orrible soddin' firm to work for — steals yer bleedin' gratooities!'

It would be difficult to imagine two brothers more dissimilar in almost every respect than John and Sidney Hodgson. John was much more worldly than his younger brother, and he kept abreast of current events to a considerable extent. Sidney would have liked to, I suppose, but he didn't really know how to go abut it.

He was an incredible man in many ways. Vague and courteous, he was an antiquary who knew a little world all his own. He could express interest, politely, in something that was happening today or had occurred yesterday, but he really had little or no interest in the age in which he lived. His whole life seemed to be in the past, and he was truly a fish out of water. He took a daily paper, the *Telegraph*, and presumably read it, but he forgot everything he read almost immediately. The most popular and absorbing talking-points of the day went over his head like the proverbial trapeze act. He reminded me, at times, of those traditional High Court judges, people I had never quite believed in, who could interrupt counsel and say: 'Who *are* the Beatles?' or '*What* is a Teddy Boy?'

He grew still vaguer as he got older. He could adjust to nothing at all mechanical. I think his son probably showed him how to switch on a radio, but I don't think he could ever have tuned in to a station. Television was quite beyond him. Sounds reached him, but even if the volume was turned high he was unable to interpret what was being said. He could take in the visuals, up to a point, but it just wasn't his medium.

I know for a fact that one evening he and his son were watching the screening of a soccer match in the mid-'sixties. Wilfrid himself told me the anecdote, and he was obviously amused by it, although he would rarely tell a story to an employee at the expense of his father. It seems that on the television screen toilet rolls, soccerdom's heavy-handed equivalent of the gala-party streamer, were coming on to the football pitch in abundance, and eventually the old man turned to his son and said: 'What *are* those things they keep throwing, Wilfrid?'

He passed from the Victorian era of leisurely elegance into an age of the mid-twentieth century which he did not understand, and to which he was never able to adapt. Literally, nothing that did not affect his own immediate comfort and well-being — things like rail strikes or frozen points, which would delay his getting up to Chancery Lane — appeared to be of very much concern to him.

Dear old Sidney — capable of the most benign and kindly procrastination where the solution to a particular problem was immediately obvious to anyone else; forgetful, absent-minded, but physically as fit as a horse for most of his life. I saw him running for a bus during the rush hour in Fleet Street when he was ninety-two!

Both John and Sidney Hodgson amused the members of their staff over the years with their particular fondnesses and predilections. John was very partial to his jar of vaseline, while Sidney just loved his paste pot.

The senior of the two was very fond of old calf bindings, and also of the gilt lettering or decoration on their spines. If ever he was in the Sale Room, talking to a client or an employee, he would frequently reach out to the shelves and take a volume from them. He would then start buffing the spine with the heel of his hand. Just as frequently, still talking, he would shuffle to a small cupboard by the door near the office, open it up and take out a small jar of vaseline and a dirty piece of somebody's old shirt, long ago discarded for wear and now cut into suitably-sized squares for further use. He would apply the vaseline, not too liberally, to the spine of the book, and then polish industriously as he talked. I don't think he did this in order to heighten the book's prospective value, necessarily. I just think he loved books, and he liked to see them as smart and as gleaming as possible.

I don't recall ever seeing his brother Sidney use the vaseline jar. He worked downstairs mostly, and one of his main jobs was to edit and prepare the copy sheets of the various cataloguers for the printers. Now, in more recent years, each cataloguer has sat at a desk with a typewriter, and every lot catalogued has been typed on to an individual sheet ruled and printed with spaces for owner's name, property number, estimated price, reserve figure, *et al*, and the whole thing in quadruplicate. Not so in the old days. Each cataloguer *stood* all day at a high and sloping desk. Lots were written out by hand on tall sheets of foolscap paper, half a dozen items or more on one sheet, if the man was working on a big property, and with the owner's name just written in at the top right-hand corner of each page.

As Sidney was going through the copy, he would quite often come across a particular lot which was in some way outstanding or remarkable, and which would quite obviously look better cheek by jowl with some other similar related item of an entirely different property elsewhere in the finished catalogue. So out would come his scissors and out would come his pot of paste. He spent hour after hour snipping and juxtaposing, happily removing here and pasting together, and then inserting there and slapping away with his brush. In the end, you might see a page or two which consisted of five or six strips of copy paper in as many as three or four quite different handwritings. I suppose it improved the final printed catalogue no end, but it caused hopeless confusion among those of the staff responsible for the administrative side of the business, because Sidney, in his enthusiasm with scissors and paste, often quite forgot, as he removed one lot from an early sheet and stuck it into the middle of a later one, to include the owner's name as well!

The old chap was blithely unaware of the trouble he caused, but very often one was able, if vigilant, to pick up these errors, and to discover, by the evidence of the handwriting, by the way the paper had been cut, or by some other means, from whose property the wayward item had been removed. Yet I am quite sure that, over the years, many a vendor eventually received less than his due and many another received a cheque considerably larger than he should have done.

Sidney had another little quirk: for some reason he absolutely hated 'tissues'. This was the name given to those very flimsy and often quite transparent sheets of paper tipped into certain nineteenth century books, usually between a printed page and an engraved or hand-coloured plate facing it. They served a useful purpose. To some extent they prevented 'set-off', that is, the ghost image of the lines of the text appearing across the plate, or the impression of the plate showing on the page of text, which sometimes resulted from damp or humid conditions.

But the old chap loathed these tissues. He destroyed every one he saw. Many, many, of course, escaped quite unscathed through Hodgson's Rooms. Thousands and millions of books were bought and sold; Sidney could not go through every one of them.

In the 'fifties, I remember that we had a pristine copy of the first edition of A. E. Housman's *The Shropshire Lad*. I saw this book when it came in, as issued. There was no dust-jacket to it, but it did have its original glassine wrapper. It certainly didn't by the time it was sold. Sidney had seen to that. Harry Mushlin, I recall, was the under-bidder. He had been quite sorry to lose the item, and during a brief post mortem on the book's unusually fine condition, I happened to mention how I had seen Sidney scrunch that transparent flimsy from the book and throw it in the direction of the waste paper basket.

'What?' gasped Mushlin incredulously. 'Blast it! I'd have gone to another tenner if that original wrapper had been on it!'

I think that the *pièce de résistance* of dear old Sidney's amiable, dithering ineptitude revolves around a most beautiful copy of one of those nineteenth century full morocco gilt topographical works with steel engravings. I can't remember now exactly which one it was. Maybe Alex Rogoyski does: he had just finished cataloguing it. In walked Sidney.

'Ah,' he said, 'what a lovely copy,' and he took it down from its shelf. Then he opened it to the frontispiece and title-page. But tipped in was his scourge, a tissue.

'Argh!' He didn't pull it out gently: his open hand descended and then closed upon a fistful of flimsy, and he jerked it out. But he also jerked out the frontispiece as well.

'Oh — dear, dear, dear! Ah, well — no problem.' Throwing away the crumpled tissue, he reached for his paste pot. He sploshed away at the margin of the frontispiece confidently. 'Soon put that right.'

Back into the book it went, but alas — he quickly discovered that he had pasted in the frontispiece upside down!

'Tut, tut, tut,' snickered Sidney. Out it came again, more paste was applied, and back in it went. But by this time both inner *and* outer margins had been daubed with paste. This did not improve the book's appearance.

'There.' He slammed the book shut with satisfaction, and reached to place it high upon the shelf from which he had taken it. But he misjudged. He let go too soon, and down it fell. It struck the floor on one corner of the binding, and as often happens in such cases with books of calf or morocco, off flew the front cover entirely.

'Oh, my!' — and a little more tut-tutting. He reached for an old piece of string, blandly wrapped it round the book, tied a slip-knot, and shoved the wreck back into its place.

'There you are,' he smiled, innocent and satisfied. 'As good as new!' Dear old Sidney was entirely oblivious that he had, within a matter of a minute or two, transformed a handsome volume into an utter ruin and had knocked many pounds off its value.

Despite all the foregoing, these two brothers, John and Sidney Hodgson, were great men, particularly so in their younger days. They were respected throughout the world for their expertise and deep knowledge of books. John will be remembered primarily for his definitive and monumental history of the subject he loved, and for his association with the Aeronautical Society over many years. Sidney will not be forgotten, either. In 1911 he had been invited to the United States to help in the cataloguing of the vast Hoe Library. It was a sale which went on for days, and he was asked to officiate at the rostrum on the evening during which a fine copy of the famous and very rare *Gutenberg Bible* was sold. It realised $50,000, and he was justly proud that for many, many years he held the world record for a book sold at auction.

I think there is not the slightest doubt that the backbone of the firm — in my time, at any rate — was Wilfrid B. Hodgson. He was Sidney's eldest child, and his pride and joy.

From childhood he must have known that he would be expected to join the firm and tread the same path of that of his father and uncle, his grandfather, and his great-grandfather, and he did not shirk his obligations. Old Sidney was a fortunate man: none had a more dutiful and loyal son.

Brought up in the same South London, middle-class tradition of all the Hodgsons before him, with the same Tonbridgian background, he was nevertheless something of an odd man out. While his father was a keen antiquary, and his uncle a great collector and scholar, Wilfrid always gave me the impression that his true interests lay elsewhere. But he applied himself diligently to his job and did it extremely capably.

When he first entered the business, as a young man before the war broke out in 1939, he went downstairs into the basement to learn to be a cataloguer. But the five or more years he spent in the army during the first half of the 'forties formed a crucial hiatus in his career — just as they did with so many millions of other young men. He came back to civilian life to find the Hodgson business marking time. Sales had continued during the war — after a fashion — but staff had necessarily been depleted. Youngsters were in the various services and the older, more experienced men who had dealt with the administration side of things were dying off or bowing out. John and Sidney had plugged on, doing as best they could and tackling every sort of job imaginable. Some elderly porters and packers were still there, but an infusion of new and young blood was desperately needed. The building, by the way, remained inviolate. It bore a charmed life. The large and lofty Sale Room, glass-roofed from front to back, survived the Battle of Britain and all the thousands of bombs which fell upon London. I have been told that throughout the whole war not one single pane of glass was broken. Blackout precautions were not ignored, but they were circumvented. Sale times were brought forward for the nonce, and everyone packed up and went home before nightfall in the winter months.

Wilfrid returned from Madagascar to post-war London and austerity to find the antiquarian book trade anxious and eager for stock. Sotheby's and Christie's were galloping forward in the fine art field, and both John and Sidney had more than enough to do in cataloguing and preparing sales to prevent their rivals from encroaching too far with rare volumes and literary property. The upshot was that Wilfrid took over the upstairs administration almost completely.

I never knew a man work harder, longer, or with such painstaking application. When I joined the firm a few years later it was already struggling hard to keep its head above water, and its palmy days were definitely over. The lion's share of the good books were going, more and more, to the now up-and-coming Sotheby's, and apart from the occasional valuable library and high spot, all we got was the residue. As the years went on, things did not improve. Had not the family owned the freehold of the building Hodgson's must have made a loss. The partners could never have afforded to rent such premises as well as accommodate wages and other overheads and still show a profit. I think that Wilfrid, almost single-handedly, kept us struggling on for nearly another twenty years.

He and I worked closely together for the whole of this time. Only a couple of paragons could have worked in such proximity day after day for so long without differences of opinion and the occasional devastating row. Paragon I certainly am not; Wilfrid came closer to being one in many respects. He was kind, considerate, and almost unbelievably honest. Vastly dissimilar as we were, I am amazed that we got on so well and worked together in such harmony, for the most part. We very rarely socialised in each other's company. While I made friends with booksellers and other buyers, he had his own select group of tennis-club and hockey-club friends in the Bromley district, but very, very few in our trade or among the book-collecting clients he served.

Between sales, when an enormous variety of callers passed through our portals, I was usually out in the Sale Room; Wilfrid was in his office, or downstairs. I acted as a sort of foil — or perhaps a sieve — and only the select got through to the inner sanctum. Although it was forever unspoken, Wilfrid was quite happy about this arrangement — or rather non-arrangement — I am quite sure. For over thirty years I encountered the most bizarre conglomeration of eccentrics, weirdies, kooks, and screwballs you could possibly imagine, quite apart from the normal callers. With very few exceptions, I enjoyed all these encounters. Wilfrid did not, and he was quite content to allow things to stay as they were.

We also had a very long-standing partnership on the rostrum during auctions. After John died in the early 'fifties, Sidney, who had begun to share taking the normal two-day sales with his son, suffered a rather bad attack of shingles, a nervous complaint no doubt brought on by his brother's death and the increased responsibility and work now thrust upon him. He tended to leave the actual auctioneering part of the business almost entirely to Wilfrid. Officiating in this position is no sinecure, I assure you. It calls for a high degree of confidence, alertness, and iron nerve, among other qualities. I have seen people, who thought the job was a doddle, get up there and try to do it. The result has often been a shambles.

Wilfrid Hodgson, a man whom I believe might have considered himself to be quite unsuited temperamentally to the position of auctioneer, over-came all obstacles and was remarkably successful. He was alert enough, but he lacked self-confidence and was not possessed of genuine iron nerve, and he forced himself into commanding a large roomful of strangers and often slightly hostile familiars. I think he had good reason to be rather proud of himself. I was proud of him, too.

It has been said that, compared with some other fast men with a gavel, he was a bit slow. This may be true, considering certain brash auctioneers only too anxious to get through an irksome chore. But it depends entirely upon your point of view. A buyer, usually a regular in the trade, waiting for that reluctant hammer to come down, often cursed him, but a vendor, sitting in the body of the room, and watching someone else take up the bidding and perhaps almost double what *might* have been the price, often blessed him.

He and I worked well together up there. While I insist that he was a good auctioneer, I must also say that he didn't remember many of his clients. If a complete stranger standing on the left side of the room bought lot number one and identified himself as Joe Bloggs, and then, perhaps half an hour later, happened to move to the right hand side of the room and start to bid again, he was *still* a complete stranger as far as Wilfrid was concerned. The man would either have to identify himself again, or else Wilfrid would mutter to me: 'Who's that?' If the unwitting Joe Bloggs decided to remove his hat during the course of a sale, or if he put one on, he was a stranger again.

For the most part, Wilfrid relied upon my memory of the sea of faces in the room, and more and more he came to leave this side of things to me. He never made very much of an attempt to retain a mental picture of a client's face or name, except the hardy annuals, and I was happy enough with such an arrangement.

But there is the reverse side to the coin. Although I don't think he could have done my job particularly well, I am absolutely certain that I couldn't have done his. It has often been said to me: 'Supposing Wilfrid was taken ill five minutes before the sale? Or what if his train broke down and he couldn't get up to town in time? There's nobody else handy. With all your experience you'd make a pretty good auctioneer in that chair.'

I disagree. I don't think I would, and I'm very glad that the occasion never arose. Having sat beside him for so many years, watching him work, I frequently wondered how the hell he did it.

Anything between fifty and a hundred men and women were sitting or standing facing him, with most of them looking directly at him. Naturally, when he called for an opening bid, he would first glance at the Pound, directly below him, for a starter, to bookselling representatives of Maggs, Edwards, Quaritch, Dawson, or Joseph, depending upon the nature of the books in the lot, but there must always be an opposing bidder. The vociferous ones, or the frantic wavers of catalogues, of course, are immediately obvious, but these are in the minority. Most bidders at auction don't want to be seen bidding. They do their best to keep the thing entirely between themselves and the man on the rostrum. Hundreds of times I watched Wilfrid Hodgson take bids from the body of the room, he noticing the merest nod of a head, the slightest flicker of an eyelid, the barest raising of a finger.

As bidding progressed, sometimes rather surprisingly, on a lot which most of us had reckoned no great shakes, I frequently tried to see which two would-be buyers were duelling. Just as frequently I failed. This could be because when the opening bids were made they were made fairly obviously, when my head was down and I was busily entering up details of the previous lot. This may well be so. Still, I did not envy Wilfrid Hodgson his job, and I never have done so — or any other auctioneer's job, for that matter. Each man to his own. I was a pretty good sale clerk, but I was not an auctioneer. Wilfrid was, and all things considered, I think he was among the best.

I have worked with a good many. Some were fast, authoritative, assured and very demanding. Others were slow, hesitant, unsure of themselves and of everyone else. They missed bids and reserves on the book before them, and they went through the sale as if in a dream. Wilfrid may not have been the fastest in the world, but he was certainly the most scrupulous. Everyone got a fair crack. I reiterate that the Conditions of Sale have always been clearly stated that in the event of a dispute the lot should be put up again: I never knew him to by-pass this rule or to show favour, although I have known others to do so.

During the whole of the nineteen-fifties, and for most of the 'sixties, the Hodgson firm and family employed me and paid my wages. I was very loyal to them, and I believe they recognised this. Looking at the whole deal quite dispassionately, I think that they probably got the better of the bargain. But, as I stressed earlier in this chronicle, I stayed because I liked what I was doing, and over the years I managed to do all right. I most definitely didn't remain just to oblige.

To wind up this section on the Hodgsons and the building in which we worked, there are just one or two things I should like to say concerning the way they and 115 Chancery Lane have gone down into history, and literary history particularly, although I doubt very much if any future historian in his delving would ever find them, or perhaps even consider them worthy of mention.

Arnold Bennett, as a young man, was a rather impoverished solicitor's clerk in Lincoln's Inn. During his lunch hours, he very often dropped into Hodgson's to search for books of French literature, of which he was particularly fond. He bought whatever he could afford at the sales, and built the foundations of his library during stolen hours in old Henry Hill Hodgson's day. You may read this in his little book, *The Truth About an Author*. Half a lifetime later, in the nineteen-twenties, he wrote that masterpiece, *Riceyman Steps*, which deals largely with a miserly Clerkenwell bookseller. Bennett had observed things closely in his early days, and the book auction house at which the bookseller buys his cheap bundles is most obviously Hodgson's, although Bennett located the sale room in the adjoining Fetter Lane.

Many years later, that eminent bookman and novelist, Frank Swinnerton, who had been a friend and protégé of Arnold Bennett's, set the scene of one of his books in Fetter Lane, too. The tale is called *Faithful Company*. It tells the story of a strange, Dickensian family publishing concern, and of how it affects all the lives of its several employees. I read this book with an uncanny fascination when I first encountered it, for here — and I have no idea how he did it — is a full-length portrait of Hodgson's, and some of those who worked there. Frank Swinnerton could never have known the place and its people terribly well, and he drew upon his imagination liberally, but how close he got to the bull's-eye!

Then there is one famous scene in Graham Greene's *The Ministry of Fear*, quite obviously set in Hodgson's Rooms, which he knew quite well, although he got his geography and topography all wrong. He put the big clock at the wrong end of the Sale Room, he located lot number one on the wrong side of the room, and he had a character spying out from the shelves towards a detective agency along Chancery Lane towards the Fleet Street end. You would have had to have had a neck about twenty yards long to do that. As it happens, there *was* a detective agency in the direction he indicated. But he put it on the wrong side of the road.

Finally, a word or two about an illustrious tenant. The adjoining premises, which were also part of the Hodgson property, next door to and partly above our Sale Room, had been rented to a firm of chartered accountants for a nominal sum for a considerable number of years. This firm was called Chenhalls and Co., and they specialised in looking after the affairs of writers, actors, and similar professional people. I always seemed to be bumping into well-known stage and film stars just outside our doors, and quite often some of these people, having concluded their business with the firm of Chenhalls, would drop into Hodgson's to view any books that might be on show. I have never ceased to be surprised at the number of actors who are either book-collectors proper, or who have taken up a profitable little sideline in dealing.

On reflection, I suppose this shouldn't be all that surprising. Some of those who earn good money while they are in work, are frequently unemployed for considerable spells. (One chap, a character-actor who is a household name and face, confessed to me that he didn't have a single job to do for eleven months out of twelve.) These people can hardly take full-time or even part-time jobs in offices or elsewhere, while waiting for their agents to ring them, but selling books by post from their homes is an ideal way of augmenting income while they are 'resting' or are 'at liberty'. The book job can be dropped almost immediately should a film part come along, and it can be picked up again just as quickly when things go slack.

Chenhalls and Co. seemed to be quite a famous firm, and lots of these people were on their files. They were very adept at sorting out the often tortuous affairs of some of their more eccentric and unbusinesslike clients. James Agate, the theatrical critic and journalist, who was forever in hot water with the Inland Revenue, makes one or two flattering references to 'the man Chenhalls' in an early *Ego*, and swore by his adroitness.

This was before the war, of course. In my time, that firm was run by other and younger people. Chenhalls himself had died in very unusual circumstances.

It appears that he bore an amazing resemblance to Winston Churchill, and wore similar headgear. He had had occasion to visit the neutral country of Portugal on business during the war, and a German agent in Lisbon thought he recognised him as the British Prime Minister. Word got back quickly to Berlin that Churchill was on neutral ground. Every move of Chenhalls was followed, and when he took a 'plane home to London a German fighter was on hand to intercept it. Chenhall's craft was full of eminent civilians, one among them being Leslie Howard, the famous actor and producer. Their 'plane was shot down over the Bay of Biscay, with the loss of everybody on board.

After I heard this story, many years ago, I related it once or twice to people whom I thought might be interested. It was laughed off as being too high-flown and fantastic to be true. I thus came to disbelieve the tale myself, but in the mid-nineteen-seventies a lady client came into Hodgson's to sell some property, and she gave her name as Chenhalls. I happened to mention that the firm in the adjoining premises bore the same rather uncommon name, and I asked if there was any connection. Yes, she said, she was a niece of old Chenhalls himself. She even knew of their connection with Hodgson and Co., which was why she had brought her property to our premises in the first place. She confirmed, too, that the story of the Winston Churchill-Chenhalls mistaken identity case was absolutely true.

I later met Ronald Howard, son of the ill-fated Leslie. This gentleman is another of that small clan of actors-cum-book-collectors-cum-dealers. The chance of further confirmation was too good to miss. His face was grim and his nod and comment were terse.

'Yes,' he said, 'but there's a lot more to the story.'

Unfortunately, he didn't proffer the rest, and I didn't pursue the matter.

The Job

Having written considerably about the people I worked for and the premises I worked in, perhaps I should now detail something of what I actually did for my living.

My specific job, the one for which I was primarily taken on, was to sit beside the auctioneer's rostrum at a raised desk, and to record all the prices and the names of the buyers as a sale progressed. These entries were made in a large, loose-leafed volume known as the Sale Book. At the same time I was to keep individual bills, or invoices, for each purchaser. These might carry one number and one price, or, in the case of firms like Maggs Bros., Joseph, Quaritch, Francis Edwards, or the Export Book Co., they might bear upwards of fifty or a hundred items. If a client came along to the desk during the sale and wished to settle his bill and clear what he had bought, I had to drop everything else, make a hasty calculation, take his cash or cheque, receipt his bill, and make an extra entry of the sum paid into my Sale Book.

One ear had to be cocked pretty attentively in case the auctioneer brought the hammer down a bit quickly on the current lot, naturally, but I soon got into the habit of this; it became second nature. I grew a bit disconcerted sometimes when people came up and started asking awkward questions, or wanted to pay for the previous sale as well, and sometimes the one before that.

During a sudden rush, when the porters had been busy attending to one or more clients, and I had just taken the cheque of another who was impatiently insisting that he had a train to catch, I have had to make a sudden dash from the desk, grab a book or two from the shelves, and thrust them into my tormentor's hands so that I could trot up again and catch the details of the next lot being knocked down. This was usually done more in order to rid myself of an irritant than in a spirit to oblige. I must record though, in passing, that the old hands, my dear friends I got to know among those men and women who attended auction sales regularly, and who fully appreciated the pressure and concentration under which all sale clerks normally work, would wait patiently until I had a second or two to attend to them, and would transact their business as unobtrusively as possible.

There was another particular distraction during the progress of a sale, but one usually far more pleasant. I very soon found out that numerous clients did not wish to spend the whole afternoon at Hodgson's, for various reasons, and would hand in commissions for us to bid on their behalf. Most of these 'marks', as they are known in the trade, went through to the auctioneer, to be entered up in his catalogue. But a select and discerning few gentlemen wanted nothing at all to do with any bosses handling their bids, and insisted upon either one of the porters or myself executing their commissions. Their reasoning was sound, I suppose. Generally speaking, it is felt that if an auctioneer holds your mark he might be tempted to open the bidding at your top figure, or at least one very close to it. On the other hand, an employee would open the bidding low, and would buy for his customer as cheaply as possible, since there was the possibility of a tip to come if the bid were successful.

As it happened, people got a straight deal at Hodgson's, and at most other reputable auction houses too, whether they left their commissions with the bosses or the hired help. It might not have looked so, at times, but you must always remember that there are the vendor's reserve figures to be taken into consideration. While I, an employee, was intent only upon buying for my man at as low a figure as I could, the auctioneer had always to look after the interests of both buyer *and* seller.

Yes, you got a fair crack of the whip with my firm, and some others, all things taken into consideration, but I can't say as much for several dubious enterprises — particularly some on the continent, where you always seem to buy at your top figure — whatever price you leave. I think this is why a great number of people had absolute confidence in Hodgson's over the years, and why a large proportion of the lots in any sale were always bought at either the desk or the rostrum. In this case, at least, honesty always proved to be the best policy.

Yes, I found this distraction a pleasant one. While it was yet another chore to attend to during the progress of a sale, I derived great satisfaction from buying advantageously for my clients, many of whom grew to be my friends and confidants over the years. Anything to come, materially, whether it was cash, a bottle of Scotch, cigarettes or tobacco, was never to be scorned, but I think I derived more enjoyment from an air letter out of the blue, quite literally, perhaps from a person I had never heard of in Australia, who said that Mr. So-and-so gave him my name and told him that I would look after his interests for him, and would I please bid up to such-and-such a figure on a particular lot?

Most people imagine that once an auction sale is over and done with, everything else is plain sailing: all you have to do is look forward to and prepare for the next one. In actuality, the sale itself is only the tip of the iceberg. (I am not speaking here at all of the *cataloguing* of properties; I am

concerned at the moment more with the administrative donkey work.)
The real graft of a sale comes afterwards, and it has to be done *immediately*
afterwards. In the present age of electronics and technology — two words,
by the way, which were in the dictionary but hardly in common use in my
young days — clerical workers have everything done for them by
machines. Many of them couldn't add up a short column of figures
correctly if their lives depended on it. As an old chap I used to know would
say disgustedly: 'Ask 'em to count up to more'n ten, an' they gotta take
their shoes an' socks orf!' Today, most auctions are aided by an ingenious
development known as the Solist System. It does all the work that is
necessary, and it is a godsend — until the computer breaks down. This is
not infrequent.

For all but part of one of the many auction seasons at which I officiated,
we all did the whole thing manually. First, once you had got rid of all petty
distractions like dallying clients intent upon doing deals with one another,
you had to total the book, and this had to agree with the tally on the
auctioneer's catalogue. Second, each of the bills had to be added up, and
these had to reach the same figure as both of the other totals. If these totals
didn't all balance — and they rarely did the first time of trying — you had
to keep at it until they did.

Why? — some people used to ask us — why all this bother? Why make
such a big deal of it? Well, for just one thing, and a very elementary one, at
that, you could sometimes have figures differing by several hundreds of
pounds. It has not been entirely unknown for an auctioneer to knock a lot
down for £2,000 and jot down the figure of £200. It was not an absolute
rarity, either, for me to note the correct digits in my book and then, in the
heat of the battle, switching to the bills, shove on an extra zero. Some
clients were rather put out, when they called for their bills while the sale
was in progress, to find a higher price than they had bid against a particular
lot, but they didn't appear to be nearly so affronted if I'd *dropped* a great
big and all important 0! A few never even mentioned it, and hoped it
wouldn't be noticed. It was, though, eventually.

This is why I have often worked very late into the evening, going over
things again and again, chasing the elusive digit. I used to wonder, years
ago, why banks always closed up so early in the afternoons. I soon
discovered that the employees inside didn't keep such short hours.

Well before the everyday use of that dirty word, inflation, and the
metrication of our currency, we had pounds, shillings and pence, and you
could advance as little as sixpence at an auction. The old tanner meant
something then, and if the man on the rostrum opened the bidding at ten
shillings, someone like Bernard Simpson, at that time working for the firm
of Joseph, would advance the bidding to half a guinea, which was ten and

sixpence. By degrees it would work up to a pound. The following bid was a guinea, or one pound and one shilling. The whole business then went up in bobs. It had to be a pretty good item up for sale, and worth quite a bit, before anyone started advancing in pounds. This meant that after the sale I had three columns of figures to add, instead of the later one, and it took all that much longer to do. It was not until the late 'sixties, when the firm of Sotheby's first occupied the Hodgson premises — which corresponded approximately with a devaluation of sterling — and both people and the press began to talk about inflation so frequently, that bidding at book auctions advanced by a minimum of one pound — and no less. (Note that I do not speak here of sales of paintings, fine jewellery, rare and valuable *objéts d'art*, and precious ceramics. I have no doubt that those concerned with the buying and selling of such merchandise raised a few eyebrows, but I do not think that they had worried much about tanners and bobs for quite a while.)

However, the pound minimum made the totalling and balancing of a book sale much simpler, but it was only to last for a matter of about ten years. Then came the controversial 'ten percent premium', about which I intend to expound later, in some detail. Just for the moment, I am more concerned about how it affected the humble clerk.

Briefly, whatever the price as that hammer came down, a purchaser had to pay the auctioneer one tenth more. We at the desk had to work it out mentally as we went along. £35 under the gavel meant £38.50 on the bill. If a client worked up the bidding to £1,750 on a good book he fancied, it was invoiced almost immediately at £1,925. And we had sales of three hundred lots, *plus*, at a time. So back again to two columns of addition. And — quite inevitably — minor errors of arithmetic crept in. Chaos is come again!

The moment a sale was over, I was usually inundated with a long queue of clients coming along to pay their bills. This was a normal procedure, and one not too difficult to handle. But there was invariably the odd man out. Looking back, I always tend to recall him as a composite figure I shall identify here as Dickie. I feel sure that many members of the book business will know the sort of person to whom I refer. He was an amiable eccentric, well-meaning, no doubt, but utterly thoughtless.

He would ask for his bill. I would hand it to him in the expectancy that he intended to pay, he would glance at it for checking, and the next client would move forward for my attention. Meanwhile, Dickie would tuck his bill into his pocket and walk off home. Later, after hours of trying to balance the books and the bills, we would eventually find one invoice missing. Dickie had an alternative gambit, by the way, when he did *not* walk off with his bill. It wasn't usually discovered until the next day, when the porters had to look out lots from the shelves, from all the remaining unpaid bills to hand. *His* lot would be missing, and if it was an expensive one, as it very often was, there would be a bit of a panic. Hours would be lost searching for the missing book. Finally, we would reluctantly telephone him, to inform the man that his purchase had somehow been mislaid. 'Oh,' he would tell us, quite blithely, 'not to worry. I've got it. I took it off the shelf!'

I could recount almost endless examples of methods by which customers prevented us from balancing after a sale, albeit unsuspectingly and unintentionally. Incorrect figures on their cheques is the one which first springs to mind, but it would be captious to stress such minor human failings. I made many a mistake, too. I should be very glad to have as many pounds in my pocket as the times I have made something like the following error: tired, dishevelled, dispirited, after having added the book and the bills for the umpteenth time, and been interrupted by telephone calls and distractions which never seemed to stop, we would find £1.12.6 in the book and £1.2.6 on the bill. Eureka! We'd been ten bob out in the balance.

Much of the foregoing, I am not unaware, may appear trite, mundane, and even dull and uninteresting. But it has not been recounted in detail without good cause. Many people have remarked to me on what a wonderfully interesting job I had, what with all those marvellous books on the shelves, the fascinating people I encountered, and the considerable drama of the average sale room cut and thrust. Well, I assure you that it wasn't roses *all* the way.

The simple, routine work of any sale clerk is, in all conscience, a humble one in itself. It is largely a bore, and it is undertaken in most auction houses by men or women who have no particular interest or enthusiasm in what they are doing. They grind away at their chores in some small office for most of their time, and for a brief but rather hectic period of an hour or two beside the auctioneer at the rostrum during the actual sale itself they come into contact with the public. They then retire to those same small offices again to pore over their bills and columns of figures. They have enough to occupy themselves without having to deal with individuals who walk in after a sale is over, who not only wish to pay for and clear their purchases but who are more often than not quite ready to talk about the wonderful buys they have made to any sympathetic listener — and often unsympathetic ones who don't care a toss. Ninety-nine out of a hundred sale clerks are content to leave the auction room assistants and porters to the volubility of the clients and to get down to the exacting work of figuring and totalling in quiet and privacy.

When I started, I would have preferred things this way. I frankly admit it. This job was quite new to me. My main concern was earning my six quid a week and getting through the day in order to attend to far more important things at home. Since balancing the sale was of the utmost importance, a modicum of quiet, concentration, and solitude were very necessary. But these things were denied me, for there was no small office to which I could retire. *My* office was the vast Sale Room, into which came all and sundry at odd times of day, and the desk at which I worked between sales was the very same one at which I laboured by the rostrum *during* sales.

It took me quite a time to cotton on to the fact that while I had been employed nominally as Sale Clerk, with capital letters to the title, I was really a General Factotum. In short, I was the man on the spot. No matter who walked in, whether he might be a client to clear his purchases, a gentleman with a book left to him by an old aunt who had told him it was worth thousands, or just the lonely and wandering eccentric who had nothing better to do than drift into an auction house and chat to a captive audience, I was his target.

In the long run, it all proved to be an asset and a boon, for remember that I first applied for this job because I was keen on books. Also, I have always got on pretty well with most of mankind.

If my only job had been to officiate as a clerk at the sales, and little or nothing else, I would have had a sinecure, indeed, at Hodgson's. In the years well before I arrived, they had held a three-day sale *every week*, and had retained a staff to match it. The sale clerk, then, had his work cut out to do a single task. But by the time I arrived it was more like a two-day sale every month, and with employees down to the minimum. Nobody did one job, and one job alone. Cataloguers naturally spent most of their time cataloguing, but if one of them happened to live in a district not too far from the home of a client who had written in about a library for sale, he dropped in and had a look at the books on his way to work. And if the property arrived, in perhaps a dozen tea-chests, when the porter was at lunch or out on another job, the cataloguer dropped his cataloguing and became a porter for the nonce. Porters could not so easily transform themselves into cataloguers, yet I have known those of an ambitious and enterprising nature who did so, and who made a pretty good fist of it.

I soon found that I was expected to do a multitude of various jobs between sales. Well, why not, I felt, as long as they paid me? I was there for eight hours a day. First, I was entrusted with the Petty Cash almost as soon as I joined the firm! I thought this remarkably trusting, since nobody knew me all that well, and I *could* have absconded. Second, I kept a cash book, I handled all incoming monies, and I paid regularly into the firm's bank; this, by the way, at a time when I didn't even aspire to a bank account myself. Third, I ran an enormous Debtors' Ledger, a vast, suede-covered folio tome which carried the details of the dealings of everybody who had ever had a credit account at Hodgson's for donkeys' years. I imagine that those clerical characters of Charles Dickens sat on their rickety stools and made entries into something similar. It had been in use long, long before I arrived at Chancery Lane, as I have suggested; I worked with it for eighteen years, and there was *still* room in it for further entries when the premises passed to Sotheby's, and a new method was employed.

The amazing thing about all this, to me, is that most of the jobs I had to do were connected with figures. I had not the very slightest knowledge of book-keeping at first. I had never been particularly good at anything at school, and my worst subject had been mathematics. I had always hated adding up columns of figures, and usually got them wrong when I had to. And here I was, doing a job which, primarily, demanded that I balance a book of some three hundred lots against bills containing the same number, and secondarily, expected me to keep account of all money that was due to the firm and all outgoing expenses.

I was appalled by the idea at first, and I felt that I could never cope. Well, I did cope. After a few years, when I grew proficient and sufficiently confident, I was able to point out to my employers that from time immemorial, apparently, they had been doing things all arse-upwards, so to speak. The Debit columns in the ledger were on the Credit side, and vice versa. What the auditors thought of it I never knew, but they never said anything.

In addition to my other tasks, I was put in charge of all catalogue subscriptions. Subscribing to *any* auctioneer's catalogues for a year now-adays is something not lightly undertaken: purchasing an individual copy of one is expensive enough, and it is amusing to recall that in the immediate post-war years the annual subscription to Hodgson's catalogues was five shillings — and half a crown only if you were in the trade. A few of the regular old buyers jibbed at being asked to pay, since all catalogues had been sent free of charge before the war. People like Jack and Sam Joseph made a token gesture of protest every year, but they stumped up reluctantly. On more than one occasion I told them that if they refused to pay they were still sure to receive their catalogues, for the firm could not afford to lose their custom, but they always paid in the end.

There was plenty of other work to do, too, should I ever find myself unoccupied. All this time I was handling and learning about books, and I grew to know an incredible number of dealers and collectors. I wrote or typed their names and addresses so often in my various chores that very soon these became engraved in my memory, and in the end there were very few that had to be checked from either subscription list or directory. If only I could have remembered title-pages, dates of publication, and current prices at auction as I remembered street numbers, postal codes, and telephone numbers!

As for the more physical side of the business, the porters, nominally, were responsible for sending up the books in the hand-operated hydraulic lift, and setting them on the shelves in numerical order for a forthcoming sale. But if the packer-cum-porter was busy with his parcels or tea-chests, and the viewing days were not too far off, I took off my coat and buckled down to the heavy graft of humping volumes.

One of my troubles was that I was over-conscientious, I suppose, but I was young and energetic as well. Further, I have always had a guilty feeling that I had a tendency towards laziness, and I didn't like this feeling. I forced myself to work in order to banish it, and in the end I finished up working harder than might have been absolutely necessary.

But I was a bit of a softie, too. Bimbo, the portly old Sale Room Assistant, found it increasingly difficult to climb ladders and to lift heavy books as the months went by. His breath grew shorter and shorter. Any observer would have had to have possessed a heart of steel to watch that old man puffing and wheezing for very long without coming to his aid. When Tom, the misanthropic numberer in the basement, went absent in his final illness and eventually died, Bimbo went downstairs and took over his work. Nobody asked him to, as far as I know, but it had to be done. So the books, in numbered lots, still came up in the lift, and I drifted into the more-or-less permanent job of getting them on to the shelves. Authority must have noticed that things continued to work quite smoothly, and for a long time Tom was not replaced. His wages were saved, I assume, for certainly we others did not get them.

Today I am rapidly approaching the same age and condition of some of these old men I have written about. Before I was finally pensioned off, I am glad to say that there were still one or two brawny youngsters about the place, still willing to lend a hand if I looked rather helplessly at a book I wanted on a high shelf, and still ready to push me aside and lift a folio with one hand while it was taking me all my strength to raise it with two.

Thirty years ago it was a quite different matter. My energy, enthusiasm, and conscience were abundant and very evident. I recall little old Jim, that ancient gnome, sitting on his stool by the fireplace, and watching me trundle a tall and heavy trolley of books past him with great effort and difficulty. He looked up and gave me a cynical grin.

'You *like* work, don't you?' he said.

*   *   *

I have now been reading, writing, illustrating, or otherwise dealing with books for something over fifty years, all told. I don't think there is another person in our trade with even half my length of service who knows *less* than I do about the finer points of the wares we are all handling. That rather sweeping statement is not a daft amalgam of false modesty and bravado: due to a combination of circumstances it happens to be a fact.

Even so, nobody can spend the length of time that I have done among books without picking up a fair general knowledge of them. And compared with that unfortunate, overworked, and oft-quoted 'man-in-the-street', of course, I must seem like a walking encyclopaedia.

But I remember my father-in-law, who was an educated and literate man, saying to me after I had been only two or three years in the antiquarian book business proper with Hodgson's, and had let drop such terms as half-title, quarto, and straight-grained morocco: 'I suppose by this time there must be very little you don't know about books?' He was perfectly serious; I must have blinded him with science! I couldn't help laughing.

When in my blithe ignorance, I replied to that advertisement for something called a Sale Clerk with a firm of book auctioneers, I really did think I knew a bit about the subject. Ah, I told myself, *this* is my cup of tea. But I hadn't been at the job more than a day or two before I realised *how* blithe, and how abysmal, my ignorance was. How very little I knew! And how much more there was to learn!

Thirty-two years later, as I write, still never a day passes without a renewed confirmation of my appalling lack of bibliographical knowledge and the amount still left to learn — and the amount most of the rest of us have left to learn, too, for that matter.

As I said earlier, my very pleasant job, primarily, was to deal with *people*, rather than with the commodity we all handled. I happen to like people very much, most of them in general and individuals in particular. And so, while I fear that my knowledge of books must forever remain limited now, I don't know of any other person who has a wider acquaintance among the men and women who buy, sell, read, write, steal and vandalise books than I have.

I spent most of my working lifetime in a large and very draughty room. It was shelved from floor to ceiling, and it was usually packed with a variety of ever-changing volumes. It was, first of all, an auction sale room, but it was also the spot where all the inspection was done on the official preceding viewing days. It happened to be a reception room for experienced vendors, too, as well as for somewhat apprehensive prospective sellers of literary property. Such properties ranged from the undesirable 'very, very *old*' Family Bible of the last century almost to the extremely desirable but — alas — never-encountered *Gutenberg Bible* of a few centuries earlier. This room was an unofficial but accepted clubroom and general meeting-house for booksellers and their clients, and also for that ever-growing and admirable breed of young dealers generally known as 'runners'. (I would call the crop of our present generation 'trotters': they certainly cover less ground, and they appear to make more money than did some of their energetic and itinerant predecessors.)

This room was my only office. Like some latter-day Bob Cratchit, with ball-point or felt pen in place of quill, but far happier in my work, I am quite sure, I sat perched upon a high chair at my scarred and sloping mahogany desk. Raised above the groundlings, who jostled, viewed and conversed, I advised and observed. If you have the imagination to forget strip-lighting and central-heating, blessings which were eventually introduced in the fullness of time, the whole atmosphere was still not far removed from the Dickensian.

Towards the end of his life, that delightful bookseller, Eric Osborne, contributed a monthly auction review to *Books and Bookmen*. On one occasion, in the early 'seventies, commenting upon the large number of people present at a particularly interesting and diverse sale, and the unusual variety of new bidders and successful buyers, he remarked: 'Even the normally omniscient Mr. Snelling had to leave his desk once or twice to check names and addresses.' A friend of mine, reading the article, seized upon this sentence.

'Ah!' he said. 'Omniscient! So *now* we know what the O in O.F. Snelling stands for!' Between the pair of them, they managed both flattery and a cherished compliment.

Over the years I have met and made friends with a host of interesting and mostly delightful people who have loved books. I am still meeting them, every day. Increasingly, I find that I tend to dredge up memories of bookmen now long gone. I should like to tell you about a few of them.

Here's a pretty interesting character for a start.

Old Jim

Jim was a diminutive cockney porter who spent no fewer than seventy years in the book trade, from start to finish with Hodgson's. He was fourteen years old at the beginning and eighty-four at the end. I would go so far as to say that more volumes passed through his hands than through those of any man of his time, but right to the last he didn't know one book from another (This is with the possible exception of sets of *Law Reports*. He put so many volumes of these in numerical order, and humped so many from the Temple and Lincoln's Inn to Chancery Lane and then back again after the sale to a new owner, that he probably experienced, with a shudder, 'the shock of recognition'.)

He could read and write, when he had to, but he kept such activities to the very minimum. I doubt if he ever read a book right through, and I don't think he wished to. Portering the damned things to and fro, and stacking enormous piles of them in the dark corners and recesses of the basement was the only contact he wanted with books, and he wasn't particularly fond of that. John Pashby, who started a long career of cataloguing with Hodgson's in the nineteen-twenties, and then went on to Sotheby's until his retirement ten years ago, knew Jim when the man was only in early middle age. The little fellow had already formed his opinions at that stage. Pashby tells of Jim's own version of *The Charge of the Light Brigade*:

> Books to the left of 'em —
> Books to the right of 'em.
> Look at the *'ight* of 'em!
> Sick o' the *sight* of 'em.

He was the filthiest man I ever met in my life. Although I only knew him for his last decade or so, admittedly, and he may well have been much cleaner in his younger days, on only one occasion could I honestly say that Jim had washed. He was due to visit a doctor later in the day, and he had given himself a lick and a polish. The change was so obvious that it was alarming. He looked positively ill. His face was several shades paler than normal.

Over the years I got to know him pretty well, although I don't think he ever fully accepted me. During a seventy-year period in one job, he saw lots of faces come and go. I have an idea that Jim tended to look upon me as one of these young fly-by-nights, even after about ten years.

However, we often worked together in close proximity — I caught a flea from him in 1953 — and once drawn out he would reminisce until the cows came home. I usually worked at the desk by the high rostrum, in the Sale Room, and two or three feet from it there used to be an open fireplace. In winter, when a coal fire was blazing there, Jim would up-end a tea-chest beside it, to serve as a table, and plonk himself on to his tiny stool behind it and proceed to fold newly-delivered catalogues into addressed wrappers. What with the book dust and dirt on his hands, and the paste he spread so liberally, I have often wondered what some of the subscribers must have thought on receipt of their catalogues, with all the smears, the thumb-prints, and the tobacco-ash.

This was one of his regular chores. I remember watching him on one occasion and saying: 'I'll bet you wish you had a penny for every one of those you've wrapped,' and he looked up at me with a wry grin.

'Wisht I 'ad a *farden*!'

Jim perennially smoked a filthy short clay pipe, for some reason always upside-down. He also smoked an equally filthy dark brown shag. It hissed and bubbled as he worked and talked, and periodically he would take a mouthful of nicotine juice and punctuate his conversation by spitting into the fire.

He told me that he had first come to Hodgson's in response to an advertisement, when he was an urchin printer's devil, at the age of fourteen. He had stood outside the office, or Counting House as it was then known, while another young cockney applicant was being interviewed. Jim related this story in the self-same spot, and he pointed. Right below the rostrum was a sort of large U-shaped table. In some auctioneers' sale rooms this is known, with perhaps unconscious irony, as the Ring. In Chancery Lane it was always called the Pound, deriving, no doubt, from the old cattle auctions, where the beasts for sale were herded. All the leading London booksellers sat around our Pound while an auction sale was in progress, and a small youth was employed to stand within this U and show each book as it came up for sale. The smaller the lad the better. This was the vacancy for which Jim had applied, and it was known in the firm as the Pound Job.

When the previous young applicant came out from the Counting House, Jim accosted him and quite naturally asked him what it had been like inside.

'Seven shillin's a week they're offerin',' he was told. 'Seven bloody bob a week, they tell me — "But of course, you'll be doing the Pound Job." Sod that for a lark, mate. I ain't takin' no seven shillin's for a pound job!'

Jim went in for his interview, knowing nothing about the Pound itself, of course, at that time. He was accepted, at seven shillings a week, and was glad to get employment. I have seen the original note-book, in which all such entries of new employees were made. 'Eight shillings a week, eventually, if he suits.' Jim suited for seventy years.

During the nineteen-fifties, I was privileged to hand him his pay-envelope, with full details and all deductions appended on the outside. They were so plain that I could not ignore them. Three pounds one shilling. It took him seventy years to reach this wage bracket. In fairness, I should add that I lived on three pounds a week myself in the 'forties, and it was a fairly average wage for an unskilled labourer or porter living in humble circumstances.

When I first came to Hodgson's Rooms, I was somewhat impressed by its Dickensian atmosphere, but far more by the imposing Law Society building hard by, and much more by the ornate Public Records Office building almost directly opposite us. This seemed to have been there since time began. Old Jim once told me that he had stood in our portals and had watched it being built!

Jim seemed to me so old that he often amazed me with some of his reminiscences. For instance, he actually remembered Charlie Chaplin as a boy, tap-dancing on the pub cellar-flaps in Lambeth for ha'pennies and pennies. Jim was at that time a fully-grown man — all four-foot nine of him.

In his youth he had been a professional boxer, bashing away at some other under-sized and under-nourished youngster after normal working hours at Hodgson's, to augment his small income with an extra bob or two. He cheerfully admitted to me that he never won a fight in his life. He didn't particularly want to. Glory and fame in the ring were not for him: he went in with both fists, put up a courageous and exciting battle which had the spectators on their feet, and then went round the house, bloody-nosed and sweating, for 'nobbins'. In this way, after a spirited exhibition, he could often pick up more than his purse-money, which was about half-a-crown. His pugilistic career came to an end when he turned up for work at Hodgson's one morning with a black eye. After authority had demanded how he had come by it, and was told, it was not a case of *The Ring and the Book*, but the ring *or* the book. Jim retired from boxing.

But although his own fighting career came to nothing, he was able, proudly, to inform me of how, in his time, his Lambeth street had boasted four British champions! I forget the names of two of them now. Johnny Curley was the third, I remember. The fourth, but first chronologically, was Jem Smith. This unsavoury character fought his last important battle in 1889 — with the bare knuckles! — versus the Australian, Frank P. Slavin. I had often read about him, and I had always thought of him as being as prehistoric as the dinosaur. Jim had actually known him.

The old man put in a lifetime of service for the firm of Hodgson's, and for the most part he worked hard. But for at least the last ten years of his life he was little more than a working pensioner. Hodgson's was a paternal firm, in the best sense of that expression. They hardly ever sacked anybody, and they would never 'put them off'. Jim would have had his wages until the day he died, during his declining years, had he never even put in an appearance at Chancery Lane except on pay-day. But he lived in a one-room hovel on the other side of the river, with a dog under the bed and himself under the feet of a nagging wife. Besides, coal wasn't cheap in winter. He found it more convenient to walk from Lambeth every morning, across Waterloo Bridge and along the Strand to Chancery Lane, and there to sit all day before a small electric fire on his nine-inch-high stool in the far corner of what was known as the Front Room. Period- ically, certain members of the trade would come in to view the books which were on show for a forthcoming auction — Harold Edwards, Jack Joseph, Gus David of Cambridge, Graham Pollard in the days when he was a dealer — and few of them would leave without dropping in to see old Jim in the Front Room, pay him their respects and hand him a shilling or two, mostly for old times' sake and long-past services.

By all the rules, Jim should have died in young manhood of malnutrition, at the very least, and he once told me a story of how he had attended hospital in his early days with a chest complaint and had been told that he had 'got the consumption' — Lambethese for tuberculosis — and a dreaded killer, with no known cure at that time. 'But I'm still 'ere,' he said with a grin. He brought up a brood of children, and he buried either three or four wives — I don't know the precise number. I do know that the last one buried *him*.

And when I learned that his local hospital was St. Thomas's, just across the Thames from the Houses of Parliament, it once amused me to work out that it is more than highly probable that one of the medical students who tapped his chest in the out-patients' department, and who as a fledgling doctor strode through the Lambeth streets at night with his little black bag as a guarantee against mugging, to deliver one or another of Jim's numerous offspring, could have been a certain young man by the name of William Somerset Maugham. The novelist has described his student days graphically in two of his books, *Liza of Lambeth* and *Of Human Bondage*. The dates certainly fit.

As far as I could ascertain, Jim's staple diet was brown ale and toasted cheese. Round about midday, in the Sale Room, a savoury smell would come wafting out from the Front Room, and anyone sufficiently inquis- itive to penetrate that region could discover little Jim on his low stool before his tiny electric fire, with his couple of bread and margarine 'doorsteps' and a thick wedge of cheddar at the end of his pen-knife hissing and spluttering away at the element. After lunch he dozed before that tiny fire, and once, at the age of about eighty-three, he weaved and nodded, and finally fell full upon it. He burned his cheek rather badly, and we were all very much concerned. But he was back at work the next day.

And sometimes, as he grew older, there would be no sound or motion from him for hours, particularly in the mornings. 'Is Jim all right?' I might ask Lew Atkinson, the packer. The reply was usually the same, shrewd and accurate: 'Boozer's gloom.' The old man was doing penance with a hangover after a hard night on the brown ale.

Jim spent much of his life at the top of enormous ladders, either putting books up on the high shelves or taking them down. Bundles of books had always to be carried up, naturally, and in the early days I imagine they were carried *down*. Not so in my experience in his old age. Jim had perfected the technique of dropping bundles of books from a height of about twenty feet or more without bruising a corner! But I don't think the purchasers of those books would have appreciated the technique had they ever seen it in action.

He was well over eighty when I saw him miss his footing at the top of a ladder. He fell as cleanly and as solidly as those bundles I had seen him drop. And Jim didn't bounce. I thought he had killed himself, or at the very least had broken a bone or two. Miraculously, he was entirely unhurt. He got up and carried on as if nothing untoward had happened.

I notice that David Low, who had known Jim when both had been employed in the basement at Hodgson's back in the 'twenties, in his book, *with all faults*, refers to the old man as a little hunchback. Here David was mistaken. Jim grew a bit round-shouldered in his old age, but nothing more. David admits that he remembers the man mainly trundling up the stairs and shuffling along the bare-boarded floors bowed over by two vast coal-buckets on his way to replenish the open fires which blazed away in winter, and formed a wrong impression.

Yet Jim was certainly little. Before the 1914 war, somebody had given him a cast-off frock coat. These items of apparel, which reached to the knees of most wearers, were at that time *de rigueur* among the professional men in the City. When Jim put it on, his hands were lost somewhere near its elbows, and the skirts flapped round his ankles. He simply cut down the sleeves to suit him and wore the thing for years as an overcoat!

He seemed to grow tinier as the years passed. Our swing-doors, which led into the Sale Room, were mahogany for about the first five feet upwards, and were then glass. From my desk you could look through as far as the street, and usually see anyone approaching along the hall. But many a time, when things were very quiet, and I worked with only the tick of the big clock to break the silence, I would suddenly see those swing-doors open as if of their own accord. Then in would drift the tiny figure of little Jim, whose head, becapped, never reached high enough to be seen through the glass upper half of the doors.

His real name was not Jim. It was Bill Hearn. When he was first taken on, the boss had asked him his first name.

'Bill,' he said.

'Oh, we've already got a Bill here,' he was told. 'We'll call you Jim.'

A few months later another young porter was engaged. He was named, truly, but incredibly, Jim Hearndon!

'What's your first name?' he was asked.

'Jim.'

'H'm...we can't have that. We've already got a Jim. We'll call *you* Tom.'

So for the rest of their working lives together, Bill Hearn and Jim Hearndon were known as Jim and Tom respectively.

In these enlightened days it is difficult for youngsters to understand why the Jims and the Toms accepted conditions of this sort — to the extent of being re-christened by their masters. Today, you have only to say a wrong word to a sensitive young book porter and he will tell you to stuff your job, and he will go off elsewhere. If he doesn't find another position in the near or immediate future he certainly won't starve.

But the Jims and the Toms grew up in a Victorian age, at a time when they felt themselves extremely lucky to find regular work, whatever the wages and whatever the demeanment. They stuck to their jobs at all costs. I am young, by comparison, but the dole money in my early manhood, if you were out of work, was eighteen shillings a week. I don't know how unemployed married men with families managed at all. People like Jim, in their old age, when they saw all around them evidence of a new affluent society and the emergence of a welfare state, were still suspicious of it and too set in their ways to change. Jim was humble and obeisant in the extreme, to the very last days of his life. Several times, on Friday afternoons, I would find him hanging about the office door, only a yard or two from where I worked myself, and this was so unusual that I would ask him what he was up to. He would jerk his head towards the office, or the Counting House, as only he still called it.

'Me wages,' was his explanation, which he gave with a resigned scowl. 'The guv'nors is in there, studyin' their books.'

The agreement and understanding, apparently, was that on Fridays he would be paid at about four o'clock, and could get off early to pick up his old age pension pittance before his local post office closed. Nine weeks out of ten there was no problem. But should there be a visitor in that office, behind a closed door, or if, for some reason, there was a conclave within, and he had been overlooked, old Jim would stand there or mooch about like a well-trained dog who has learned that he should have a bone at this time but mustn't bark or he might lose it altogether.

In all fairness, I must admit that when I tumbled to the situation, and on several occasions more or less burst in and diplomatically enquired: 'Have you forgotten Jim?', the guv'nors were always most contrite and apologetic about the whole business. The paymaster was positively embarrassed. It was just that there were more pressing problems at the moment, and that it was Friday afternoon had been entirely forgotten.

Jim talked to me about former pay-days, donkeys' years before. In the old days, you worked on till about eight in the evening for most of the week. Saturday was different. You not only knocked off early — four o'clock! — that was when you got your money. At about five minutes to four you all lined up in front of the office door and waited for the big pay-out. But if anything untoward was happening within you just waited. If the bosses forgot, you still just waited, until in the course of time somebody either remembered or came out for some reason and saw you waiting. You never knocked and demanded what was rightfully yours.

That had been the position with old Jim in the latter decades of the nineteenth century. It was still the same halfway through the twentieth.

Fred Karno's Army

Gordon Wright was a very young man who started work at Hodgson's in the year 1929, at the princely sum of one guinea per week. I never knew him very well, for he had left the place long before I arrived, but I recognise him as having been an extraordinary and capable man. (I don't think the Hodgson brothers were aware of this when they engaged him, but he had attended the Stationers' School, so as far as Sidney was concerned the lad was a white-haired boy from his initial interview.)

I understand that Gordon began more or less as an office boy and junior clerk. He later went downstairs into the basement and developed into a good cataloguer. He left the firm and went to work for a London bookseller in the nineteen-forties, and eventually he became an extremely successful bookseller in his own right. It was over fifty years after he had first started with Hodgson's, in a letter to another old Chancery Lane *alumnus*, David Low, that he waxed reminiscent about some of the strange characters he had encountered, and the unlikely occurrences that he had experienced during his days with the firm. I saw that letter, and one sentence in it sticks in my memory.

'I could write a book on the Fred Karno happenings,' he said, 'but no-one would believe me today.'

I would — *every word*. After all, I knew many of the odd-bods and eccentrics he had worked with myself. But his relatively brief tenure, interrupted by the war years, did not really compare with my own lengthy stay at those premises. I had the privilege and leisure to watch a never-ending parade of comedy characters he never even knew. And a Fred Karno's Army it was, indeed. I thank Gordon Wright for quite unwittingly giving me an ideal heading to this section on some of the Hodgson employees who passed through 115 Chancery Lane.

When I first joined the firm most of the other people there appeared to be permanent fixtures. Old Jim had then put in about sixty years, and was to serve quite a few more yet. Tom Wheaton, that surly old curmudgeon, wasn't far behind him, with about sixty years to *his* credit. Of the cataloguers, Alfred Sims, another sore-head, had chalked up some thirty-five or more. Millward, the Sale Clerk before last, had had a similar term. Lew Atkinson, the very efficient packer, was something of a new boy: he had only done about a quarter of a century. Abie Osborne, who died shortly before I arrived, had still been in harness after two score. I knew of him only as the truculent and domineering Head Porter. Thornton, the Confidential Clerk, another man I never knew, had spent what was virtually a lifetime in the Counting House.

'Our employees seem to stay with us for a long time,' old John Hodgson had told me at my interview, intimating that the conditions of his domain must obviously be very congenial, and that if I came I would want to stay, too.

I did. But after Tom and Jim died, the rot seemed to set in. The new and younger cataloguers, for the most part, could not exactly be called transient, for both Martin Orskey and Alex Rogoyski, lads a few years younger than myself, stuck it for fifteen and twelve years respectively. But I now seem to look back on many of the staff who followed the old Victorians and Edwardians as a succession of fleeting grotesques and eccentrics. There *were* some fairly normal employees, naturally, but the Hodgson family seemed to possess an uncanny knack of taking on the most outrageous odd-balls.

I have never kept any regular sort of diary or journal in my life, so I cannot list these people in strict order of arrival or departure. I must try to rely on my memory.

Alfred Sims had long been in residence as the senior cataloguer in 1950. He was a white-haired man in his late sixties, quiet and uncommunicative. He never mixed socially with any of us, and at first he rarely spoke to me. We were never introduced, but after several months he would start drifting upstairs very occasionally, button-holing me at my desk and airing his grievances. Only very recently did I learn that many years previously he had been given the opportunity to move on to Sotheby's, a firm who even then was showing signs of developing into the enormous and influential concern it was to become. But John Hodgson had somehow talked Sims out of the idea of changing jobs, and when the chance was gone, the man had seen that he had made a mistake. He regretted it for the rest of his life. He felt that Hodgson's had held him back, and he did not look upon the members of that family very kindly.

As a young man Sims had begun his career among books as an assistant librarian in a south coast town. Among his colleagues there had been another young man, one Edgar Osborne. While Sims had come to London and had spent a short period with the famous bookselling firm of Henry Stevens, Son and Stiles before moving on to his long sojourn at Chancery Lane, Osborne had stayed in librarianship, and not only had he carved a successful niche for himself in a very good job at Derby, but he had grown quite famous as the collector of one of the very finest accumulations of children's books ever put together. After his retirement he would often come into Hodgson's to negotiate the sale by auction of certain rare books he had bought advantageously. Old Sims would have been blind indeed not to have compared his own situation with that of his erstwhile colleague. If he wasn't jealous, he was certainly envious. For some reason, his employers bore the brunt of this, too.

He very strongly resented Sidney editing his copy. With a good book or an unusual binding he was inclined to spread, and give it a good description, but his employer, ever aware of printing costs, would blue-pencil his cataloguing drastically. While John Hodgson was alive Sims could always go to him with a petty grievance here and there, and the senior partner would often side with him. But after the old man died, Sims found himself without an ally, and with Sidney and his son, Wilfrid, actively in opposition to him. He brooded and festered.

There came the time when he had a particularly large property to catalogue of the most dull and uninteresting quarto and folio volumes of theology, all in dusty and broken calf. The task seemed never-ending. He slogged at it for day after day and for week after week, and he grew more morose and nervous as the time passed. The poor old chap must have had nightmares about those books. But eventually the moment came when the whole lot had all been written down, and he was able to give a sigh of relief. But almost to the minute, as he turned to apply himself to more interesting things, the chute flap opened, there was a vanful of the same sort of thing, sent in from Maggs Bros., and down the slide came hundreds upon hundreds of dry and dirty old folios. Alfred Sims put on his hat and coat and tottered off home to a complete breakdown.

I must say that his employers sympathised. They really felt sorry for him, although Sidney could not forbear a chuckle at the funny side of it all, as he explained it to me. But it wasn't quite so amusing as the months went on and Sims showed no signs of returning. His wages were being sent to him every week, and Sims seemed quite content with the *status quo*. But it could not go on forever, and finally Wilfrid wrote to him and asked if he had any intention of *ever* coming back to work. Only then did Sims put in a reappearance, but he had ideas.

At the age of almost seventy he started looking about for another job! This might never have come to anything, had not he seen an advertisement in *The Clique* for the position of curator of the Gilbert White Natural History Museum at Selborne. He applied, and despite his age, he was successful! But first he went to the Hodgsons, and made all sorts of outrageous demands and stipulations if they wanted him to stay on at Chancery Lane.

This marked one of the very few occasions I ever saw Sidney put out. I recall his exact expression.

'The man's quite impossible! He's holding a gun to our heads — *and* in the middle of the season!'

This was the ultimate insult. For Sims to let them down and threaten to walk out while so much was still to be done was what really cooked his goose. Although it was extremely inconvenient, and getting anybody to replace him was not going to be easy, the bosses simply refused to discuss it with him. They let him go.

Alfred Sims did not stay very long at Selborne. It was already common knowledge within the book trade that the gentleman to whom he was answerable there, and with whom he would come into close contact, was rather impossible himself. It was generally agreed that Sims would not be able to stick it for long. Sure enough, in only a matter of months back he came, cap in hand, so to speak, and with his tail definitely between his legs.

He could not have picked a worse moment. It was the day of a sale, the auction was just over, and everybody — porters, cataloguers, and all clerical staff — were up to their ears in work and harrassment. Nobody had a moment to spare for him, and old Sidney was trotting about all over the building in an effort to get away. He finally went downstairs and locked himself in the lavatory until he had been told that Sims had gone!

Poor old Alfred. He didn't last very long after that. The balance of his mind became disturbed, and within a short time he passed away.

John Hodgson was still alive and fairly active when he interviewed an impressive and very respectable-looking man of middle age, so this would have been in 1950 or early 1951. Their conversation took place in the Sale Room, where I was working, and I heard every word. The gentleman had called on behalf of his son, who was interested in books and wished to make his livelihood among them. Big Daddy was a prepossessing figure: here I had my initial experience of how easily any member of the kindly, trusting, but gullible Hodgson family could be conned. The son had the job sewn up for him well before he himself came in for his token interview. With hindsight, I can see now that the young man could never have landed a job on his own initiative, even with the Hodgsons.

I never did know the boy's first name, but for the purposes of this narrative I shall call him Luke. He arrived late for his interview, and shuffled in breathlessly and with apologies. Despite this, he was taken on, and was requested to report for work on the following Monday. He arrived late again, on his very first working day. I cannot recall now exactly how long he stayed with us: it was certainly several months, but *never once* reported on time. Indeed, he turned up later and later each day. Our hours were nine-thirty to five-thirty: I am not exaggerating in the slightest when I say that I frequently saw him arrive — in a taxi, no less — at about four-thirty or five o'clock.

He always had a brand new excuse for his tardiness, as far as the guv'nors were concerned. I think that they were just as embarrassed about the whole business as he was, otherwise he could never have lasted as long as he did, and it wasn't all *that* long.

To the other employees he confessed that he was simply incapable of waking up on time. His life must have been sheer hell when he was in the army, and I imagine that most of the period he spent in uniform he was 'on jankers'. Now, in peace-time, dwelling alone in a bed-sitter, and living much alone — which is often an entirely different thing — he spent most of his solitary leisure in the cinemas. It never occurred to him, apparently, to have what we usually refer to as an early night. If I am mistaken, and it did occur to him, obviously he couldn't drop off. But when he *did* eventually do so, he couldn't wake up! Things got to the point where he lived a waking life all night and slept all day.

Had the Hodgsons tolerated him a little longer — for it literally got to the point where we were all knocking off as he arrived — it is just possible that things would have turned full circle. Luke could have awakened so late after his slumbers that it would have been early morning. He could have arrived on time, done a full day's stint, and would have put in an appearance more or less punctually the following day.

The matter never reached this interesting stage. Delightful old Sidney Hodgson, extremely indulgent, and inclined to humour in his way, at times, on one occasion suggested to his downstairs staff: 'Perhaps we should all club together and buy Luke an alarum clock!' He thought this a great joke. I am amused by his use of the archaic 'alarum'. But not even the most modern and the loudest alarm clock could have awakened Luke in full slumber.

I suppose it was something or other in the man's metabolism. But quite apart from that, he was absolutely impossible as a cataloguer of books. Most of his work had to be gone over by somebody else. He also had the most strange handwriting. I found it not unattractive: it was something like Corvo's script, and quite intelligible. But I think it drove old Sidney half dotty, with his own standard copperplate. 'The man's got a *kink*, you see,' was the extent of his explanation for Luke's unusualness and eccentricity.

Poor Luke. He was a gnome-like creature living in a world of alien humans, a poor and lonely little misfit who just couldn't wake up. He must have been the despair of his father, who I am sure subsidised him. The lad was quite unable to make a living of his own for any length of time.

It was something of a cliff-hanger for us all, waiting for Luke to get his quittance. When he did eventually get it — a very rare thing with our firm — he got it with a month's notice. 'Don't bother to try to come in to work any more. Just drop in for the next four Friday afternoons and pick up your money.' I don't know why the Hodgsons insisted on this method of payment, unless they disliked the idea of forking out a whole month's money in one go. But perhaps I am being unkind, and they wanted to give him the chance of finding other employment while they doled out a weekly stipend, not trusting him with too much cash in one lump.

True to form, little Luke put in his appearance regularly every Friday and collected his money, but he was *always* late. After that, we saw him no more. But a few months later, seeking out a job somewhere in the west country, he had the *chutzpah* to write to the Hodgsons for a reference!

Concurrently with the many odd-balls who passed through our portals at about this time was Arthur Mumford. He, I must stress, was a perfectly normal being, and a great asset to Hodgson's during his stay of some ten years or so. He had been a post office worker for most of his life, and after he had been pensioned off he applied for some menial position with us in order to supplement his small income and to work among the books he loved. It transpired that he had been a client of the firm's in previous years. This was an unusual turn-up: many an employee later graduated to buying books from the Hodgson shelves for business or pleasure, but Mumford was the first collector I ever knew who reversed the procedure.

Never in his life had he much money to buy books and the topographical engravings of which he was so fond, and nothing he ever accumulated was of any great value, but the man derived a great deal of pleasure from his modest collection. He was a nice old chap, but like all members of the working class, he would be ribald and familiar with his fellow-employees while offering the utmost deference and respect to the guv'nors.

Bimbo, the Sale Room Assistant, who had now gone downstairs to take on old Tom Wheaton's job of numbering the lots, had a terrible hacking and wheezing cough. He smoked Gold Flakes, and every time he lit one up we were all in store for the bout of red-faced panting and acute distress that inevitably followed. He knew quite well that he was doing himself no good, and Mumford told him in no uncertain terms to give it up. They used to have a running discourse about it in the basement, all in good humour, with plenty of obscene expletives flying about.

One day Mumford was going about his job behind a shelf of books, in silence, when quite suddenly from behind another shelf, came a spasm of coughing. Mumford, without breaking off from what he was doing, offered a quite audible comment.

'*Die*, then — you silly old bugger — *die!*' he said.

All the cataloguers heard it, as did the recipient of the advice. It was Sidney Hodgson. Bimbo was out at lunch.

Bimbo was a man for whom I had great affection. He had been given that odd nickname, for some reason, in very early childhood, and it stuck with him among both friends and family for the whole of his life. He was benign, avuncular, and of an extremely dignified appearance. Portly, white-haired, and moustached, he strode with a slow and even gait. He carried a large paunch before him, across which was draped a gold watch-chain. Bimbo had spent almost the whole of his working life as a minor civil servant at the Victoria and Albert Museum, in a sinecure with the Ceramics Department.

As a young man he had been fortunate enough to make a connection at the Royal Albert Hall, not too far away from the V. & A., and there he often worked in the evenings as a steward, augmenting his income considerably. Like the other stewards, he had access to a great many complimentary tickets to various concerts and other functions, and had he wished he could have made quite a bit of money by selling these at a reduced rate. But he never did. These were *free tickets*, he insisted, donated by the owners of the private boxes, to be distributed gratis as the recipient wished, and Bimbo would have thought it immoral to have made money from them. When I first knew him at Hodgson's, he seemed to have a constant stream of callers, who appeared to have been regulars of his for years, and he would never accept any form of payment from anybody.

Naturally, when I got to know him well, and he offered me complimentary tickets to Albert Hall concerts, I would try to show my appreciation afterwards with a packet of his favourite Gold Flakes, at least, but he soon put a stop to that. 'I hope this isn't going to be a regular occurrence,' he said, 'or the tickets must stop.' Those that he gave me, by the way, were *always* for Lord Spencer's private box, a person whom I had never heard of at that time. This is my one very tenuous connection with our present Royal Family!

When Bimbo was compulsorily retired from the Museum, I think he would have had enough to live on, normally, what with his pension and the few pounds he picked up in the evenings at the Albert Hall. But the man was an inveterate gambler. He must have squandered a fortune, in his time, with the few bob he put on here and there on the various horses running each day. He was obliged to find another job to keep things going, and the Hodgsons took him on at £5 a week in 1949 when their Head Porter, Abie Osborne, died rather suddenly after a lifetime of service behind him.

Bimbo didn't like being called the Head Porter, and he did as little portering as possible. Either he was dubbed, or dubbed himself, the Sale Room Assistant. The position had never existed before, and it never existed later. True, he always wore the dark grey overall-smock which stamped him as a menial, or labouring type, but his silvery hair, his most dignified bearing, and his advancing years prevented too many people from requesting him to hump heavy piles of folios to the doors. He was always willing to advise, to help, or to execute commissions during a sale, but you had to treat him with respect and not look upon him as a mere pack-horse or bearer of burdens.

He had a strict routine between sale days, occasions when he was always fully engaged. This was long before the present era of betting shops, an age when you can go out and back your fancy any time you like in almost every major thoroughfare. In the 'fifties, Bimbo had to sneak into the telephone booth in the corner of the Sale Room at about lunch time, ring his bookie, and make his investments for the afternoon. At half past three or so he would divest himself of his overall, put on his jacket, and march off with his measured tread ostensibly for his afternoon tea. Actually, it was to buy the latest edition of the *Evening Standard*, to see the fate of his 'interests', as he called them. Later on, when he knocked off at five-thirty, he would buy another paper, and immediately turn to the Stop Press to see how his later horses had fared.

He never stopped castigating himself for being such a bloody fool with his betting, but he never stopped it, either. His brother, also in retirement, who occasionally came in to see him, had been a bank manager, and was well fixed financially. He also possessed a very valuable stamp collection. Bimbo, the black sheep of the family, possessed nothing.

Apparently he had a pretty hopeless home life. He was barely on speaking terms with his wife, and his job at the Albert Hall on several nights of the week gave him ample opportunity to absent himself from the fireside whenever he wished to do so. His conjugal life, in the accepted sense of that term, had been nil, he confessed to me, for well over ten years. I shouldn't have thought that this would have worried him a great deal, at his age, but it so happened that Bimbo was a very randy man.

Periodically, he would treat me to details of his extra-curricular sexual exploits. He pursued a waitress who worked in the buffet at the Albert Hall, for many years. Finally, patience was rewarded, or so he told me. He also professed undying love for the headmistress of a girls' school, who used to pop in sporadically for tickets to concerts. It seems that he had 'made' her, just once, many years previously, when she was in a weak moment, and she had said: 'This must never happen again. I have girls to look after, and I constantly warn them about things like this.' It didn't stop him trying, though, and he never gave up hope entirely. Intermittently, he would pick up with a prostitute in the Edgware or Bayswater Roads, and later regale me with tales of mirrors on the ceiling, over the bed.

In the last year or so of his life he met a sort of skivvy, or back-room worker, in the Lyons' tea-shop in Fleet Street. She wasn't presentable enough to be employed out front, where meals and drinks were provided, but toiled behind and out of sight, among the steam, the dirty dishes, and all the washing-up. Actually, she wasn't all that bad, once she was tarted up a bit and away from that environment. She and Bimbo took an instant liking to each other, and an autumn romance of sorts blossomed. Both were unhappily and unsatisfactorily married. They used to meet every Friday for a carnal evening in the flat of an indulgent friend of hers.

This went on for several months. But by this time Bimbo was getting more and more wheezy. He had now given up smoking completely, but he had chronic bronchitis, and the slightest effort made him pant. Sexual intercourse with his paramour must have been a great physical ordeal, but he persisted. The spirit was still willing, even if the flesh was weak.

Came a day in November, when we had one of the last of those terrible London pea-souper fogs. Traffic was almost at a standstill, and visibility was practically nil. By coincidence, it was a sale day, when the poor old chap was taxed more than usual. It was also a Friday, and he had a date to serve his lady friend later that evening.

In those times, after a Thursday and Friday sale, the busiest time of the week at Hodgson's was the Saturday morning following. Here every hand was at the pump. All lots had to be 'looked out', all commission successes advised by post, and there was a constant stream of buyers calling in to pay for and to clear their purchases of the days before. I met poor old Bimbo coming down Chancery Lane that morning, plodding his steady way to work, but hardly capable of putting one foot before the other. The fog still swirled around us, and he wheezed painfully. Being well aware of the importance of the occasion, he had somehow dragged himself up to work, but he was really past all effort. He confessed that his physical exertions of the evening before, plus the fog, had done for him.

I am not a callous man, but I was largely preoccupied with the important and immediate work I had to do that morning concerning the sale that had taken place, and I cannot recall seeing a lot more of old Bimbo that day. I never saw him again. I believe he knocked off early; he either went home or was sent home. We all thought he would get over it in time and would soon be back as usual. But he went straight to bed, and he stayed there. He lingered for quite a long while. I heard that his wife, whom he had told me had done nothing but nag him while he was on his feet, nursed him faithfully and devotedly while he was on his back.

In due course, poor old Bimbo expired. It fell to me to clear out his desk.

I found a Post Office Savings Book: it had many deposits at the start, and many more withdrawals at the end. There was no money left. I also found a letter from a lady in West London, telling him that their relationship must cease. I was able to return this to her and tell her that Bimbo had died.

After his funeral, his daughter asked me if I had any idea who the distinguished-looking lady in the background might have been. She had not come forward and spoken to any of the family. I said that she was probably one of the old V. & A. Museum colleagues to whom he had given free tickets to the Albert Hall concerts. But from her description I recognised her as the headmistress of the girls' school to whom I had returned the letter, with the place and date of the funeral.

Mumford and Bimbo had worked together fairly closely, and when the old chap finally went, a lot of his work fell upon Mumford, while I did the rest. Things carried on like this for some while. But in course of time, Mumford felt that things were getting too much for him, and after he had departed to a well-earned retirement in Chelmsford, one of his immediate successors was Turpin. I shall write a little more of him elsewhere in these pages.

Turpin was a cadaverous man in his sixties when he forsook the precarious living he had earned in Great Russell Street under bookseller George Salby and applied for the vacant job of a porter at Chancery Lane, presumably in order to 'better himself'.

It was a perpetual source of wonderment to me at the sort of people the Hodgsons were prepared to take on. As far as I have been able to ascertain, all Turpin was ever able to offer as a credential for employment was that he had once been requested to, and therefore could, collate a book! It took some time for the downstairs staff, with whom he usually worked, to tumble that Turpin was a clandestine alcoholic. He would glide about the basement, with a perpetual dew-drop on the end of his big, hooked nose, and periodically he would disappear behind the thick pillars which supported the building. Here one could hear him coughing and snuffling, and one day Alex Rogoyski found him there spraying his throat — but with methylated spirit! The place reeked of the stuff.

As the months passed, Turpin grew more erratic and eccentric. For instance, we tried to teach him how to tie a slip-knot, which was essential on the bundles of books which had to be sent upstairs. But he could never grasp it. He certainly tried hard enough, and wouldn't give up. I remember him spending the best part of a whole day trying to learn the simple knack, standing there with a piece of string in his hands, throwing left over right, right under left, shaking his head in bewilderment and tut-tutting every time he failed. Again, his attendance could not be relied upon, and we could never be sure when he was going to go absent for several days at a stretch. Presumably he was off on one of his meths jags. I think most of his money went on booze, and his clothes were second-hand remnants someone or other had handed to him. I recall him turning up for work one morning in a long, shabby raincoat, cavalry twill slacks, and white cricket boots!

Then there was the period when he announced to all of us of his impending marriage! We were incredulous. Who on earth would every marry Turpin? Only the scrubbiest of the old scrubbers, we were sure, but he insisted that he would be marrying an attractive young chick in her twenties. It never happened, of course. Either the prospective wedding was in his mind alone or, more likely, some heartless trollop had strung him along just for laughs. One week he was full of it all, and the next he didn't even mention it. The subject was allowed to lapse. I never had the heart to ask him what had occurred.

Turpin was rapidly becoming a terrible embarrassment, even to the indulgent and long-suffering Hodgsons, who must have been wondering how to get rid of him, when once again he failed to turn up for work. We all thought that this was another of his brief sabbaticals, but we never saw him again at Chancery Lane. He didn't even bother to collect his cards. I think I did catch a brief glimpse of him a few years later, in the King's Road one day, outside a pub. I think he recognised me a second or so before I saw him, and he rapidly turned away. He needn't have bothered; I had no real desire to renew his acquaintance.

I think that the next of the screwballs to come to Chancery Lane was Bert. I forget his surname. It occurs to me now that there was no rhyme or reason why some of the employees were always known by their first names, and others always by the second. It wasn't a case of growing familiar with the more affable: Turpin, for instance, was always a more approachable person than Bert, and yet if the old drunk *had* a first name, then none of us ever heard it.

Bert was a grim, taciturn misogynist. He lived a solitary, one-room existence as a lodger somewhere south of the river in his sister's home. She was the only woman he ever seemed to have any time for at all, and I never heard him utter a good word for *her*. He spoke seldom enough, it is true, but when he did he would often launch into an impassioned diatribe against womankind. He usually finished with a paraphrase of the same pronouncement: '*Wimmin*! Got no time for 'em. Chuck 'em all aht the winder!'

Like many another near-illiterate, Bert had a great respect for education and the printed word. He had spent most of his life as a packer, but a packer of glass-ware and ceramics. Now, for the first time in his career, he was putting on to shelves, and into tea-chests and cartons, hundreds and thousands of books. He had never known that so many existed. He spent most of his leisure, and all of his lunch hours, browsing through the dullest of tomes. 'Litrachoor', as such, held no appeal for him at all. But request him to place on to a top shelf a run of — shall we say? — two hundred and one volumes of the *Transactions of the Society of Chemical Engineers*, or some such title — almost unsaleable, and only taken in because of other worthier stock in the same property — and Bert was in his element. He couldn't shelve it quickly enough. The sooner it was done, the more time he would have to plough through, in his thorough and painstaking way, the details of the mysteries he had now discovered and only fractionally understood. As for myself, I understood even less than he did, simply because I had no interest at all in the subjects that absorbed him. But in his infrequent confrontations with me — the others downstairs got the worst of it — he would bore my backside off about the importance of a paper he had read, perhaps, on the gas turbine engine.

Bert had a good job; he was never overworked. According to his lights, it amounted to a sinecure. But he, like Turpin, departed suddenly, and without explanation. We never discovered why. There may have been a domestic upheaval with his sister, during which she became defenestrated; it is possible that he grew to dislike us all, for he was certainly kidded unmercifully, particularly by the cataloguers in the bowels of the establishment; he might even have been knocked down and killed. I don't know. But Hodgson's and Chancery Lane knew him no more. Then came Harry.

Oh, what a scintillating gem was Harry! Wilfrid showed me his hand-written letter of application when the job was advertised. It was in neat copperplate on cheap, ruled notepaper. He had worked in the British Museum Reading Room, it seemed, and was very highly thought of by Sir Frank Francis there. 'I am fifty-three years of age and a life-long non-smoker and tee-totaller.'

Actually, he must have been sixty-three if he was a day, he periodically got stoned out of his mind on cider, and although he said that Sir Frank Francis had had to let him go because he got dizzy at the top of high ladders, it was very soon evident that his dizzy spells were always the result of excessive imbibing. Several times I had to restrain him forcibly from climbing aloft with armfuls of books when he was in no condition at all to walk a straight path through the Sale Room.

Harry was short and rotund, he perenially wore a flat, cloth cap, and he carried a voluminous carpet shopping-bag which dragged on the ground, and in winter he wore an old grey overcoat which reached to his ankles. He had no friends that we knew of, no apparent family, and he had no actual fixed place of abode.

He spent most of his nights at a Rowton House in Camden Town. Being something of a regular, it seems that he often got the same bed, and I think he was looked upon as something of a star boarder. But if he didn't turn up at a certain time each evening and claim his bed he didn't have to pay for his night's doss. It was a long time before we discovered that most winter weekends he came back to Chancery Lane after everybody else had gone, turned on every gas and electric fire in the place, and spent the Saturday and Sunday in solitary splendour, warmth, and comfort. Wilfrid didn't tumble for many months, even when his bills came in and proved to be something like double the amount of the comparable quarter the previous year.

Harry was a fantastic worker when he eschewed the cider, and for this reason alone he held his job for the length of time he did. He was always repentant after a bout of insobriety, and eventually Wilfrid induced him to let the firm hold all his spare cash in the safe. In this way Harry built up savings of some forty or fifty pounds at one time — more than he had ever accumulated in one lump for years. Then he went off the rails, demanded that his money be returned to him, and in a bout of drunken generosity tried in vain to distribute largesse among the other employees.

I can see him now, reeling about that basement with a quart bottle of cider in his fist, his brawny little arms tattooed to the elbows. He looked the typical drunken sailor — which was what he had been. There is no doubt that he had the steel plate in his head, which he claimed was a legacy from a wound in submarines during the war, and which possibly contributed to his present eccentricity. My memory grows dim: I remember that one moment he was chasing Wilfrid round a table and demanding his money, but I seem to recall that at another he was pressing five pound notes upon his employer. There is one distinct moment I shall never forget: Harry drunkenly throwing his arm about his very staid and correct boss's shoulder, looking earnestly into his eyes, and telling him, to the embarrassment of everyone watching and the recipient of this quite unexpected affection too, I'm sure: 'You're a nice man, Mr. Wilfrid — a *very* nice man.'

Harry survived this episode. 'He's extremely useful downstairs,' Wilfrid told me, and he certainly was — as long as he was sober. Then came another happening.

During the winters, Wilfrid's relaxation was to play for Bromley Hockey Club on Saturday afternoons, and most of their engagements were south of the river. They did, however, play one or two fixtures north of the Thames. Wilfrid had been out to play in a match at Southgate, I believe, and he decided to break his journey home and drop into his office to pick up some papers he had forgotten. It was a bitter, frozen day in January or February. Imagine his surprise when he walked into the gloom of the premises and found Harry lying blind drunk and completely passed out on the carpet of the office, before the roaring gas fire! Both Harry and the carpet were extremely damp. The carpet was stained only temporarily; Harry's character, already indelibly stained, now stained even darker. Still, he got away with a caution.

Some months later I arrived one Monday morning at my usual time of nine-thirty to find the place locked up and empty. This was very unusual: Harry should have been in a full hour earlier to clean the place up and to attend to various other chores. For some reason, I didn't have a key with me at the time, and I was unable to gain access. I turned back up Chancery Lane to go and have a cup of tea until someone with a key made an appearance. Halfway up the street I bumped into Harry. He was still stoned out of his mind, after a very heavy weekend. His eyes were glazed, the corners of his mouth were stuck together, and I'm quite sure he hadn't washed once over the weekend. He mumbled some excuse about having forgotten his key, and having had to go back for it.

'Oh — give it to me, Harry,' I said impatiently, and recognising the situation immediately. 'I'll open the door.'

I should have remained silent. He fumbled a bit and sheepishly fished it from his trouser pocket: it was wet, stained, and covered with rust. I hastily opened the door, returned the key to him quickly, and rushed to wash my hands.

As an act of contrition, Harry immediately got to work, and started to weave up a ladder with an armful of books. I hastily put a stop to that. When Wilfrid came in later on and saw the man's condition, Harry got sent off for the day, although where he went I haven't an idea. He couldn't claim his bed till evening. But still he wasn't sacked.

He grew worse and worse, as time passed, and the point eventually came when the position grew quite untenable. He had long been talking about getting out of London, and returning to a certain town in the midlands, where he had always claimed to have some relatives. He boasted that a certain job awaited him in a factory up there. So Wilfrid finally let him go. Months later, he received a letter from a solicitor in the midlands: Harry was claiming two weeks' 'holiday money', which he said had never been paid!

For years afterwards I used to reminisce about such old prize employees to some of the younger cataloguers who came from school or university to grace the Hodgson coterie. One of these was Alan Gillitt, who had

himself come from the midlands. After I had told him about Harry he
asked me what had happened to him in the end.

'Oh,' I said, and I mentioned the place to which Harry had departed, 'he
went back home — to work in a pork pie factory.'

'What?' said Alan. 'Why, my uncle *owns* that factory!' If Alan had ever
eaten one of his uncle's pork pies in previous years, I'll bet he never did so
afterwards, if he remembered some of the things I told him about Harry.

Tucker was the most unlikely-looking member of the book trade you
might ever encounter. He stood about six feet or more, and he must have
weighed about fifteen or sixteen stone, at least. He was fat, florid, and
very, very blond. He had a hulking jaw, a thick red neck, and a bullet head.
This latter feature was emphasised by a fancy which led him to wear his
hair in that fashion known *many* years ago as 'short back and sides' — quite
literally: not that expression as interpreted today by those who normally
sport their locks rather long. Tucker's barber went over that skull with the
clippers. On top, the man allowed himself a couple of inches of yellow hair
on either side of a severe centre parting. He looked extremely 'butch': the
tough sort of customer who might have been a great asset in a rugby
scrum. He also wore spectacles. These gave him the general appearance of
a somewhat aggressive and pugnacious owl.

Actually, despite his bulk and appearance, he was normally very mild
and gentle. Far from being a rugby type, he was a rabid soccer buff, and he
told me that he had been a goalkeeper in league football in his younger
days. I had no reason to dispute his claim, and he certainly knew his stuff
when he talked of the game. He informed me that he was a talent scout for
Brentford in his spare time, but I suspect that his duties were largely
voluntary. But he was eager to impress, and it was obvious that that was
where his main interest lay.

He got the job of portering books mainly on the strength of the fact that
he said he had formerly been in the trade. I later discovered that he had
earlier been a door-to-door commission salesman on behalf of the Caxton
Book Co! That beat Turpin's booksy experience in collating by a mile.

Tucker came to Hodgson's direct from a mental hospital, where he had
been employed as a sort of male nurse and strong-arm man to quieten
violent lunatics. Apparently he had grown tired of this sort of work, and
he sought something rather more sedentary, like humping immobile folios
and tea-chests. But his duties with us also entailed the numbering of lots, a
semi-clerical job which taxed him no end.

He also had to identify each item from the shelves as it came up for sale
during the auctions, and it was pathetic and pitiful to watch him running
backwards and forwards, desperately attempting to keep one jump ahead

of the auctioneer. He simply didn't have the capacity to go to lots one, two, three and four, take them from the shelves and present each at his leisure as it came up for sale. No amount of coaching could teach him: it had to be one at a time. Thus, in a summer afternoon's sale of some three hundred and fifty lots he would be forever running to and fro, red-faced and panting, with the sweat streaming from his brows. He was not particularly intelligent, and yet he was just intelligent enough to grasp that he hadn't got the abilities needed to cope with a job of this kind. He wasn't sacked. Once or twice he walked off in high dudgeon, claiming that he was being put upon, and asking for his cards to be sent on to him, but Wilfrid usually managed to cajole him into returning.

But in the end he left us — in quite good humour, as it happened. He dropped in once or twice later on to see how things were going, and I asked him how matters fared with him. He seemed happy enough with his lot: he had gone back to wrestling with the patients at the hospital, and he could still travel out to some obscure evening soccer match between Southern League nonentities and pass through the turnstiles free of charge and with a swell of pride by saying that he was a scout for Brentford.

Young John was a man in his middle twenties. He had intelligence, and some learning. Naivety and the normal youthful idea of 'going his own way' had led him to kick over the traces of the parental harness. When he came to us he had already had his year or two of Soho and Bloomsbury. I think he had had a bellyful, too, but he wasn't quite ready to admit it.

The man *should* have come to us as a learner-cataloguer. Most certainly, I have known youngsters with lesser academic qualifications than he possessed who made good in this direction. But young John came as a porter, the vacancy that was open, with the *possible* prospect of advancement.

I would be lapsing into the realms of sheer truism and mere cliché were I to start talking about the fall of the dice, or the way the cookie crumbles. But *my* life has been affected one way or another by a chance happening, and so has yours and everybody's. I was privileged to witness it happen with John.

He hadn't been with us a week. The boy was keen: he had been fiddling a living one way or another for quite a long time, and now, on the recommendation of an older member of the staff, he had got into a job which looked good. He liked books and literature: he was determined to make a go of it and to advance.

John had been instructed to put number slips into certain volumes which were located on dim shelves under a staircase by the office. Two particular books were adjacent, and one looked very much like the other. Being quite new to the job, and not looking too closely, the items were wrongly numbered by John. Very few people happened to view these lots, for they were of a high specialisation, but one who did so was a very well-respected lady in the book trade, acting on commission for a client abroad, who wanted to know the condition of the book in which he was interested. The lady, his agent, didn't peruse the volume's title and contents. In that light she could hardly have done so, anyway. She saw that the book was in good state, and a day or two later she bought it at auction on what she had seen. After it had been delivered it was found to be the wrong thing entirely, and a considerable sum of money was involved.

I don't think I ever saw Sidney Hodgson angry. But I saw him put out — just once or twice. Let's say this was once. The lady was a valued friend and client, and a member of his staff had caused her embarrassment, so he took the blame. Quite in vain I tried to explain to him that young John had only just started, that such an elementary mistake could happen to anyone, but — *no*. Poor John was on Sidney's shit-list from the very beginning. He never got off it.

He was a likeable boy. He was enthusiastic, he was anxious to improve, and I defended him staunchly. *No* — said authority. He was a poor timekeeper, for a start. No — he had made that grave mistake with numbering. He was careless. No — he would never amount to anything at all.

I grew a bit worried about young John. By this time he was beginning to look upon me as Big Daddy. I confess that I rather relished the role. I'd never had a protégé before. It felt good. His wage was seven pounds a week, and he couldn't quite manage. All he needed, he explained, was a few bob extra, to make ends meet. So I took him to the White City one evening. It is easy enough to make a small profit and get out quickly while you're still ahead, if you have the 'know how'. John did all right, he made a few quid, and he solved his immediate problems. He was immensely grateful to me, and I went up a notch or two extra in his estimation. I frankly admit that I now took advantage of my position, for young John had another pressing problem. He still couldn't get up in the mornings. He wasn't another Luke, by any means, turning up when others were going home, but he was always late for work. This did not endear him to authority.

At this particular period in my life I was extremely interested in hypnotism, which was having a vogue with certain stage performers like Peter Casson. Successful amateur hypnotists were writing fascinating books on the subject. One of these, I recall, was the absorbing *Search for Bridie Murphy*. While I was a mere 'armchair' hypnotist, limiting myself to interesting case histories and music-hall shows where members of the audience volunteered to be put to sleep, my young brother-in-law, Julian, had steeped himself in the subject in a more practical way, and had had considerable success in hypnotising one or two of his young colleagues. He was now looking for more subjects, but they weren't easy to find. You can't normally 'put under' a close friend or relative, or someone who knows just as much about the technique of the business as you do, but it's quite different with strangers.

I remember that one day I was having a cup of tea with young John in Lyons', and he continued to bemoan the fact that he just couldn't get up in the mornings and report to work on time.

'I could clear that up for you in no time at all,' I said airily.

'How?'

'Light hypnotism,' I informed him, with authority. 'My brother-in-law's a hypnotist. He could put you under like *that* —' and I snapped my fingers in the approved fashion, ' — and merely by suggestion he could clear up your problem easily.'

John was the ideal subject. He was gullible, young, trusting, impressionable and inexperienced. He also worshipped the water I walked upon. I was considerably older and more experienced, although I admit to being somewhat gullible and trusting myself. Perhaps I should have known better than to take advantage, but both Julian and I were pretty sure of ourselves, and this was a heaven-sent opportunity.

The upshot was that we got him back to my flat one evening very shortly afterwards. He knew me too well, so I doubt if I could have hypnotised him. But he was meeting Julian for the first time. Further, Julian was then working at the Royal College of Surgeons building in Lincoln's Inn Fields: he was a technician for the Imperial Cancer Research Fund. This in itself impressed John no end. In short, he went out like a light. A coin was placed on the back of his hand, and he was told that the area it covered had no feeling. When he came to, he was invited to stick pins into it. He did so, and felt nothing.

Thus convinced, it was child's play to put him under again, to inform him that henceforth he would have no difficulty at all in getting up in the mornings, and to send him on his way. It wasn't quite as abrupt as all that, of course. We had a cup of tea and a chat about the whole thing before he left. I retain a distinct memory of John sitting there and repeatedly sticking a pin into the back of his hand, and with an incredulous look on his open-mouthed face.

There was another thing that I will always remember about young John. He was given to excessive perspiring; when most people sweat, beads usually break out upon their brows, but John, for some reason, sweated through his nose. He sat there that evening, still jabbing pins ineffectually into the back of his hand, while sweat dripped down to the end of his proboscis like mucus dew-drops.

I arrived for work the following morning at my usual time, and heard excited voices downstairs. I listened over the open lift-shaft. John had already arrived! This was the first time he had ever turned up on time, and nobody could believe it. They wanted to know why. And there he was, hardly believing it himself, extolling the virtues of hypnotism and the powers of his good friends Fred and Julian.

The suggestion continued to work for some time. I do not know how long it would have been before it worked off and he needed putting under again, for two reasons. One was that now Julian had successfully demonstrated with several people that hypnotism worked, he suddenly lost all interest in the business. A good thing, perhaps: I don't think he would have fancied having John as a permanent patient. The other was that John had put in for a rise in wages from seven pounds a week to seven pounds ten shillings, to make ends meet, and he had been turned down. He was disgruntled, to say the very least.

Then, quite out of the blue, a dusky young chick from Harlem arrived in London, intent upon a couple of weeks' holiday in Europe. She knew nobody at all over here, but had been given John's name and address by a friend in New York. I think she literally turned up on his doorstep, if he had one. The girl was a very liberated young lady: she was into his bed with him on that very first evening. This was in the late nineteen-fifties, mark you. No-one had heard of the permissive society, and free sex of this sort was hard to come by among impoverished young book porters. John just couldn't believe his luck. And she wanted him to come with her to Paris, and then to squire her round the continent. She would foot the bill.

John made a rapid calculation and a decision. His passport was outdated: it would mean going to Petty France immediately, getting it validated, and then off to ecstasy for a week or two and no job to come back to; but the alternative was his seven quid a week at Hodgson's quite regularly, with that ten bob rise that had been refused still rankling. It was no contest. Young John just disappeared that weekend. I haven't seen him from that day to this. I'll bet he didn't get up very early in the mornings for quite some time.

I think that Bill and Les were the next ones to come, although I cannot be absolutely sure. Certainly they came almost together, the one as a packer and the other as a porter. They formed a rapport immediately, simply because they were both new boys, and didn't quite know their way about. Further, they were both musicians.

It has always been difficult for me, flattering myself that I am literate and also able to enjoy music — without being able to play it or fully appreciate its finer points — to understand how there can be people who can play music so easily, appreciate it so well, and still at the same time be almost completely illiterate. I have come across this situation many times in my life. For instance, the very few letters extant penned by Bix Beiderbecke are ungrammatical and all but indecipherable, he learned absolutely nothing at school and college, yet we are told on good authority that he could tell you 'the pitch of a belch'.

For a living, Bill packed parcels, cartons, and tea-chests with short, stubby fingers that were scarred and calloused; he had no interest at all in the contents of any of the books he handled. For relaxation, he played classical violin in symphony orchestras. Les, who would hump books and boxes all day long if the occasion demanded it, would read only very reluctantly. He confined himself to the headlines of a tabloid newspaper each morning, cutting out the more delectable female photographs displaying ample bosoms, and to the more pertinent paragraphs of the *Melody Maker* each week. He looked into no other periodicals. Les wrote not at all — he shunned the task. Whenever he had a letter that *had* to be written for some reason or other, or an official form to fill in, he left it to the weekend, and then got his wife to attend to it for him. This man, barely capable of writing his own name, and quite incapable of penning a coherent letter or reading a book, was a brilliant jazz saxophonist. He had played with Joe Loss's orchestra, and had done arrangements for the band.

It sometimes occurred to me to wonder why Les couldn't take down a simple name and address correctly over the 'phone, when a client was ringing in for a catalogue. Did it ever occur to him to wonder why other people couldn't just look at a page of horizontal lines, interspersed with black dots, and embellished with bass and treble clefs, sharps and flats, and still not see *and* hear the wonderful sounds thereon? If it ever did occur to him, he certainly never mentioned it to me, for he was also inarticulate. I used to think he must be missing a hell of a lot, but nowadays I am not so sure.

Rex was a big, black African, one of the very first 'gentlemen of colour' to get a job, even of a humble nature, in the somewhat hide-bound and conservative premises of any London auction house. Even then — and this must have been in the late 'sixties — after he had been provisionally taken on as a porter we were all first approached and asked if any of us had an objection to working with a black man!

Nobody had, of course, and if jobs were retained merely by an ability to do the work required, Rex might have stayed on for as long as he liked. But he was forever being caught out in minor transgressions, and it very soon became evident that his days were numbered. He was warned, over and over again. Authority did its damnedest to be fair to the man. Quite apart from that, Rex had a chip on his shoulder about his complexion, and those in charge had to tread warily. There *was* such a thing as the Race Relations Act.

On one occasion I came across him crouched over my typewriter, tapping hesitantly. I asked him if I could be of any help, for I knew quite well that he was unable to type. He grinned in a somewhat cunning and conspiratorial manner.

'How do you work this thing?'

'Well — what are you trying to do?' I asked.

In the machine, precariously held by the rollers, was a very small and rather flimsy piece of paper. Close inspection revealed it to be the counterfoil of a five shilling postal order. He admitted to me that his father, back home, was subsidising him to some extent, and was prepared to reimburse his son for any legitimate expenses he might incur. But the old man wanted proof of those expenses, and in black and white.

'Well?' I asked.

'I'm trying to put a pound sign in front of where it says 5s.,' he explained. 'Will you give me a hand?'

'*What?*' I was not outraged by the man's duplicity: I was simply appalled at his stupidity. I refused flatly to have anything at all to do with this attempted deception. If he really believed that it was going to fool his father, then his old man must have been even dafter than Rex.

I have known men to be sacked for a variety of reasons. Some were very unusual, but I venture to suggest that when Rex finally got the boot it was for a reason quite unique at Chancery Lane. It was a viewing day, preceding an important sale. I will not pile it on and say that a great many clients were present. As a matter of fact the Sale Room was almost empty. Perhaps it is a good thing that it was, for taking advantage of the situation, Rex sat himself down on a chair in the middle of the room, took off his shoes and socks, and spent some ten to fifteen minutes trimming his toenails with an old razor-blade I used up at the desk to sharpen pencils!

I have never quite believed in the image of the thick, dumb, and pig-ignorant Irishman, although I have heard dozens of jokes and stories about him, and who hasn't? But I can recall only one tale which revolves around an example of the tradition that I know to be true.

Mick was an affable young Paddy who was quite prepared to do any job at all you might ask him to undertake. I never knew a lad more willing. The only trouble was that the jobs mustn't be too taxing on his brain. But ask him to take a forty-foot row of books which were on a shelf at waist level, and tell him to transfer them to a shelf above which was chest-high, an' he could do t'at all roight, all roight. It'd take a bit of toime, now, but you musn't rush t'is sort of t'ing. Why, he could even put 'em up above eye-livil, *and* all in duh same order, wit' niver a one out of place.

But the job Mick did best of all was morning tea. He had this one down pat, so to speak. He knew exactly how many of us there were, he knew who took sugar and who didn't, and he rarely gave only one spoonful to them as took two. But one morning, immediately after we had all been doled out with our cuppas and were sipping them appreciatively, in walked dear old Alfred Lenton, that most well-liked of booksellers, fresh down from Leicester for the day's sale. There was an immediate chorus of 'hulloos' from all the young porters, but I knew the welcome my old friend would *most* appreciate.

'Mick,' I called. 'Run down and make a cup of tea for Mr. Lenton too, will you?'

'No.'

Quite literally, there was a stunned silence. What was this? Mutiny?

'Why not?' I said.

'I can't,' Mick explained. 'The kettle's empty now!'

The above anecdotes, related somewhat selectively, might give a reader the impression that none but eccentrics and weirdies ever passed through the portals of Hodgson's Rooms as packers and porters. This would not be true. Some of them proved to be perfectly normal people; maybe this is why I have forgotten most of them, or have found little about them worth repeating. I can't, for example, think of anything amusing I observed about the long-serving packer, Lew Atkinson. He had been there long before I arrived, and I worked in close proximity to him for many years. He looked a bit like Mr. Punch, particularly when he grew older and lost his teeth: his nose and chin seemed to be forever trying to meet each other. I think he might be recalled by many *habitués* of our premises for this alone.

But he did tell me one story, against himself, which might have some bearing on this general narrative. After Abie Osborne, the Head Porter, had died, occasional clients might leave the odd bid or two with Atkinson. It was then an accepted thing for porters to bid in most sale rooms. One day, during the progress of an auction, while he was busy looking out the next lot to come under the hammer, he heard a figure called from the rostrum, and he suddenly realised that he had a commission for this item.

'Twenty-five I am bid,' he heard.

'Twenty-eight,' he called hastily.

'Twenty-eight,' came the acknowledging response. 'Thirty.'

'Thirty-two,' called Lew.

A pause, and then down came the hammer.

'Thirty-two pounds!'

'What?' cried the dismayed Atkinson. 'I was bidding thirty-two shillings!'

Forever afterwards he was forbidden to execute any bids on his own account, and none of the other porters were ever allowed to do so, either, with the exception of the more reliable Bimbo. Any commission handed to Lew Atkinson he passed on to me. It was when I asked him why he did this that he related the tale.

He died eventually, of some strange sort of cancer. I was utterly surprised when he went. He had long been a sort of star exhibit at Guy's Hospital, and was asked to medical lectures, with his various bumps and protuberances being pointed out to the students. He was rather proud of it. He didn't seem to know what was wrong with him, and I never guessed.

Millward, Hatry, and Wise

During the nineteen-twenties, the 'thirties, and the rather lean period of the war years, the Sale Clerk at Hodgson's Rooms was one J. G. Millward. He was a very shrewd and capable man who eventually became something of an institution east of Trafalgar Square — a sort of counterpart of the famous Sam Patch of Sotheby's in the West End.

For a great many years Millward held the bids for numerous private collectors, as well as those of certain members of the trade who could not attend a sale personally. He always kept the identities of his clients a close secret, by calling out the name 'Mackenzie' whenever a lot was knocked down to him. A number of those people for whom he was acting *in absentia* were under the impression that he used this pseudonym for themselves alone; some were flattered, and felt not a little important. What they did not know was that in addition to bidding on behalf of all his customers, Millward was also buying for himself any worthwhile lots which looked like going cheaply and below their true value, also under the same name of Mackenzie. In this way he built up a pretty useful stock of books over the years.

He was trusted implicitly by a great many people. Personally speaking, I always found him a pleasant and affable enough acquaintance, although I didn't have a lot to do with him professionally. He had long gone to 'fresh woods and pastures new' in a different job when I came on the scene to take over his former chair. But from what I have been told, his ethics were sometimes questionable, although I suppose that all depends upon the way you look at things, or — to put it another way — your *standard* of ethics.

It seems that occasionally, if a client happened to leave him a moderate bid on a lot in which he was particularly interested himself, he would very conveniently 'forget' the commission he had been given, or would otherwise avoid executing it. Eric Osborne, that delightful and erudite man who used to trade from St. Leonards-on-Sea when he was not working for any one of a dozen different dealers, once told me of how he had left a bid of a fiver or so with Millward on one particular item. A day or two later he came in and asked Millward how much the lot had made.

'Three quid,' he was told.

'Oh, good,' said Osborne. 'I got it, then?'

'No,' replied Millward. 'I had a higher bid from someone else. There was no point in pushing the price up, was there? *You* wouldn't have got it, anyway.'

Osborne was a bit put out, of course, but he saw the logic in the answer. 'Who took it, then?'

'Fellow named Mackenzie,' Millward told him.

This incident still rankled with Eric Osborne many years later, when he told me the story, for he had seen the very same book in a shop a few days afterwards, and he knew the proprietor well enough to learn from whom it had been purchased.

'*Millward* was bloody Mackenzie! I wonder how often he pulled that stunt?'

J. G. Millward accumulated a very respectable knowledge of books over the years, as well as a very respectable stock. Much of this he salted away, although he did a bit of dealing on the side when it was advantageous. Such a practice was not frowned upon by the more indulgent employers in the book trade as it is today. I am writing of the early 'thirties: wages were none too high, good men were hard to find, and if they chose to augment their incomes with a few extra-curricular activities, well — if a blind eye wasn't actually turned the practice was at least winked at.

After the war, when Millward was middle-aged, white-haired, and might have been expected to stay at this particular job for ever, he was approached by one Clarence Hatry.

I think this is a name which will not mean much at all to those of the younger generation, and certainly not in the connection of antiquarian books, but I think veterans like Bernard Simpson, Charlie Traylen, and Tom Thorp might allow themselves a chuckle in recollection. Hatry was an infamous crooked financier, who had been sentenced to fourteen years in prison after a long *cause célèbre* back in the early 'thirties. It appears that he had got the idea of making a 'corner' in rare books after his release! Now, anyone who has even the slightest knowledge of our trade will realise how ridiculous such an idea must be. You can acquire a *lot* of good books, yes, if you have the means, and you can get hold of *some* of the best, perhaps, but it would take untold millions and a lifetime of experience to grab even a lion cub's share of them *all*.

I had always thought of Clarence Hatry as a clever rogue who had been unfortunate enough to get caught — a sort of latter-day Horatio Bottomley *sans panache et chutzpah*, so to speak — but after I heard about this pipe-dream of his, even in my early days in the business, I didn't think him clever at all. He probably got everything that was coming to him. At any rate, he set his sights pretty high after the authorities deincarcerated him, and he somehow acquired a major interest in the business of Hatchard's, the famous old firm in Piccadilly. It was the Royal Family's favourite bookshop. I remember bumping into old Queen Mary there, in her regal mauve and purple, as she 'browsed' — if that's the word, with bowler-hatted heavies behind her and hand-rinsing assistants backing before her. But she would only deal with one trusted old employee there, and he was kept on long after retirement age in order to attend to this occasional but exalted and profitable client. (I used to think of him as Scrotum, the wrinkled old retainer.)

This sort of thing obviously appealed to Clarence Hatry, but after he had settled in he wanted somebody in charge whom he knew and could trust, and he invited Millward to take over as manager of the antiquarian and rare book side of the business. So off went my predecessor to the West End.

I suppose I should really thank both Hatry and Millward, for this eventually opened the way for me to take up the position I held and enjoyed for so long. Millward was not my immediate predecessor at Hodgson's, but I am very well aware of the fact that had he never gone I would never even have started.

In the early nineteen-fifties, J. G. Millward thus became a client of mine, sometimes coming to bid on behalf of his new master, and very occasionally leaving me his marks, and our acquaintance ripened somewhat. But the time arrived, perhaps inevitably, when Millward came to understand that there was no future in Clarence Hatry's fantastic schemes and grandiose ambitions for Hatchard's. He was no mug: he had probably tumbled very early on, and was just marking time. At all events, he struck out on his own. But originally, he informed me one day, Hatry had wished him to sign an agreement to the effect that should he ever start up in business personally, he would not do so within a twenty-five mile radius of Piccadilly! Millward had jibbed at this: rightly so — as I say, he was no mug. And anyway, he lived at Purley, in Surrey. He got the agreement altered to a five-mile radius before he signed. It was just as well he did. Once on his own, Millward conducted a thriving business from his home during his declining years.

The name of Clarence Hatry faded from the scene of books. But not the name of Hatchard's. On and on it went; it has been going on for well nigh two hundred years, and may it go on for at least another two hundred. J. G. Millward has long since gone, but I still very occasionally bid for elderly clients who passed their marks to him some forty or fifty years ago and either won — or lost — their bids to one Mackenzie.

A good friend of Millward's I inherited was that very large but naive and nervous old bookseller from Liverpool, the late Gilbert Jamieson. He had been a victim of poison gas in the First World War, and his physical health had been poor thereafter. You would never have guessed it, to look at him: he was a big, fat man of the most imposing appearance. But he was meek and as docile as a month-old kitten — and scared of every other man-jack in the book trade. He once confessed to me that when he first came to London to bid at auction he had walked round the block three times before he had summoned sufficient courage to enter Hodgson's.

Now, public auctions are exactly what they are stated as being: *public* auctions, but you might be surprised at the number of people who believe that they have no right, really, to attend them, and feel that they are encroaching upon the more regular bidders' preserves. Did it never occur to these lambs that each and every one of those now hardened bidders once had a first time? The chances are that *they* were just as apprehensive and uncertain about everything on the initial occasion, but persevered.

Gilbert Jamieson persevered, too, yet in all the years he came south to London to buy his stock he felt that he was resented by the local members of the trade. I never heard a word against him. When Millward befriended him and used to go out with him for a cup of tea or a sandwich he felt that he had a buttress or bulwark against his imagined foes: a trusted ally in the enemy camp! He felt lost when Millward left, and then, after a few years he gained the confidence of the next Sale Clerk, until finally, when I was established and he felt able to take me into his trust and confidence he was happy again.

I have one story about Millward which is too good to miss. He told it to me himself. Back in the 'thirties, two young booksellers came into Hodgson's. Their names were John Carter and Graham Pollard. For some time they had suspected the authenticity of certain publications purporting to be first editions. These were usually slim books and pamphlets which pre-dated the hitherto acknowledged original printings. By sheer detective work and painstaking research it appeared to them that these items might, more than probably, be forgeries. Further, all lanes and trails seemed to lead back to one man. He was a wealthy and autocratic collector and bibliophile, named Thomas J. Wise. But both libel and slander were hazards never far from their thoughts, and they had to tread warily.

When they came into Hodgson's that day, one of these suspected forgeries was on the shelves: it was Elizabeth Barrett Browning's *Sonnets*, dated Reading, 1847. Carter and Pollard induced Millward to allow them to take this book and with a razor-blade, cut off a very narrow sliver — no more than the merest fraction of an inch — from the outer margin of one of the pages. It did not, ostensibly at any rate, deface the book. The two young men then took their sliver away and had it analysed. The paper proved to contain esparto grass, an ingredient not used in the making of paper at the time the book was purported to have been printed. Carter and

Pollard added one more fact to their now very impressive dossier, and knocked one more nail into the coffin of Thomas J. Wise.

In 1935 this enterprising pair published their now famous *An Enquiry into the Nature of Certain Nineteenth-Century Pamphlets*. It caused what is, perhaps, the greatest literary scandal and sensation of all time. It was the making of both of them, and it was also the ruination of Thomas J. Wise. Carter and Pollard never directly accused the man, but the implications in their book were obvious. Wise was never arraigned or prosecuted, but he never set foot outside his Hampstead home again.

The *Enquiry* is a scholarly work. It is fascinating, no doubt, to the bibliographer and erudite book-lover, but it could hardly be called popular reading for the layman, despite the intriguing tale it tells. Those sufficiently interested to pursue the strange life and career of the man responsible for this whole bombshell should seek out Wilfred Partington's biography of him, *Thomas J. Wise in the Original Cloth*. This is a title with allusions immediately obvious to the bookman, but it is one as obscure as David Low's *with all faults* as far as the uninitiated are concerned. The much racier title given to Partington's American edition of his book, *Forging Ahead*, displeased the pedants and blue-stockings of both sexes, who thought it pandered to the masses. But what's wrong with that? It induced far more people to read the book and learn than the English title might have done. That's not a bad thing, surely? Quite a few who did read it were encouraged to progress to Carter and Pollard's *Enquiry*.

I never knew Wise personally: he was just before my time. But I have heard a lot about him from those who did and who saw him frequent the various book auction houses. He used to stand at the back of the room, glowering, with his big moon face and bald dome, bidding in an authoritative and bullying manner. From all accounts he was not a particularly pleasant person.

One of his ploys, long before he was tumbled, was to send into an auctioneer for sale a copy of one of his forgeries. Of course, it would be sold anonymously, coming under the heading of 'The Property of a Gentleman', or under that more miscellaneous description: 'Other Properties'. He would then go to bookseller A, let us say, and instruct him to bid on commission for him for the item, up to fifty pounds. But he would also instruct bookseller B, perhaps, to act on his behalf for the same lot to the extent of sixty pounds. A and B, of course, would sit in the auction room and bid against each other, never dreaming that the two clients they were representing were in fact singular: one and the same man. A would drop out at his limit of fifty, and B would take the book at, say, fifty-five. Wise himself would gladly pay the auctioneer's commission and that of the bookseller to whom he had entrusted his bid. Why not? He got the book back, and he had also established an undisputed if exaggerated price at auction! He had dozens of other copies of his forgeries tucked away in various places, and with the precedent he had created artificially he surreptitiously sold many of them to good advantage.

The dubious activities of this strange bibliophile, scholar, and crook still came to light many years after he was dead. He would go to the British Museum Reading Room, ask for a particular book, and sit at one of the tables perusing it. In his mouth would be a short length of string, which he chewed and impregnated with saliva. In due course he would take this string from his mouth unobtrusively and place it into the fold of the open book before him. He would then gently close the book, put it aside and take up another for a short spell. After his saliva had done its work he would open up the first book, lightly pull away the saturated page he wanted, and secrete it upon his person. Many a time he thus made up imperfect copies in his own possession, books which either lacked a particular leaf or had wormed or defaced pages which offended him.

It is a remarkable thing that he seldom bothered to remove the tell-tale piece of string. Many, many years later, some of these copies were asked for again. They were found to be mutilated and imperfect, naturally, complete with evidence. The previous handler was always found to be Thomas J. Wise.

Perhaps an even more remarkable thing is that in his will he left a proportion of his collection of books to the British Museum!

Knock and Ring

Most people who have had anything at all to do with auction sales have heard of the Ring. A good proportion of these have also heard of something known as the Knockout. The two go together. These activities appear, by their very nomenclature, to have strong connotations of pugilism, but actually those who have indulged in them have often been the most unpugnacious people you could imagine.

Briefly, and as simply as possible, I will try to explain what occurs. Two or more people will get together before an auction sale and will compare those lots in which they are interested. Then, instead of bidding against each other competitively, and thus forcing up the price, one man will be delegated to bid alone for a particular lot or lots. The lack of opposition among the group *could* find some of the items coming down cheaply, but there is never any guarantee of this. One or two outside bidders among what used to be called the gentry could cause a lot to be knocked down at its right value, and sometimes a maverick dealer will force things up. Often, the lot will even exceed its true value.

After the sale is over, the members of the Ring — which is the name given to the group who have collaborated — adjourn to a local place of refreshment, and sometimes a private room free from prying eyes and curling ears, and then conduct another and more serious little auction among themselves. This is known as the Knockout, or settlement. On this occasion, everybody who is interested in acquiring certain items will bid. Thus, a lot which might have realised a mere £10 at the first auction might perhaps make £60 or £70, or even more, at the second one. The successful bidder then 'holds' the lot, and pays his money into the 'kitty'. If the lot has finally been bought at £70 there is now a sum of £60 in cash over and above the original auctioneer's 'hammer price'. At the conclusion of the Knockout there could be an accumulation of either a few pounds or several thousands, depending upon the importance of the sale and the goods which have come up for auction.

There is then a shareout, or 'divvy', among all those persons who have been members of the particular Ring. Some are happy with their cut and some are not. I should imagine that the happiest are usually those who have put in an appearance at the sale primarily in the hope of being invited into the Ring, without having had much intention of bidding seriously or holding any of the lots. I have known one or two people who claimed to have made a pretty good living in this way at the country auctions or in the premises of the smaller London sales.

Now, this practice of the Ring and the Knockout is strictly illegal. It has been so ever since the Auctions (Bidding Agreement) Act of 1927 was passed. But the fact that I have heard of only one prosecution and no conviction at all — as far as book sales are concerned — suggests that there is a strong difference of opinion as to whether it is also *unethical*, even among those in the legal profession. Further, it is an extremely difficult thing to catch anyone at it, since nobody can condemn a man openly for not bidding publicly, and that man is going to make damned sure that there are no outside eyes about when he bids privately, later on.

I can speak for the book trade only, of course, since I know little about others, but within our business I would say that the difference of opinion as to whether or not the practice is unethical is rather equally divided. Some of those — shall we say? — 'honest' booksellers who would not think of joining a Ring or entering a Knockout, and who stubbornly resist all efforts and invitations to get them to take part, often look upon the participants as blatant crooks and thieves.

Be this as it may, it is my own experience that, with a few exceptions, the so-called crooks are as pleasant people to deal with, socially and professionally, as the apparently upright and virtuous booksellers. I am fairly tolerant, and I have never had anything against a mild rogue, particularly, provided he is a decent enough sort and doesn't try to cut my throat or stick a knife into my back, figuratively, every time he encounters me.

That needs a little elucidation, for never forget this: some of the very people who are dead against the Ring in their pronouncements are, in fact, Ringsters of a sort themselves! Many a time a specialised bookseller has walked into a sale room, with his eye on one particular book or lot in the catalogue, and to his dismay has seen that a colleague in the same line of specialisation has noticed that item, too. I have watched such people, and have known what they were after. I have seen them nod and exchange a few pleasantries, ostensibly, and then drift apart. I have also seen that when the lot in question has come up for sale, only one of them has bid for it. Weeks or months later the same item has appeared in the *other* man's catalogue or shop.

If it seems to these people that a Ring at auction can be comprised of twenty, ten, or even far fewer prospective buyers, why doesn't it occur to them that they are equally as guilty of dishonesty, a mere couple, as the others? It's all a matter of degree, obviously.

I have also seen a pair of private collectors, close friends, sit together at a sale. One has said to the other: 'Look here, I'm only interested in one or two lots. I want them. Don't run me up on these, will you?' His friend has agreed, although on one such occasion that friend's enthusiasm got the better of him, and he began bidding away like mad, much to the other's dismay. Now, according to *my* understanding of that 1927 Act, these people were not dealers, and had no intention of reselling their acquisitions, so they were not acting illegally. But were they not acting unethically? They were certainly defrauding the vendor just as much as the hardened veteran dealers who made a regular practice of abstaining. A vendor who is out of pocket isn't very likely to appreciate the point if you start splitting hairs.

Broadly speaking, the argument of the ethical contingent is that Ringsters are cheating the owner of the goods of his true and just reward. The argument of the unethical is that we are in a dog-eat-dog competitive world, and that the vendor possesses ample protection by going to an experienced and worthwhile auctioneer who should know the true value of the goods and who is ready to suggest a reasonable reserve price for them. Then, the auctioneer bids up to an agreed figure on behalf of his client, if there is little response from the body of the room, and should nobody exceed this reserve figure the lot is 'bought in'. It reverts to the vendor, usually for a nominal charge to cover the costs of handling and cataloguing.

Although I became aware of the existence of the Ring very soon after I entered the book trade, I have naturally had very little to do with it, happening to have been employed by auctioneers, primarily, rather than by booksellers. Yet I am flattered that many Ringsters have trusted me enough to talk to me about the practice fairly frankly in the distant past, when there was more of it going on — but they were not *too* trusting, and not *too* frank, I am quite sure. Rings and Knockouts can be a lot more devious and complicated than my brief description of them, I assure you.

For the the most part, the dealers have trusted me, as I say, but one or two have never been able, quite, to look upon me as anything other than a member of the enemy camp — or even as a spy and informer! I have met them socially, and I know them quite well, but while they are normally loquacious there is always an air of aloofness and 'clamming-up' whenever I join their group. Better safe, I suppose, than sorry.

Those readers who believe that all major booksellers are regular members of an established Ring are completely mistaken. In fact, I would go so far as to say that there is comparatively little settling in the book trade these days. I am not speaking for other trades: one or two of them have quite wicked reputations, and to see some of their members in an auction house, during the viewing and while a sale is in progress, could give an impressionable onlooker the idea that he had stumbled into a conclave of the Mafia.

Further, there are certain book dealers who regularly attend auctions largely on behalf of important and influential private clients: people who leave them commissions to view, advise, and buy. These particular dealers, in accepting the commissions, are duty-bound to buy the lots for their principals at the cheapest possible price 'under the hammer', and therefore cannot enter into any agreement or settlement with their colleagues, even were they so inclined. On the other hand, I am not so naive as to deny the possibility that there are those English booksellers who will often accept a commission from one of their counterparts from New York, California, or the European continent, and that the dealer from across the water is well aware in advance that the price he will have to pay might vary greatly from the figure eventually printed in the Prices and Buyers Lists later issued by the auctioneer. After all, the Ring is not solely a British institution.

A famous character in the trade, and one who had a foot in both the camp of the auctioneer and that of the bookseller, was Abie Osborne, who was for some forty years or so Hodgson's Head Porter. Trusted implicitly by the dealers until his death in the late 'forties, he 'held' the bids of many of those members of the London and provincial trade. After they had visited the Rooms and had completed their viewing, they would pass their marks to Osborne, who entered them into his catalogue in his beautiful and meticulous copperplate script until the pages were literally black with bids. By leaving the job to him, the booksellers and their assistants were thus free to go about their business and save a whole afternoon spent in Hodgson's Rooms.

Now Osborne's actual job — the one for which the guv'nors employed him — was primarily to look out the lots as they came up for sale and to hold them up for identification while they were being sold. But simultaneously with this activity he would be bidding for anything up to a dozen or two dozen different booksellers during the progress of the auction. While I think it very possible that old John Hodgson didn't very much like the idea, there wasn't a lot he could do about it. It seemed to me that the Hodgson philosophy was always quietism, even if unconsciously formed. Anyway, John recognised the value of having the trade's competition against the private buyers in the room and the proxy bids on the book, even if they were often underbidders.

In this way, Osborne became something of a petty dictator in the Chancery Lane Sale Room. While he was paid a few pounds a week by the firm in a fairly menial occupation, he recognised the power he wielded, and he grew increasingly saucy and impudent over the years. He would make perfectly audible remarks about his employer on the rostrum during the progress of a sale — quite often to the amusement of everyone present apart from the butt of his somewhat blunt wit.

'Git on with it — you silly old sod!' he might call to the auctioneer, if that gentleman paused before knocking a lot down to Osborne, and hopefully looked round the assembly for a further bid. 'Bring that bloody 'ammer dahn!'

John Hodgson, who was a most benign-looking and gentle-mannered man — when the occasion suited him in his professional capacity — would be sitting high up above the bidders, with a smile on his patriarchal countenance as the sale went on. He ignored Ossie's remarks. If he had a high reserve on a particular lot and the bidding was not too brisk, he would naturally bid against any offers from the room in order to protect his client's interests: a perfectly legal and accepted procedure. But it seems he was not above 'trotting 'em up', even when there was little or no response from those present.

Shillings were important in those days, and the bidding advanced very gradually.

'Twenty-five shillings I am bid,' he would say with a mild nod. 'Thank you, sir. Twenty-five ... twenty-eight ... thirty — thirty-two — thirty-four — thirty-six — thirty-eight ...' His head would move from left to right, and back again, as the price increased.

Suddenly, there would be heard Osborne's voice from the back of the room as he moved about his job.

'There 'e goes — the wicked old bugger: bouncin' 'em off the bloody walls!'

Osborne considered his employer's tactics highly unethical, and he made no bones about saying so. But he saw nothing wrong at all in retiring to his cubby-hole in the Front Room immediately after the last lot of the sale was knocked down and working out the highly-complicated details of the one-man Knockout he was now holding for the benefit of his clients.

He would then ring them up and inform all and sundry who had got what, and how much could be expected from the 'divvy'. His own cut was traditionally 'a bob a lot', but I think he often did considerably better than that.

I have been told by some of the old-timers that Osborne was amazingly accurate, and that he never missed a lot. Knowing the length of time he was at this work, and appreciating the difficulties of having to do more than one job at a time, I have my doubts about that. He was certainly not infallible in all respects, as I was one informed by a particular man. This bookseller, one in a small way of business who did not normally have much to do with the other London dealers and who had never collaborated with them in any sale room, once gave a commission to Osborne to try to buy a particular lot in a sale he was unable to attend. A day or two later he came into Hodgson's Rooms and asked Ossie if he had been successful in obtaining the lot.

'No,' he was told, 'but you've got seventeen-and-six to come.'

Osborne was lucky in his choice of customer when he committed this gaffe. I know one or two who would have made things very unpleasant for all concerned.

When this unforgettable character died his little business died with him. His successor at Hodgson's, Bimbo, the highly respectable-looking pensioner from the Victoria and Albert Museum, was entirely unknown to the general run of booksellers, and could not be approached in this direction. In any case, I don't think he had much idea of what had been going on.

Of course, it was a traditional thing in those days to leave bids with the porter — or the Sale Room Assistant, as the new man preferred to be called — and the trade and private collectors still did so, but there was never any question of leaving him to attend to the settlement. Yet he had his regulars, and for several years he conducted a profitable little sideline, but most of the dealers who had previously left it all to Ossie now drifted back to attending the auctions personally. They only left their bids with any of the porters when they were either too busy to come along themselves or wanted to nip out for a quick drink before closing time.

I think it worth mentioning here that among those dealers who have sat in at the Knockout after a sale, there are quite a few of them who are unaware that there is such a thing as a Knockout *before* a sale.

I well remember two of the old 'barrow boys', most of them long gone even when I was a young man, who made a regular habit of conducting their settlements well before the auction date. They would come into our Rooms to view the cheaper lots: those stacks and bundles of anything up to a couple of hundred volumes, mostly pocket editions of no great value. They would assess the lots quite separately and individually, then retire quietly to our Front Room and have their own little private auction. After one or the other 'stood dahn', and their business was concluded, they would each hand their commissions privately to the porter, confident in the honouring of this 'gentleman's agreement', knowing that the other would not try the old double-cross by slipping the porter a higher bid on the quiet. It must have occurred to the man who was handling these commissions, at some time or another in his career, that these two lists of 'marks' from these old-stagers never seemed to bear the same lot numbers. If it did, he never mentioned it, even to me. To tell the truth, it was quite a long time before I tumbled what they were up to.

Although Bimbo and I often bid against each other during the course of a sale, each for our regular customers, booksellers and collectors, he never suggested that we collaborate. Nor, for that matter, did I. Our bids had been left in the strictest confidence. As a point of interest, the very large majority of the people who entrusted their bids to us took that matter of strict confidence for granted. I think in all my many years of bidding at auction only two people ever said to me: 'You won't let anyone else see these figures, will you?' A few more *have* remarked: 'You'll buy for as low a price as you can, I hope? You won't start at my top figure?' There were not many of such clients, and they were usually types I would rather not have acted for, anyway.

Potty

It was during my very first week in the book auction business that a strange apparition of a man walked into Hodgson's Sale Room. He wore a flat cloth cap on his head and an inane grin on his face. From this grin protruded two buck teeth, which hung over his lower lip like an inverted V sign. He sported a dark brown shirt and a 'kipper' tie with an enormous knot. He also carried a voluminous shopping bag. Anyone less like a bibliophile or book dealer I could not imagine.

'Is *he* a bookseller?' I asked somebody. 'He looks more like a junk dealer.'

'Yes. Well—that's what he is, actually,' I was told.

I found that a great many other people subscribed to this opinion of him, and I did so myself for a time. It arose, I expect from his habit at that time of usually buying only the cheaper lots, some of which frequently contained imperfect books. He looked as if he didn't have two ha'pennies to rub together. As it happened, he was quite a wealthy man, with a remarkably valuable collection of early-printed books.

He was, in fact, Pottesman, known to us in Hodgson's, Sotheby's, and Christie's, who knew his name, as 'Potty'. He was 'Inky' to those in the trade who didn't. This was a nickname he had earned because of his obsession with *incunabula*: books printed before the year 1500. I think that almost every antiquarian bookseller in London and district must at some time have been faced with his Grock-like grin and the perennial query: 'Got any 'Inkies' for me today?'

Potty was a middle-aged and already grey-haired man when I first knew him. At that time he was still living with his mother, who must have been approaching eighty. I never met her, but I have been told that she looked like a female equivalent of her son, plus clownish lipstick, rouge, and white face-powder. He professed undying devotion to her, but he often used that semi-private telephone booth which used to be installed in the far corner of the Sale Room at Chancery Lane, just behind my desk, and from their conversations I couldn't help overhearing they seemed to live a cat-and-dog existence, forever wrangling.

He lived at various addresses in the Bloomsbury area, never very far from the British Museum. He haunted the Reading Room, and he knew the reference works and bibliographies there better than the assistants. He did his best to keep his home addresses secret from most of his acquaintances, and he always had his catalogues posted either to an obscure relative, who would pass them on to him, or to his bank in Piccadilly. I only knew one man who gained his confidence sufficiently to be invited into his home. This was a Bloomsbury bookseller. The visitor was unexpected, and he was asked in very reluctantly. He had a gruesome tale to tell.

The place was full of books, of course, but incredibly squalid. The host offered a cup of tea, and it was reluctantly accepted. But when the tea had brewed, Potty apologised for only having one cup, and he drank *his* portion from a half-pint milk bottle. But he did observe the niceties: he wiped out the visitor's cup with a filthy washing-up rag.

It was only in retrospect that the unexpected guest came to realise that there was only one bed in the place, and no other item of furniture upon which a person might recline. Did Potty and his old mum, then, share the same bed? At first there seemed to be no other conclusion. It later transpired, however, that *he* slept in the kitchen!

As this cockney scholar and pedant grew older — and particularly after his mother died — he grew stranger, and he was strange enough to start with. His grey hair turned quite white, and those two distinctive front teeth fell out or were pulled out. They improved his appearance, certainly, but not his table manners. I remember him once, during a sale at Hodgson's, sitting at the Pound, below the rostrum. He took out a greasy, brown-paper package, opened it up to reveal some sort of sandwich, and proceeded to munch this crumby lunch as the bidding progressed. One of my most vivid recollections is the look on old Frank Maggs' face as he turned to observe this gourmet beside him.

Potty's dirty shirts grew no cleaner over the years. We had always suspected that he favoured dark brown or dark grey ones for economy's sake, so to speak, but he carried that economy too far. And when his neckwear grew too soiled at the knot, he would tie it a little higher, and that knot grew a little bigger. Finally, the knot was so large and the front hanging portion so small, with the underhanging narrow part reaching down past his navel, that he would discard it and get a new one. What with the decrepitude of the rest of his attire, it looked like a rose on a slag-heap. During his last few years he gave up the unequal struggle and renounced neck-ties completely.

I recall, too, when he walked in one day with a new pair of shoes which had obviously caught his fancy. He probably thought himself Beau Brummell — no less — but they were incongruous. They looked like crocodile skin, with brass buckles and scintillating toe-caps to knock your eye out. I think he must have passed through Carnaby Street one day. No self-respecting co-respondent of the nineteen-twenties would have been found dead in them.

Potty was an extremely irritating man in our Sale Room, and I understand that he acted no differently in other similar premises. In all his years of bidding he never learned exactly *how* to bid. He would forever start an opening offer with a nod or the raising of his catalogue, and then, in his anxiety to get the lot, fall out of step or bid against himself. This was seldom evident to anyone in the body of the room, of course, but it was very evident to the auctioneer and the clerk up at the rostrum. And inevitably, once he had bought an item, and felt pleased with himself, he would turn to his nearest neighbour and start a conversation about his success and the merits of his purchase.

Sod's Law, which decrees that if ever you drop of slice of bread and butter it will always land butter side downwards, invariably came into effect the moment Potty was successful in the auction room. You may be sure that his immediate neighbour was desperately trying to buy the *next* lot, and as unobtrusively as possible. Potty would easily put the mockers on that. He could disrupt anyone's attention without even trying. Further, he was a great mover-abouter, an oh-most-nonchalant stroller from one side of the room to the other. If someone raised his arm to catch the auctioneer's eye, Potty could usually be relied upon to be crossing the room to hide that gesture.

People were always complaining about him, naturally, and very often *to* him. But he was incredibly thick-skinned, and very difficult to insult or even to annoy. His usual response was that ugly but good-tempered grin.

He was always the first to come up to me after a sale was over to ask for the total of his purchases, but he was also always the last to pay. It literally took him about a quarter of an hour to write out a cheque, elaborately scrawled in his big, schoolboyish hand, and once he had passed it to me he was always reluctant to let it go. He usually wanted it back for a final perusal, to make sure he hadn't miswritten something, dated it incorrectly, or forgotten to sign it. His explanation was always the same whine: 'I once made a mistake in writing out a cheque.'

Naturally, I was anxious to get this part of the day's business concluded, in order that I could start the lengthy and painstaking job of totting up the sale's proceeds and balancing them against the bills. Ours was never the most commodious of auction houses: I had no quiet cubby-hole to which I could retire. My office was always the Sale Room desk, but I could never concentrate while Potty was mooching about.

Now came the time for his famous String and Brown Paper routine. He always insisted upon wrapping up his own purchases, and always brought his own materials. This act was usually accompanied by good-natured badinage with one of the porters and excessive rustling and attempted smoothing of his paper. All this was never a help to my concentration. And although, as I say, he always brought his own string and wrapping, it was never quite enough. He could usually be relied upon to come up to me to cadge a piece of string, a further piece of paper, or the use of a razor blade while I was halfway through adding up a long column. Many a time I have dashed down my pencil and shouted at him in rage: 'Oh, bugger off, Potty, for Christ's sake!'

Sometimes I used much stronger expletives, but I rarely offended. He took it all as a great joke, and yet there was one occasion, in the 'fifties, when our relations were at a very low point. He had annoyed and irritated me so much, and I had insulted him so badly — I am no slouch at invective — that Potty finally took offence.

'There's no need to talk to me like that, Snelling,' he said with unusual heat. 'You always treat me very badly here! I'm never spoken to like that in any of the other auction rooms or in any bookshops!'

I felt more than a little contrite, and I wondered if I had been too short-tempered with him. But my contrition didn't last long. Shortly afterwards, George McLeish told me that he had quite literally kicked Potty down the steps and out of his Little Russell Street bookshop.

In the early days of my job at Hodgson's old Pottesman would run up a bill of about six or seven lots, usually of no more than two or three pounds each, and would then ask for a bill listing only one or two of the items he had bought.

'I'll just pay for these now,' he would tell me, 'and I'll come back for the others later.'

He would come back for those others much, much later. It took us some time to tumble what he was up to. Obviously, he was prepared to pay immediately for those books which he knew he would be able to sell at once to a local dealer. As far as the others were concerned, he would scout around for weeks and months, trying to talk various booksellers into the idea of buying them. Only when he had made a definite sale — and he must have been remarkably persuasive to talk anyone into buying a book which had not been seen — would he come back to Chancery Lane, pay for the item in question, and trot off to deliver it to his customer. In the end, we had to put a stop to this practice, otherwise those books for which he could find no market might never have been paid for and collected. But he was not being wilfully dishonest, and once things had been made plain to him we had no more trouble in this direction: he paid up and took his purchases away *in toto*.

Strangely, there was never any need for this eccentric behaviour. He was not a poor man: quite the contrary. But he just could not bear to part with money which did not show evidence of netting him an almost immediate return.

Potty was almost infantile in much of his conversation and day to day social encounters, although when he talked about early-printed books he could leave you open-mouthed with awe and astonishment at the extent of his knowledge. Also, despite this knowledge, he was quite unemployable by any bookseller. He had never had a job, as such, in the whole of his life, except for one period when he had to go into a factory and do war work. He once admitted this to me quite cheerfully. I am perfectly sure that had it been in peacetime he would have been sacked within a matter of days. No guv'nor could possibly have tolerated him. He did things at *his* pace, and in *his* way, and no man on earth could change him.

Yet, in this own way of his, the man was nothing short of brilliant. I believe that he had a knowledge of *incunabula* and early-printed books far surpassing that of all but the most learned of scholars. Had he been less of a penny-pinching 'cheapy', and more of an adventurous type, willing to take a chance and back his judgement, he would have done much better than he did — and he did all right as it was, by most booksellers' standards.

Not that more money in his bank account would have changed his way of life. He bought and sold some books to pay his rent and to buy a little food, but the best things he usually kept, and I believe that he had an ever-present and irrational fear that if he spent he might not have the money to acquire the gems and high-spots for which he was forever seeking. Mere accumulation was all he ever seemed to want: the accumulation of rare books very few people ever saw. Spending money was anathema to him, and he lived like a pig to avoid it.

I called him a penny-pincher. That is not literally true, of course. I don't think Potty actually *pinched* a penny from anyone — or anything else for that matter — in the whole of his life. The man was scrupulously honest. He had a certain code of honour and ethics, for all his eccentricities and strange appearance, both of which made people tend to distrust him.

He kept most of his valuable books in various safe deposits and vaults, dotted about in London. They were not for reading, not for perusing, seldom even to be boasted about or discussed, except to or with a privileged few. He had them; and he knew he had them. That was enough. This did not prevent him from living in an agony of apprehension, continually fearing floods and burst pipes, which might ruin his valuable books housed deep below ground level and all too near the treacherous river, which one day might overflow. I have even heard that he suspected that the cistern in his flat might burst. He had it disconnected, and flushed the loo with a bucket!

I have been told that his aim was to collect one example, at least, of the work of every printer practising before the year 1500. It was an impossible task, perhaps, but Potty probably came nearer to realising his dream than any individual who attempted such a thing, although certain libraries and wealthy institutions surpassed his collection. But he owned a most formidable, albeit dispersed, library of *incunabula*.

There was one short period — all too brief for some booksellers and auction houses — when the man ceased to frequent his usual haunts. Word quickly got round that he had sequestered himself from the world, for the nonce, and was writing a book! This took a bit of believing. What on earth could he be writing about? Who would publish this work? It transpired, in course of time, that his 'book' was actually a pamphlet of a psychological nature and that he was having it printed privately. It was called *Time and the Playground Phenomenon*. When it was ready he sent out copies to several hundred people, acquaintances of his, mostly, who might be interested. But his *magnum opus* was still born. I have heard that not one person to whom he sent his pamphlet even acknowledged its receipt. This is rather difficult to believe, but if it is true, then surely that massive silence fell not because the pamphlet's recipients were callous, but rather because they were kind? No comment at all seemed preferable to the embarrassment of insincere praise and flattery.

I think Solomon Pottesman will be remembered in our trade generally, and by myself in particular, for a remarkable discovery he made in the 'fifties. It appears that the old binders, working on a stiffening or reinforcement for their calf or vellum covers, would use any convenient paper material or printers' waste that came to hand. Potty was always ferreting for this sort of thing, and he pulled out a manuscript sheet from one particular broken binding. I can do no better than to quote verbatim from Alan Thomas's obituary in *The Times*, later extended in *The Book Collector*.

> ... Francis Meres, writing in 1598, stated that Shakespeare had followed *Love's Labour Lost* with another play, *Love's Labour Won*. Scholars have searched for this ever since, but no copy has ever been seen or even recorded. In 1953 Pottesman removed from a copy of Thomas Gataker's *Certain Sermons*, 1637, some sheets from the ledger of Christopher Hunt, a bookseller working in Exeter in 1603, recording his transactions and stock. And there, among other plays by Shakespeare, adjacent to *Love's Labour Lost*, was *Love's Labour Won*.

Potty could have made a lot of money from that find, had he wanted to, and had he gone the right way about it. I know more than one or two dealers who would have hit the jackpot. Not Potty. I can't help admiring him for what he did — what he told me himself he did. It was quixotic and also enigmatic. This miser-cum-altruist told me he sold it for barely more than a token payment to a scholar working to prove the very point.

But he certainly got good publicity. One day he walked into the Chancery Lane 'clubroom' and proudly pulled out a letter he had recently received from the BBC. They wished to do a television programme on the subject. I don't think that he chose to show the letter to *me*, particularly — it was pretty well-thumbed, and I'm sure that it went the rounds, for he had good reason for his pride — but he gained considerable satisfaction from allowing me to see it. I had always shown him scant respect. He could never understand that my attitude had nothing at all to do with my opinion of his scholarship, which I respected, but only with the difficulties and frustrations he always presented at auction and afterwards, when I was harrassed to the extreme.

Still, the very idea of the old Potty we all knew actually going on the box and being interviewed was something that couldn't be missed. This I must see, I thought to myself. And everyone in the trade who got to know about it was incredulous, and looked forward to a sort of documentary *Comedy Playhouse.*

I admit that I misjudged the poor old chap entirely. On he went, in his usual dark shirt — we didn't have colour telly in those days — and with his cap removed, for once. He spent half an hour talking to Andrew Sinclair, and he put up a very good show. The whole thing was absorbing. It must have been rehearsed and edited, to some extent, I suppose. Pottesman, given his head, would have been impossible.

It was a very specialised programme, and I won't say that it appealed to the masses. Not many people of my acquaintance even heard about it. Most viewers probably watched a cowboy shoot-out or a comedy show on the other channel. Under different circumstances I might have elected to watch something a little more exciting and visually entertaining. As it happened, I wouldn't have flipped that knob for 'Star Wars on Ice'.

'And fools who came to scoff, remain'd to pray,' quoth Goldsmith. I, for one, remained to pray forgiveness — to Potty — for having laughed and joked about his appearance, for having sneered about him for his oddities and eccentricities, for having figuratively kicked his backside through our portals many, many a time for his infuriating ways.

The best buy he ever made more or less took place within the precincts of his beloved British Museum. Stories get garbled in the telling, quite naturally, and some details of the following may not be accurate. Certainly, the deal was a little more extended, but I think the gist is fairly true. Here, in the Reading Room one day, Potty met a bookseller who was just producing his first catalogue. He was deep in research when our man sidled up to him. He was quite naturally proud of the particular book he was working on, and Pottesman latched on to it immediately. He tried to buy it then and there, but the bookseller wasn't having any; he knew it would be the best thing in his catalogue.

The book was John Lathbury's *Liber Moralium Super Threnis Ieremie*, dated 1482, in a contemporary Oxford binding of blindstamped calf over wooden boards. Potty did his best to hide his enthusiasm, but he kept tabs on that bookseller nevertheless, and the minute his catalogue was printed and about to be distributed, Potty was on his doorstep. He snapped up the book at its price of £650. The story is embellished by the rider that he got a ten percent dealer's discount, of course, and it decorates an already fascinating anecdote immensely, but I have it on the best authority that it is not so.

Now, periodically, Pottesman would get some independent authority and expert to visit his vaults to value his major possessions for the purpose of insurance. He had this book down in his own list as being worth some £8,000, but the insurance company couldn't believe a book was worth that much, and they wouldn't accept his valuation. Michael Morton-Smith, who was called upon by Pottesman on more than one occasion to assess his rarities, has told me himself that *he* put a figure of £10,000 on this book alone, the first time he saw it, a good many years ago. When Potty died, Michael estimated that it might be worth double that figure, or more, with increasing trends. He wasn't far wrong. It realised £25,000 at auction. But Michael didn't know the half of it!

Paraphrase has its uses, at times, but why should I, with a very limited knowledge of the details of this matter, even attempt to offer my own version of what came to pass when my friend and colleague, Will Ward, first picked up this volume for detailed examination? It is far better that I go to Alan Thomas again and recount, in part, what he had to say in a postscript to his obituary and article on Pottesman after the collection had been sold.

> While preparing the catalogue the Hon. William Ward made a remarkable discovery. Examining the Oxford Lathbury, 1482, he noticed that vellum sewing-guards inserted in the middle of each quire consist of lateral fragments in three type-settings of John Kendale's Indulgence, licensed by Sixtus IV, to raise money for the defence of Rhodes against the Turks: one of 21 lines (only about 18 words of approximately 280 are missing) was printed by Caxton in 1480, and hitherto known only from two fragments at Trinity College, Cambridge ... a further 3½ lines (of 17) were printed at London by Lettou, 1480 ... And finally, 4½ lines printed by Caxton ... *hitherto unrecorded*, probably printed not much before or after what has been called up to now his second edition of 1480. The book ... therefore contains material printed by the prototypographers of Westminster, London and Oxford.

It is ironic that Pottesman, the master of the hidden fragments, should have kept this book (in his private strongroom below Harrods) for nine years without being aware of this exciting aspect. Had he kept it at home, poring over it, sooner or later, he must have realised that his most treasured volume was greater than even he had hoped.

Ironic indeed. I know of no more perverse an example of circumstance in all my dealings with buyers and sellers of books over the years. Conscious as he was of cash, the actual monetary value of that volume would have been of secondary importance to Potty. What delight he would have experienced had he only known that he *possessed* it!

I have dealt with him harshly, perhaps rather cruelly, in this short reminiscence. Yet I now remember the old chap with fondness, and while I have not exaggerated at all, I have tried to picture him as I saw and felt about him half a lifetime ago in order to highlight my own young intolerance.

When he died, he left his collection to one or two of his relatives of whom he was fond, and of whom he always spoke well. His niece, I remember, had always been particularly kind to him, when most of the people he encountered had given him short shrift. But I think he knew that nobody close to him cared a jot about his books, and he was desirous that the collection should be sold by Sotheby's, the firm with which I was then working.

An excellent catalogue of the *incunabula* and sixteenth-century books was produced by the aforementioned William Ward. The sale took place on 15 and 16 October, 1979. It realised close to £200,000. The catalogue also bore a photographic frontispiece of Potty, snapped by Keith Fletcher at a Book Fair. It is the only picture of him I have ever seen. Opposite, at the foot of the title-page, is the following information:

In Sending Commissions
this Catalogue may be referred to as

'INKY'

I honestly don't think he would have asked for a better epitaph.

When Potty arrives at his Valhalla, if he hasn't already got there, may it be chock-full of old bookshops he has never penetrated, all of them with unrecorded *incunabula*. I can see that grin now as he steps over each phantom threshold.

'Got any "Inkys" for me today?'

The Grey Man

I shall call the gentleman Patrick Upcott. That wasn't actually what he called himself. It's near enough, but the name which he went by was exactly the same as that of a very well-known person. To use it here would be rather confusing. I'm not at all sure that that was his real name, either. It was very British-sounding, and yet he had a slight foreign accent which was difficult to place. But he was not easily approachable, and was most certainly not the sort of man of whom you asked personal questions. He was perhaps the first of the slightly larger-than-life characters among book-collectors I had the privilege of encountering.

Looking back, I suppose that he might have been probably nothing more than just a rather reserved if unusually affluent business-man who accepted the possession of wealth as an everyday fact of life. He had the stuff in abundance, it was for use, and so he spent it. To us, all very humble and impecunious young men working at Hodgson's, and then drawing a weekly wage-packet the contents in pounds of which could be counted on a single hand, he was Croesus and Midas rolled into one.

Quite naturally, we often wondered what Patrick Upcott did for a living. We visualised sumptuous office accommodation at the very least, but in this, as in almost everything else, he proved to be an enigma. An enterprising colleague of mine, intent upon selling this unusual collector a particular book he felt might well be acceptable, once penetrated the man's premises. These held a simple desk, a tall green-metal filing cabinet, an imperturbable female secretary in an ante-room, and virtually nothing else. The nature of the business he conducted was a somewhat non-committal Import-Export.

We always thought and spoke of him as the Grey Man. There was good reason for this. For a start, he had greying hair and a decidedly greyish personality. Also, apart from his immaculate and highly-polished brown shoes, he always dressed entirely in grey: hat, shirt, tie, suit and socks. I have an idea he couldn't find any grey cigars about anywhere, although I'll bet he tried, but the expensive-looking cylinders of silvery ash which formed on the ends of those he was always smoking well made up for that.

He quite obviously had a great deal of the grey stuff. Brains certainly, but in addition he always carried many more than a considerable number of those crisp and crackling large five-pound notes of yore with the black copperplate engraving on a white and deceptively flimsy background.

From a distance these looked pale grey, and — please believe me — until well after the war was over people like myself only did see them from a distance: from across the footlights or on cinema screens. Unless you had a very lucky day at the races, which was unlikely, you rarely possessed them. Even then, you were anxious to be rid of the things, and any humble clerk or artisan trying to pass one in a local pub or in a grocer's shop might be asked to write his name and address on the back! They were legitimate currency, but hardly normal currency in our work-a-day world.

The gentleman I am dealing with here apparently disdained to use anything else. I never knew him to write a cheque. Further, I never knew him to handle mere pounds, shillings and pence, except when I gave him change for his purchases. Even this was rare: he bought costly books which normally came to a fairly round figure. But in those days of guineas and half-guineas there were one or two occasions when I had to hand him silver and copper.

I have no idea what he did with this dross. I have imagined him casting it into the gutter as he left our premises, but I admit that my imagination is warped with regard to Patrick Upcott. He probably took all his small change to his bank as soon as possible and got it all back in newly-minted fivers. Once or twice I caught a glimpse of him in places like Harrod's, or the much more convenient Gamage's, which was not far from his office. He was always as grey as usual, and always with that aromatic cigar, impassively paying out at the cash desk for large and expensive-looking parcels. I was sufficiently intrigued to watch this process and see if he came up to my expectations. He did: always those crisp fivers! Nobody ever asked *him* to write on them.

Until this time I had never before met an individual like Patrick Upcott. The nearest I had come to it was in reading A. J. A. Symons's brilliant pen-portrait in *The Quest for Corvo* of that real-life but most unlikely book-collector, J. Maundy Gregory. This most extravagant gentleman kept *his own taxi* to run him about London. He could have afforded a couple of Rolls-Royces, but his explanation was that a waiting taxi attracted less attention. Patrick Upcott did not go that far, but he clocked up a great deal more on the meter at the kerbside than ever he did on his journeys. He would always command the taxi-driver to wait, and would then walk into the auction room and quite calmly and leisurely spend anything up to an hour or two viewing the books for a forthcoming sale. Presumably he acted similarly in his other jaunts and dealings around town. Once, I walked out for a morning cuppa and found an impatient and apprehensive driver watching our front door.

'That bloke — the one with the cigar on — is 'e still in there?' he asked me.

'Don't worry,' I informed him. 'He's still there. He won't run away.'

But on another occasion the taxi-man was not so trusting. He must have been bilked in the not-too-distant past. After a very long wait, which was disturbing Patrick Upcott not at all as he viewed the books, in burst a very disturbed taxi-driver who looked wildly round the crowded room before approaching my desk.

''Ere, guv'nor,' he said, 'there ain't a back way out of this place, is there?'

I cottoned on immediately, and jerked my thumb in Patrick Upcott's direction. The driver made an effort to bluster his fare into either hurrying up with what he was doing or else paying off the taxi, but Upcott hardly looked up from the book he was perusing. The man had advertised himself and his vehicle for hire, he had been hired, and as far as Patrick Upcott was concerned both the man and his cab were his till Doomsday or until he chose to relinquish them. 'Just wait outside for me,' he said, turning his back. 'I shan't be long.' He was, though.

I cannot recall the Grey Man ever dropping out of the bidding for a lot, or even being the final unsuccessful under-bidder. Once he had latched on to an item he always stayed with it until the lot was his.

Well, all very interesting, I can imagine you thinking. But what sort of books did this unusual man collect? Was he a general buyer, or did he specialise? Well, that's a fair enough query. He did specialise, and very much so. And in what else but early-printed volumes entirely devoted to alchemy?

Alice in Plunderland

'The poor always ye have with you.' But rampant inflation, unlike the poor, was not always with us. It only seems like it. In earlier days there were certain standard books which, while not exactly scarce or rare, had long been out of print. There was always a ready market for them whenever they turned up. To some extent they were the bread and butter of the trade, and you could nearly always reckon, within a matter of a few shillings, how much they were going to make at a book auction.

Tombleson's *Thames*, for instance, is a good example. Full of rather dull and gloomy steel engravings, booksellers had once chucked it aside as unsaleable. It was now an eight pound book. An exceptionally clean copy might even realise as much as eight pounds ten! It had become a 'breaker'. The plates were cleaned up and coloured by an industrious horde of ladies and gentlemen working all over the country, and were then mounted or framed and sold individually. Nobody was interested in the text. Booksellers laughed their heads off at this sudden change of fortune, except those who had handled dozens of copies and had thrown them out. It's pretty scarce today, and makes well over its 'double century'.

The Yellow Book, a handsome set of thirteen volumes in a canary-hued binding — if the dust hadn't been allowed to get at it — was reckoned at about ten bob per tome. This made the full set worth about six and a half quid. A particularly fine set might even fetch seven. I coveted a run of this remarkable periodical publication, a sort of late Victorian *Saturday Book,* with contributions by Aubrey Beardsley, Max Beerbohm, Baron Corvo, and contemporaries. But I could never afford it. It would have cost me the better part of a week's wages. Today a fine set might make well over £200, and it's still going up. This is a good example of how prices have outstripped earnings: £10,500 per annum is a bit more than the present national average.

There was another good set which always made roughly the same price. This was Bury's edition of Gibbon's *Decline and Fall*. It bore excellent notes, and it was beautifully illustrated. It was also nicely cased in blue cloth gilt. The set ran to seven volumes, and the trade reckoned them as being worth at least a pound each. Under the hammer, Bury never made less than its full seven pounds, but it had to be a pristine set to reach seven and a half or eight.

Do not imagine that I am suggesting that those halcyon days would have stayed with us forever had galloping inflation not set in pretty soon afterwards. But I am writing here of the early and mid-'fifties. Halcyon they may have seemed; in retrospect we realise they were austere. However, I was privileged to be a close observer of one of the events which first started to send prices wild in the second-hand and antiquarian book business. I'm sure that even some of the hardened veterans are not even aware that they played their own part in it — not consciously and admittedly, anyway.

At the particular time I am writing about, the London trade was dominated largely by a few select names. Most of them, I am most happy to say, are still flourishing. One or two seemed to be remarkably fortunate in their contacts. They were quite able to fill their shelves from advantageous private purchases, and they seldom seemed to be obliged to have recourse to the auction rooms for stock. But other firms had a rather larger turnover than that fortunate few. They sold so many books each week that they simply *had* to use the various sale rooms in order to replenish their continually dwindling stock. I will mention a few of these businesses by name.

There was Maggs Bros., that famous family firm in the magnificent house in Berkeley Square, with the fathers, the uncles, the sons and nephews, all known by their first names but all respectfully awarded the prefix of Mr. by employees and clients alike. Then there was the fine shop of Francis Edwards, with its double windows and its long and galleried rooms in Marylebone High Street. There were also the imposing premises of both Bernard Quaritch and Chas. J. Sawyer, at that time next door to each other in Grafton Street. Three others who never missed a sale were Thorp's of Albemarle Street, and Joseph's and Marks & Co., both of Charing Cross Road. Represented by the senior employees Wally Harris, Bernard Simpson, and Frank Doel respectively, three of the most knowledgeable bookmen who ever lived, these firms *really* viewed a sale, no matter whether it was large or small. If any mixed lot in an auction room harboured a 'sleeper', then one or more of this trio smelt it out.

But came the day when a new face began to appear in Hodgson's Rooms — and probably in others, too. There was a certain prosperous business which was established in the West End of London. Hitherto, this expanding enterprise had confined itself almost exclusively to the sale of *new* books. It was now opening up all sorts of specialised departments in various parts of town. One of them, in a spacious and well-located basement, was to devote itself to second-hand and antiquarian books.

The gentleman employed to run this side of the business was an amiable maverick whom I shall refer to here as Donovan. He was intelligent and educated, and to a considerable extent he knew what he was up to. But he lacked that asset which had been acquired in an abundance by those firms I have mentioned, and for which there is no substitute — not even with whizz-kids: experience.

Apparently Donovan was given *carte-blanche* to buy. He also had a firm behind him with plenty of cash. Further, I think he had primed himself by diligently reading all the manuals on auction procedure. Most of these inform the prospective buyer that if he does not wish to do the bidding himself this job will always be readily undertaken by somebody else, usually a dealer, at ten percent. Obviously, he couldn't ask his rivals in the trade; for one thing, he didn't know any of them well enough. He didn't fancy any of the auctioneers handling his commissions, either. So he came to the Sale Clerks. I was in this particular position at Hodgson's. So for some months I did all of his bidding, and extremely successful I was. I also received, in cash, a strict ten percent of all Donovan's bills! (I think I should add here that I have been acting at the desk on behalf of various clients *in absentia* for well over thirty years, and I have now bought many, many thousands of pounds worth of books. If my customers had all paid me a strict ten percent on successes I should today be a very rich man indeed.)

When Donovan grew a little elated and confident with his continuing success — a success which wasn't surprising, since he was paying over the odds — and when a particularly good sale came along, he elected to attend Hodgson's Rooms himself and buy. This was a mistake. Hitherto, when I had been holding his marks, nobody had known whom I might be representing. I could have been bidding on behalf of any one of twenty or thirty clients, both trade and private, and nobody would have known the identity of the successful buyer until the lot was knocked down and I called a name. Even then, I could have used a pseudonym. Only the more courageous would have dared to run me up too far, for fear of being landed with an over-priced lot. But when Donovan plonked himself down at a conspicuous spot in the Sale Room and started bidding recklessly on all the good items in an effort to stock his shelves, more than one or two of his rivals refused to let him have a cheap lot. He ran up an impressive bill, it is true, and he got most of the good books, but he had to pay at least half as much more than they had previously made. In some cases, where his opponents had been unusually wicked, he paid nearly twice their earlier value.

'*You* went a bit mad, didn't you?' I said to Donovan after the sale was over.

He shrugged. 'Can't be helped. I've got to have the stock.'

Unfortunately, it is one thing to buy books at high prices; it is quite another to sell them at even higher figures and to show a profit at the end of the financial year. Also, he had established new prices for worthwhile books, and these prices were being noted in the annual volumes of the sale room transactions. Most booksellers would recognise that the high figures shown in *Book Auction Records* were inflated ones, but private collectors and amateurs wouldn't do so quite as quickly. Next time they would be prepared to spend even a little more to get what they wanted.

Inevitably, the time arrived when Donovan's firm must have come to the conclusion that he was a bit too much of a luxury. The antiquarian side of this particular business continued, but in different and less profligate hands. Donovan himself got a job with another firm of booksellers, who dealt almost exclusively in new publications bearing a net price on their glossy wrappers. This was an entirely different kettle of fish. But the damage had been done.

Presumably Donovan prospered, but I saw no more of him in our Sale Room for some years. I might never have seen him again, but for a rather remarkable occurrence. I think it makes an interesting anecdote, and it is certainly a most unusual sequel to all the foregoing. One day, in he walked.

'Hullo, stranger,' I said to him. 'Come to buy some old books?'

'No. I've come to sell one.'

He handed it to me. It was instantly recognisable. There is no other book quite like it. It was a copy of *Alice in Wonderland*.

'A first?' I asked doubtfully.

'Yes.'

'Ah — but the *right* one?'

He nodded. I opened it at the title-page, and sure enough, there was the date: 1865. It was a terribly dilapidated copy, but there was no doubt about it. It was the first copy I had ever touched or even seen.

I should explain here that Charles Lutwidge Dodgson, the author, who wrote this book under the name of Lewis Carroll, financed the production of the famous classic himself. He had the last word in all the phases of its printing and binding, although he employed Macmillan's for its publication and distribution. The story goes that when he first received a pristine copy of the book in 1865 he was dissatisfied with the appearance of Sir John Tenniel's illustrations, although I have heard, too, that Tenniel himself didn't like their reproduction, which might have influenced Dodgson. At any rate, the author ordered the whole job to be done again.

Since he was footing the bill the job *was* done again, but *Alice in Wonderland* didn't come out until the end of the year, and a new date appeared at the foot of the title-page: 1866. But since Macmillan's had never anticipated anything quite so fastidious from this very fastidious man, they had already jumped the gun, so to speak. A number of advance copies had already been despatched. They called them all in, of course, and many came back to be replaced. But a few — nobody knows quite how many — did not. So that today, while the official 1866 first edition of *Alice* remains a rare and desirable enough item in itself, the very, very scarce 1865 printing is even more desirable and extremely valuable. The known copies of it some twenty or so years ago could almost be counted on the fingers of two hands.

And here I was, holding yet another copy of it!

'What's it worth?' asked Donovan.

'In this condition, who knows? Two — three hundred? Maybe more.'

I should point out that in my experience relatively few 'juveniles', or books produced for children, were ever retained in good condition. The youngsters read them with jammy hands, scrawled in them and dropped them, and sometimes successive generations wore them to pieces. This one was no exception. It was bent and dog-eared at every corner, far from clean inside, and only a strip of the front end-paper remained. Even so, it was still an 1865 *Alice*.

It seems that it had been bought in a collection from an overseas client who had, in turn, picked it up for the equivalent of about two shillings and threepence in an Indian bookshop! How it had ever got there I suppose we shall never know. Before that, as I gathered from information inside the book, it had been in the library of a children's convalescent institution. Dodgson is known to have presented a number of these withdrawn books to similar establishments: 'hospital copies', as they are known to the bibliographers of *Alice*.

The day arrived when the volume was put up for sale. On the morning of the auction, while the books were still being viewed, who should walk in but the great Lew D. Feldman. Big, shrewd, and taciturn, Lew was an extremely successful American bookseller, although with his expensive camel-hair coat and his hand-stitched suit he looked more like the popular image of a successful bookmaker. Come to that, he gave the impression of Hollywood's idea of a nineteen-twenties gangster, too. I think he fostered these ideas.

This singular gentleman had earlier taken his three initials and had incorporated them into the name of his firm: The House of El Dieff, New York City.

Now, the verb 'to plunder' suggests robbery, theft, and even embezzlement. It would be quite unfair to ascribe such terms to Lew, but plundering carries its onomatopoeiac suggestions, too. Although he paid his bills, the man was quite inclined, like Byron's Assyrian, to 'come down like a wolf on the fold' at any really prestigious sale of rare books at auction. I have known him to take virtually every important lot in a catalogue. He left in his wake an impression of disaster, pillage and rape, and many, many a sorry heart in the book trade.

I knew immediately what Lew was after, naturally, when he visited our otherwise somewhat ordinary sale that day. He seldom deigned to visit us, and then only to look at the high spots. A dealer of his stature and status could only have come for one thing. I walked into the office and took the book from the safe the moment I saw him walk through the doors.

He glanced at it with his dead pan and those puffy, menacing eyes, and handed it back to me rather disdainfully.

'What time'll it be comin' up?' he asked.

'Oh — about three o'clock,' I told him, after a hasty calculation.

'I got an appointment.' He glowered for a moment. 'Not at all sure I can make it.' He turned and started to walk away.

Then, as if as an afterthought, he stopped and said: 'Bid for me up to five hundred. An' don't use *my* name — use your own. But . . . I may be back.' And off went Lew, without a please or a thank you.

I didn't want the man to come back. *I* wanted to buy that book. There would be nothing in it financially, I knew quite well. I was aware from the experience of earlier dealings that Lew D. Feldman didn't pay menials for executing his commissions. But the kudos of buying an 1865 *Alice in Wonderland* in my own name, with full details in *Book Auction Records* and *American Book Prices Current* would do me no harm at all for the future. And I must say that I felt pretty confident of securing the lot. £500 seemed a hell of a lot of money for that tatty copy.

So you may imagine how my heart sank when at about five minutes to three o'clock, and only a short time before the book was due to come under the hammer, I saw Lew walk in through the swing doors. More than one or two other hearts sank, too, when their owners glimpsed him. He came up quietly behind me and said: 'Drop it.' He would be bidding for the lot himself.

When the *Alice* came up for sale, it transpired that there were only two bidders in it. I watched as Lew Feldman and the young John Maggs bid against each other impassively. I saw them both pass that figure of £500 with expressionless faces, and I gawped as the New Yorker finally took the book at the almost incredible price of £880.

Remember, he had seen this book, he had valued it at £500, and he would have been prepared to pay up to this figure had he sent me a 'phoned or postal commission from the States, or had he left *me* to try to buy it in *my* name for him. I was the only person in that Sale Room, apart from Lew himself, who was aware of the value he had placed upon it. But here he was at the sale himself, which is quite a different thing.

The point of my anecdote is that Lew D. Feldman was too big a fish in our small pond of antiquarian books to be seen to be the loser or under-bidder on an 1865 *Alice in Wonderland*. I think that John Maggs was more than probably bidding on commission up to the figure of £850, but this makes no difference at all. I believe that had he received instructions to go up to £1,000, or had his firm decided to buy the book for stock up to the same figure, Lew would still have taken it at £1,100.

I heard later, via a devious route, that Feldman sat on his purchase for quite a time, but that he eventually sold the book at a very handsome profit. I know how much he made. I wonder what that battered little volume would make today? Considerably more than his eventual selling price, I am quite certain.

A cautionary word to ambitious young booksellers who might be reading these lines: I have related how Donovan changed the 'giving' price of some certain standard books almost overnight and then found that he couldn't sell them. I have also told of how Lew D. Feldman gave a lot more for an item than he felt it was worth and still cashed in. But there is a hell of a difference between the Donovans and the Feldmans in *our* little world of rare and antiquarian books.

The Little Doctor

There was a time when he was known to almost every bookseller in the country — of volumes both new and second-hand. He was a small, frail, and elderly man of benign countenance and disposition. He was also the meekest of all the earth-inheritors. He lived in retirement with his maiden sister, in a very pleasant block of mansion flats just across the river, facing Battersea Park. After I had got to know him well I visited him several times, and there wasn't a book to be seen in the place, although I was aware that he was an indefatigable collector. He appeared to be quite dominated by his prim sister and a somewhat autocratic manservant. These two had ganged up against him, and both of them bullied him unmercifully. I don't think they allowed such dust-gathering things as books in that spacious flat.

But he had overcome this problem. He must have got on extremely well with his next-door neighbour, whose own flat was a bit too large for *his* needs. The little doctor had arranged to have a hole knocked in the far wall of his bedroom, which flanked the adjoining premises, and he had a door put in, to which only he held the key. Thus, with private access to a fairly large room in his neighbour's abode, which neither the doctor's sister nor his employee ever entered to pry into or to clean, he was able to house one of the most remarkable collections of books, prints, and ephemera it has ever been my privilege to see.

Many years previously, I gathered, he had been responsible for a great deal of successful research involving respiratory diseases contracted by chimney-sweeps and other similar unfortunates. Somehow it brought him a great deal of money in the form of a grant, award or honorarium. I don't know the details, for he was always extremely reticent about his achievements in the medical profession. Personally — although I loved the little man, for he was extremely engaging — I don't think I would have trusted him to bandage a cut finger or prescribe an aspirin. He did not exactly inspire confidence. Obviously, his talents lay in a quite different direction.

At any rate, he lived very comfortably — as did his sister, who seemed to be entirely dependent upon him financially — on a pretty handsome income. He had, early on, begun his book-collecting career with Charles Dickens in the original parts — pristine condition only, naturally — but after his success he started to accumulate *everything* he could lay his hands

117

on which referred to, either in detail or in the slightest way, with chimney-sweeps!

If there are any middle-aged or elderly London booksellers reading these lines who have wondered, up to this point, what on earth I might be getting at, I am sure they will now immediately remember him. He was, indeed, Dr. Sidney Henry, dome-pated, bowler-hatted, and mittened.

I doubt if there was a single book, story, article, print or snippet even mentioning sweeps which he did not possess, in all editions or states. If he didn't have it he certainly knew about it, and the pursuit was never-ending. He spent every weekend at it, and his collection was racked all round that room on those very convenient but most hideous adjustable units of dark green metal shelving, with all the holes, the nuts, and the bolts. The solitary window in that adjunct hadn't been opened for many years, and its panes were never cleaned. But the place wasn't particularly dirty, since the only dust that ever got a chance to penetrate it was that which came in with the books he bought. But it was airless, musty and gloomy.

The little old chap and I got on wonderfully together. I don't know why, exactly, for I had not the slightest interest in chimney-sweeps. I didn't 'fancy' him, either, although I was fond of him. I had very early on guessed, or rather suspected, that he might be of a homosexual inclination. This was not my first close encounter with the third kind. But it was a long time before I knew him well enough even to broach that subject.

It finally came about after he had told me of his rather stern, stolidly Victorian home up-bringing, of how as a young man at table one day he had happened to mention the name of the current 'man in the news', the scandalous Oscar Wilde. His father had clamped down immediately, forbidding mention forever in his household of this most wicked, de-praved, and criminal of beings. I'm quite sure little sister didn't know *then* what Oscar had been getting up to, and I feel pretty sure she had only the very vaguest idea in the 'fifties, when I knew her — if the thought ever crossed her chaste and delicate mind. Bodily functions of *any* sort were rarely broached by ladies of her generation and upbringing, particularly with those of the opposite gender. Even in the mid-twentieth century, when both she and my young wife were discussing the best food for cats, a species they were both fond of, my wife happened to mention raw liver. The lady paused, waited until my attention was attracted by her brother's conversation, and then shook her head furtively, and silently but exag-geratedly mouthed the fact to my wife that 'Liver's too *opening*!'

The little doctor confessed to me, after his Oscar Wilde story, of having felt a certain affinity and comradeship with that pariah of the 'nineties, but he had lived in silence with his predilections. I do not think he was much of a practising invert, if he ever lapsed at all. Surely there must be celibate homosexuals as well as celibate heterosexuals, albeit extremely few?

Over the years, as I got to know him much better, he tended to confide in me more and more. His pursuit of the chimney-sweep in literature remained unabated, even to the extent of that enormous seventy-odd-volume set of Voltaire's *Works*, which contains, I believe, one short reference to the subject of his interest. But our social acquaintance ripened, mostly in Lyons' Teashops or ABCs, after I had finished work. Here he expanded. He was a lonely little soul, and he seemed really delighted to have found a sympathetic listener: somebody with whom he could joke about his rather solitary plight and know that I would not censure him or turn away in disgust or misunderstanding. Today, of course, sexual inversion is not only accepted but is barely given a second thought. Throughout this poor old chap's life to be queer was virtually a crime. You weren't gay then: the word was not yet in common usage. He didn't live to see the day when those of his ilk would become emancipated, and a relationship 'between consenting adults' would no longer be frowned upon by the law and so-called respectable society.

For all that, as close and as confidential with each other as we grew, I never felt able to mention to him another thing I had suspected. It was my opinion that his overwhelming and absorbing interest in chimney-sweeps, and particularly those urchin ones of the last century, exemplified in books like *The Water Babies*, had a morbid basis, and that the rather obvious Freudian symbolism of the sweeps going up the dirty chimneys was entirely lost upon him.

One day, a cataloguing colleague of mine, a sophisticated young man who eventually grew almost as close to our old friend as I was myself, was sorting through an enormous private library which had recently come into us for sale by auction. Now, it should be understood that in many collections of this sort, while most of the books are saleable and often very valuable, there is much of very little worth. On one side of the room was a shelf or two of the 'chuck-outs': rather worthless books and pamphlets which would eventually have to be sold off before the auction sale proper to any small market dealer or barrow-boy who made the best offer. My colleague tossed me a slim volume from this shelf, just for a laugh.

It was a privately-printed little book of verses. I am no great judge of poetry, but even *I* could see that most of the stuff in this *opus* was little more than flowery and sentimental doggerel. The most interesting things in the book, as far as I was concerned, were a number of pasted-in and rather excellent sepia photographs of adolescent boys, all in the nude, all in leafy surroundings with sunlight shining through the trees, and all with beautifully slim limbs and well-rounded buttocks.

'Ha!' I said, with great amusement, 'this is delicious! The little doctor would love it. Let's send it to him — just for a joke?'

I don't recall who bought that stack. Whichever one of the dealers it was who got it, he didn't 'reckon' the book at all. He wouldn't take a penny from me for it, and passed it over for nothing.

It was duly sent to the little doctor. The recipient was just as amused and delighted by it as we had been, for the title, the illustrations, and the verses of the poetaster. The most engaging thing about the doctor was an ability to see the pathos *and* the bathos of the whole situation. The book was eventually absorbed into his enormous collection, I suppose. Where it resides today I do not know, although I am aware that his exhaustive accumulation of books and ephemera on chimney-sweeps found a resting-place, before his death, in a special room in the library of a well-known northern university.

The pay-off to my anecdote is that many years later, long after the little doctor had departed, I read an essay by Donald Weeks. It was called 'A Corvo Collection'. It may be found in Cecil Woolf's and Brocard Sewell's *New Quests for Corvo*. This is a number of contributions by various hands: a most admirable anthology which supplements the famous A.J.A. Symons biography of that enigmatic and improbable character know as Fr. Rolfe. The piece under discussion refers to a slight book of verses, by one John Gambril Nicholson, entitled *A Garland of Ladslove*, issued in 1911. It contains a poem, 'From the Italian of Baron Corvo'. Nicholson and Rolfe had been to school together in the eighteen-eighties, and had been acquaintances until after the turn of the century. The book now makes quite a bit of money.

This was the little book that had been lightly tossed aside, had been just as lightly tossed back, and had been passed on for a laugh to the indulgent butt of our humour.

A Garland of Ladslove, if not exactly an extremely rare book, is not all that easily obtainable. It is definitely an essential item in any Corvo collection. And the photos — those with the deliciously-rounded boys' bottoms — who took those? After all, Frederick Rolfe Baron Corvo, artist, translator, poet, biographer, novelist, was no mean photographer, either.

A Salutary Story

I do not think that there can be a great many people reading these lines who will remember George Salby. Admittedly, there are a few old-timers still knocking about who couldn't possibly forget him, but he wasn't exactly what you would call a good mixer with other members of the book trade, and he didn't have a lot of time for customers in his shop, unless they were heavy spenders.

He was a big, lean, and taciturn man whom some might have called downright surly. He was quite unlike a bookseller — whatever a bookseller is like, and I'm sure I don't know that. I had long heard that he was of Scandinavian origin, and I am indebted to J. G. Garratt, who worked for the man for a couple of years before the war, for informing me that Salby actually came from Aarhus, in Denmark, and that his real name was actually Georg Satrup.

For much of his early life he had been a merchant seaman, and a most unlikely candidate to open up a bookshop in Great Russell Street, hard by the British Museum. But this is what he did, and here he flourished for many years. He specialised in books on the Far East, and in archaeology and exploration. He had a pretty good pitch.

David Low has told us of Salby's frugality, of how he used to save paper and string from the incoming parcels, to be used again for his outgoing ones. I have known more than one or two people equally frugal in this respect — it is not at all unusual in the book trade, where overheads seem disproportionately large and profits all too small — and I can certainly bear David out as far as old George Salby was concerned. For one of the many manual employees who passed through Hodgson's Rooms as a porter during the 'fifties and 'sixties was that engaging but grotesque and furtive alcoholic imbiber named Turpin, of whom I have already written.

He had worked for Salby before he came to us. But not, it transpired, on a monthly basis, or even a weekly one. No, Salby wanted value for money, and he paid Turpin by the day. The man was unreliable, to say the least, as he himself was only too ready to admit. His wages were ten bob a day, and he didn't get *that* all in one lump. Salby gave him five shillings for his morning's work of packing and humping folios, and if he came back after his liquid luncheon and was able to do an afternoon stint he got another five bob in the evening.

It seems that George Salby was a very violent man when he was put out, and had been known to assault his assistants physically. Perhaps, quite naturally, nobody stayed with him for very long. He also had some very strange and unusual ideas. One was that the only time one should have intercourse with one's wife was solely to procreate. Harold Edwards, who learned this as a young man soon after the First World War, has an amusing remark on the subject: 'In my early twenties I thought this very odd. In my early eighties I still do...'

I knew George Salby for many, many years, and yet I *really* only got to know him on the very last occasion I ever saw him. I shall never forget it.

It was late afternoon on the day before Christmas Eve, and our last working day before the holiday. There was nothing on view in our Rooms, and the spacious shelves were gaunt and empty but for a few uncollected lots from a recent sale. The staff had knocked off early. The guv'nors, the cataloguers, and all the porters were away for the coming Christmas spree. The pubs had now closed, twilight had already descended, and noisy revellers were wending their way up and down the narrow Chancery Lane to their buses and stations.

I was just about ready to shut up and lock up when in walked George Salby with an enormous empty portmanteau! He had come in to collect a load of books he had bought in the sale we had held about a week or so before.

Now, he did not exactly qualify for the Popularity Stakes at that precise moment, as you can imagine, but the spirit of Christmas was strong upon me, and I not only helped him to fill up his roomy case but chatted to him about things in general for some time. I only wish now that I could remember more of what we talked about, but I can't. I do recall that I was amazed at his geniality: he appeared to have mellowed tremendously in his old age.

On reflection, it occurs to me that *he* must have been equally amazed. He seemed agreeably surprised to be treated with courtesy and consideration. Hitherto, I should add, he had never been treated with anything else as far as I was concerned, but our previous dealings, over what seemed donkeys' years to a fairly young man, had been brief and sporadic. They had been largely confined to his presentation of a cheque up at the desk while a sale was in progress and his business was done, my hasty receipt stamping of his sale-bill, with a quick 'Thank you, sir — see the porter,' and my rapid return to the next lot that was being knocked down by the auctioneer. I had watched him viewing a sale many times in the past, close to some of his near-neighbours like young Sawers, at that time with Kegan Paul, the Wheeler brothers of George Harding's, and Don Berry, then with Edward G. Allen's — in those days businesses of considerable consequence — but he, as well as those experienced individuals, was an old hand at the job of viewing a sale and had never had to approach me for aid in locating any odd lots. We had had the minimum to do with each other.

'Where on earth are you lugging this load to?' I asked him, as we filled up his case and squeezed the lid closed. 'Great Russell Street?'

'No,' he said. 'I'm taking it home.'

'Are you sure you can manage?' I was really concerned. It was a hell of a weight, and the man must have been pushing eighty. But he assured me that everything was all right, and he tottered out with his burden as I wished him a Merry Christmas.

It was now some time after four-thirty. I turned off all the lights, locked up the premises, and then wandered up the gloomy yet high-spirited and raucous Lane towards my bus in Holborn. Halfway up I encountered Salby again. He was taking a rest, and breathing heavily.

'Here,' I said to him, 'you can't manage this. How far have you got to go? Where do you live?'

'Barnet,' he told me. 'Once I get it to the station I'll be all right.'

'Hold this!' I thrust my light brief-case into his hand and picked up his load of books. I admit that it nearly creased me getting that burden to Chancery Lane tube station at the Holborn end of Gray's Inn Road. I left him with it at the top of the escalator, after he had bought his ticket. He wouldn't let me take it any further, and he insisted that the worst of his journey was done. I took his word for it. I waved the old chap goodbye as he descended from sight. I don't know to this day if he had to drag that case up Barnet Hill at the other end.

But I do know this. George Salby dropped dead the very next day, Christmas Eve, from a heart attack. He was standing in line to buy stamps at the Barnet Post Office. I'm sure I know what killed him, too. The man had lived by books — and he died by them as well. Some of the more uncharitable members of our trade suggested that his death coincided with a sudden rise in parcel post rates, of which he had been unaware.

It's funny how you remember certain things: in my mind's eye I can still see that cheque of his — held over for payment until his estate was finally settled. I even remember the amount. It was for eighteen pounds.

Dear healthy young booksellers, and emerging enthusiastic collectors, quietly convinced in your twenties and thirties that you are immortal — take note. You are not! And simply picking up a copy of Dylan Thomas's slim *Eighteen Poems* will one day feel as if you're hoisting a volume of Camden's *Britannia* — if there are any of them left intact — and well before you know it!

The Worst Bidder in the World

Apsley Cherry-Garrard was a book-collector, apparently with plenty of money to indulge his tastes. He was a rather extraordinary but simple man. A gentleman, in the original and now rather old-fashioned sense of that term, he was also a mild and somewhat naive amateur who stood very little chance at all with the professional sharks of our trade.

He had been a member of Captain Scott's famous and ill-fated expedition to the South Pole, before the first World War, and he was the author of the standard work about that adventure: *The Worst Journey in the World*. It is a rather remarkable thing, perhaps, but it is certainly a fact that a man who had braved all the physical and mental vicissitudes of a hazardous Polar Exploration shouldn't really have been allowed out alone in London, and particularly not into the book auction rooms of New Bond Street, King Street, and Chancery Lane.

He appeared to be quite oblivious that he was often being made the 'fall-guy' when he attended a sale. Once, he informed me that he deliberately wore a shabby old raincoat, and told his wife that he would be wearing his 'auction hat' when he came up to town to do his bidding — it was a battered old thing — being quite mistakenly under the impression that his competitors would thus not think that he was a man of means. The truth is that his cover was blown on the very first occasion he ever attended and bought at a really important auction.

There was a handsome set of the four *Shakespeare Folios* at Hodgson's: a most desirable acquisition for anyone. Naturally, there was a room full of hopeful prospective purchasers, and a chorus of rubber-necking onlookers as well, to say nothing of the BBC's Radio Newsreel — this was well before the regular television coverage of the more important auction sales.

The bidding went up and up, as old John Hodgson took the nods. Eventually came the offer of £7,000, which was already a record, at that time, for a lot sold at Chancery Lane, and the bidding stopped. John was just about to knock it down when from the crowd at the back of the room came the words: 'Seven thousand, one hundred!'

A pause, and then down came the gavel. Both Wilfrid and Sidney Hodgson, who were keen observers, understandably, were out there very quickly to find out who this nondescript buyer in the dirty coat and shabby hat might be. The trade didn't get to know immediately, but they very soon came to recognise him whenever he showed his face again in the various major sale rooms, and I don't think he ever bought a bargain afterwards — auction hat notwithstanding.

This is not to suggest that the trade made a particular point of 'running him up' whenever it came apparent that he had latched on to a certain book. That is a most unwise and dangerous practice, as most of my experienced confrères know only too well, but I am sure that one or two of them exceeded their pencilled marks, in desperation, once they came to know who was bidding against them. But there *was* one bookseller who became dead-set against Apsley Cherry-Garrard, and this calls for a slight digression.

This man, Raphael King, has been dead now for many years. Although he was admired universally as a great bookman, I never knew anyone who had a charitable word to say about him purely as a person. He was a rogue, but quite unlike most of the other genial rogues I have met in this trade, he was a very unpleasant piece of work.

He hated the idea of anyone else buying a book that he coveted, and he was jealous of the success of any of his colleagues. He strongly resented any dealer bidding against him at auction — 'Lay off, that's *my* book,' — and he was absolutely thumbs down against a private collector opposing him.

He particularly disliked Cherry-Garrard. He would quite regularly oppose the collector on any book that had taken that gentleman's fancy, and Cherry-Garrard paid through the nose for many an item.

'I don't like the look of his bloody face,' the bookseller told me once in explanation of his regular attitude.

Now, *I* didn't particularly mind anybody forcing up the price against someone he didn't care for. Why should I? The higher the prices at auction, the more prosperous the firm became. And, of course, in logical sequence, the more stable my position and the better my prospects. But I didn't like King's attitude when he got stuck with a lot he had never really wanted, after someone else had 'dropped' him with it. Other booksellers have confessed to me many a time that they might have paid too much for an item, but they have shrugged it off with a grin and have taken a loss — or else have held on to it, and sometimes surprisingly made a handsome and unexpected profit in course of time.

My man's response after paying over the odds was often quite different. He had no compunction about defacing a volume in some way, and then returning it, under the Conditions of Sale, as imperfect or defective. He couldn't put in unmentioned worm-holes or things of that sort, which a cataloguer might easily have missed, but he had other and most ingenious methods. I shall not relate or describe them here — I should hate to put temptation in anybody's way — but they certainly *were* ingenious.

And now, to return to Cherry-Garrard. I tried, on many more than one occasion, to point out to him that he would save himself money by leaving commissions either with the auctioneer, who would bid on his behalf from the rostrum, or with one of the more reputable bookselling firms, who would act for him with integrity for ten percent, and with his name never being mentioned. But I could not convince him. I think he had a persecution complex. He appeared to believe that the whole world was in some sort of conspiracy to get money out of him. I admit I was rather flattered, when he confided this opinion to me. At least he didn't think that *I* was one of those on the make!

I don't know the full extent or truth of his suspicions — they might have had some basis of fact, and thus contributed towards his increasing eccentricity and so eventually sent him a bit 'funny' — but certainly, as far as book-buying is concerned he would have saved himself hundreds of pounds, and maybe even thousands, if he had never shown his face in the auction rooms.

The book trade in London used to be enriched and embellished by a certain rather colourful doctor of dentistry, who had long before given up extracting the teeth in favour of extracting the urine — figuratively-speaking — from almost everybody he encountered in the day-to-day business of buying and selling Modern First Editions. As well as being an extremely knowledgeable dealer in his particular field, he was a master of that art universally known as bullshitting. I was once privileged to witness a most remarkable session — purely as a disinterested and impartial observer. He had come into Hodgson's Rooms to pay for and to clear a mixed lot he had bought in a recent sale. Among his books were certain volumes which he knew nothing at all about and for which he had no use at all. It happened that the next sale to come was then on view, and Cherry-Garrard also happened to be present, browsing round the shelves.

Our man recognised him immediately, having seen him in action at previous sales. The doctor got into conversation with the collector, and then proceeded to flatter him with the most magnificent piece of ex-tempore bullshit I have ever listened to. When Cherry-Garrard was either utterly hypnotised, or else completely convinced that he must surely be the greatest book-collector who had ever lived, the doctor slipped subtly into his sales talk. With two large, pig-skin, blind-stamped folios under his arm, the contents of which I am perfectly sure he knew absolutely nothing at all, he brain-washed that simple man into believing that here were books no self-respecting bibliophile should be without. I made no attempt to eavesdrop. Whenever the dear doctor held forth in public *everyone* knew about it. I just sat and admired, as cash and books changed hands.

I was told that in the end Cherry-Garrard grew rather too unstable for his own sake, and was eventually confined to a nursing home. He later died.

But long before that I had many an interesting chat with him. In the 'fifties he saw through for publication the new paper-backed Pelican edition of his now famous *Worst Journey*. He had written a special new preface. 'The whole thing is now definitive,' he told me. 'It will scotch all stories — false rumours — *canards*. It will tell the full truth.' (I went to the trouble of reading this preface; I honestly don't know what he was on about.) I wonder what the old chap would have thought, had he lived, to read the latest 'full truth', published only in 1979!

The first printing of his *Worst Journey in the World* has two quite distinct and different states of binding. The one more often seen is in a full light blue casing. The other, and earlier, is half-bound in a whitish simulated vellum or holland back — I forget which, since it's years ago I last handled it. Most interested dealers and collectors are aware of this, naturally, but it was Cherry-Garrard himself who told me why this variant exists.

He had gone to Bernard Shaw, when the book had been written, and had asked his advice about a publisher. Shaw told him that *he* actually published all his own books himself, but merely employed the firm of Constable's for details like printing, binding, distribution and accounting — all largely at his own final say. Apsley Cherry-Garrard felt that what was good enough for the great and successful Shaw was also good enough for him. He entrusted the job to the same firm, but footed the bill for all production costs himself and chose the book's external appearance. Against all experienced and professional advice, I am quite sure, he insisted upon that white half-binding, since he wanted his book to look as handsome and as 'Polar' as possible.

The result was that none of the regular and established circulating libraries of the time would touch it! Within a few weeks of handling, every copy would have grown so grubby it would have had to be recased. Fortunately, only relatively few copies of the first edition were actually bound up. (I think Constable's knew pretty well what was going to happen.) Intent upon the widest circulation for his *magnum opus*, Cherry-Garrard bowed to commercial common-sense.

He lived outside London, not very far from Ayot St. Lawrence, in fact, just over the hill from Bernard Shaw. He was a close neighbour and acquaintance of that remarkable man. Two people holding more diametrically-opposed political views you could not possibly imagine. Yet, Cherry-Garrard told me shortly after Shaw's death that the famous dramatist and pamphleteer had finally seen the error of his ways, and had become completely disillusioned with the socialist theory! The inference was that he, Apsley Cherry-Garrard, had been responsible for causing Shaw to see the light.

I do not, of course, know the full facts of this momentous matter. But I very much doubt if a rather naive and simple man like Cherry-Garrard could have had any lasting influence on a mind like that of Bernard Shaw. Yet I do know that Shaw had some tiny influence upon Cherry-Garrard.

The playwright had the habit of always addressing his letters in the bottom right-hand corner of his envelopes. 'To leave plenty of room for the postman's thumb!' was the rather typical Shavian explanation for his idiosyncracy. Cherry-Garrard once begged a sheet of Hodgson's note-paper and an envelope from me after he had found something on our shelves which he thought might be of interest to his friend, and after he had sealed his letter he left it with me to post. I noticed that he had addressed it in exactly the same way, but exaggeratedly. Shaw's name and address had been penned *far* down in the bottom right-hand corner.

It occurs to me now that this *could* have been a code: an agreed sign to inform the recipient or his secretary that here was a note worthy of the sage's personal and immediate attention. After all, Shaw's daily correspondence was voluminous, to and from the exalted and worthy and to and from the most outrageous crack-pots. He kept the Ayot St. Lawrence village post office a solvent concern. On the other hand, Cherry-Garrard might have adopted this calligraphic quirk for all of his letters, vainly but hopefully waiting for someone, some day, to ask him why he did it. The second-hand Shavian witticism would have been ready and bubbling on his lips.

Mr Poonawallah

Mr. Poonawallah was a roly-poly little Indian gentleman, a man of business resident in London for many years. He was near-sighted and chubby-cheeked, and he had the tiniest, pursed-up 'stewed prune' mouth I have ever seen on any person. He could manage to get words out of it, but I often wondered how he was able to get food into it.

He lived in a large block of mansions in the Holland Park area, and one of his hobbies was collecting books. His main interests in this direction appeared to be the East India Company, India itself, and the Mahatma Gandhi. He bought a good deal in the auction rooms, often in bulk, and his greatest difficulty was in getting his books home. Once he asked me to call him a taxi, at about five-thirty in the evening, which I did — no mean feat in the Chancery Lane and Fleet Street district at that time of day.

After we had stuffed the cab with octavos, quartos, and folios it was just about my knocking-off time, and he graciously asked me if he could drop me off anywhere. As it happened, he could. I had just then come to live in the unfashionable part of Ladbroke Grove, and this was more or less on his way. I got a free lift to Notting Hill Gate — not at all an unconsidered trifle in those impecunious days, but that buckshee ride was my undoing.

Thereafter he would frequently ring me from the City and ask if I would be good enough to drop off the books he had purchased, on my way home. He always tipped me, and paid my fare, of course, but he never suggested that *I* take a taxi. Being a very obliging young fellow in those days, I often lugged his heavy cartons the whole length of Chancery Lane, did my stint of strap-hanging on the Central to Holland Park Station, and then had about another three quarters of a mile to go on foot. Once the job was done, there was another mile or two for me to walk home, unless I chose a crazy zig-zag journey involving two or three bus changes. What a mug!

Whenever I rang his door-bell, he was always most apologetic for having given me so much trouble, but he would ask me in and offer me a straight-backed chair in his drawing-room while he trotted off to write me a cheque in settlement of his purchases. His mansion flat was opulent and spacious. In my early visits I only ever saw the inside of this one drawing-room, but it was filled with Indian paintings, curios, well-stocked bookcases and sumptuous Oriental carpets. Mr. Poonawallah was obviously a man of means.

He did not live alone. I heard female voices twittering in other parts of that roomy flat, and once I caught a glimpse of the back end of a sari-clad figure disappearing into what might possibly have been the kitchen. In all the time I knew him he never introduced me to his wife, if such there was, or to his daughter, if he had one. Not that I was particularly bothered.

Mr. Poonawallah was diffident, aloof, even secretive — at home. But visiting us in the auction room, and viewing the books for sale, he was effusive and affable. He took a great liking to the porters, to the cataloguers, and to myself in particular.

One day in the Sale Room he asked me if I would like to catalogue his books. My heart sank. For one thing, after an eight-hour day I didn't relish the idea of another three or four hours hard at it in the evenings. I valued my leisure. For another thing, I wasn't a cataloguer. My official title was Sale Clerk, but I did a multiplicity of jobs which were mostly administrative.

I told him this, and suggested that if he wanted his library catalogued he should approach Martin Orskey or Alex Rogoyski. These two very competent gentlemen were then 'making their bones', as *The Godfather* has it, in Hodgson's basement.

'Nonononono,' quoth Mr. Poonawallah from his tiny pursed-up chops. 'You are not understanding my meaning, my dear sir. I am not wanting my books *properly* catalogued.'

Well, thanks very much, thought I.

'What I am requiring,' he went on, 'is a card index, as you might say. For filing. Mere author, title, date. And at the foot of these cards a room and shelf number. A1, A2, A3. And in the next room B1, B2, etc., etc. . . You are seeing my meaning?'

Yes, I was now seeing his meaning. I could do that job all right, but I still wasn't all that keen, and I said I'd think about it. But every time I saw him he kept on about the job, and finally I knew I was lumbered. And by that time, too, I was in need of a few extra quid. It was summer, I hoped to get to Paris at the end of the auction season for a week or two, and I wasn't all that flush.

'Have you a typewriter?' I asked.

'Yes, a very good typewriter. All the cards, too. Everything is in readiness.'

'All right, then,' I told him. 'I'll do the job.'

'How much?' he asked immediately.

I hadn't a clue. I am probably the world's worst business-man, and also one of the most naive. I made a hasty mental calculation. How long would

it take me to type out an author's name, a book's title and its date of
publication on a standard-sized index card? A minute or so? What on
earth should I say?

'Oh, I don't know,' I sighed, completely defeated. 'A penny a card?'

I don't remember if Mr. Poonawallah's eyebrows shot up. They
probably did.

'Are you sure?'

'No. Not at all. But how many books have you got?'

'Oh, several hundreds, of course... Perhaps a thousand or two. I do not
know exactly. I have not been counting them, you see?'

Hasty mental arithmetic has never been one of my stronger points. But
in those far-off days there were two hundred and forty pennies to the
pound, the pound itself went a long way, and he had hundreds and
hundreds of books.

'Oh, all right,' I said with resignation. 'I'll do it for you at a penny a
card.'

As I look back, I might quite aptly be referred to as a right berk. So off
trotted I, every evening at six-thirty to seven, up that hard and very steep
slope of lengthy Ladbroke Grove — that more respectable end where no
vultures fly and no buses run — across Holland Park Avenue and into the
purlieus of Addison- and Abbotsbury-Land. And night after night, for
three or four hours, I knocked out Mr. Poonawallah's card index for him.

The routine each evening was more or less the same. I would be shown
into a room, be seated at a table on which his typewriter and cards were
ready and waiting, and he would then disappear. I was up and down from
the chair all evening long, of course, with half a dozen to a full dozen books
at a time, and I would tap on persistently, mounting up my pence. At
about half past eight or nine o'clock in would waft a vision in pink or
jasmine sari, and silently place by my side a cup of Nescafé, and would
then waft out again with no response to my muttered 'Thank you'. I
couldn't tell you to this day if it was the same person each evening. It
probably was — just a different sari.

Mr. Poonawallah was very strict and prompt about paying me every
night for what I had done. I would count up the cards I had typed, do my
sums on the back of one I had botched, and inform him in pounds, shillings
and pence — probably incorrectly — of the nightly reckoning.

At first the job was pretty hard going, and I was rather slow. But as the
evenings passed I grew more adept. I moved from one room to another —
I had never dreamed that these mansion flats were so spacious, and I never
even entered kitchen, living-room or bedrooms — and after perhaps a
couple of weeks of evenings I completed this rather ridiculous job. I
became my own time and motion expert, getting it down to a fine art with

sheer economy of motion, and I whipped through those books like the proverbial knife through butter.

That was well over a quarter of a century ago. I've done some pretty daft things in my time, mainly in the army during the war — things like white-washing coal stacks for appearance's sake — but that was because I was told to. But what led me to take on that unrewarding task in the conscientious manner I did? Was it just the money, or did I wish to oblige?

I shall not easily forget my very last evening at Mr. Poonawallah's. On this occasion he led me into that large and most sumptuous drawing-room into which I had originally been taken.

Not *here* again, I thought. I've already done this lot. But he produced a key from his pocket, and quietly bent to a cupboard at the foot of an enormous bookcase, the upper contents of which I had already worked upon.

'*These* I keep privately,' he whispered. I detected a rather shame-faced look upon his countenance. I will admit to a certain degree of gullibility, but I am not absolutely daft. I suspected what might be coming, and I wasn't wrong. 'Not quite suitable for the ladies to see. You understand?'

Yes, I understood all right. I spent the last evening of my chore card-indexing the most colourful, extensive, outrageous, and probably valuable collection of erotica, curiosa, and sheer hard pornography I have ever seen in my life, and I've seen more than one or two.

I saw more of Mr. Poonawallah, too, that evening, than I had seen in the whole preceding fortnight. He popped in every five or ten minutes, ostensibly to see how I was getting on. Of course, he could have been doing his best to make sure that I didn't knock anything off. On the other hand, I am reminded of a rather grandiose notice one used to see in foodstuff emporiums, and which has now gone with the wind. 'Kindly do not handle the merchandise if you have no intention to consume.' Well, in my case, I must admit that the intention to consume was not entirely absent. Chance would have been a fine thing. I didn't have the opportunity to get past the title-pages.

Well, finally the job was done. Mr. Poonawallah locked up his lower cupboard and he put his key away into his pocket. He was grateful, and I was paid in full. Here was a job well done, and he was happy that it was completed. He was also probably more than just a little bit confused. He knew that he had put one over on me, the callow and impecunious dupe who had done this job for him for mere peanuts, but what might I now be thinking of him? He grew rather loquacious and unusually expansive. In the course of conversation he eventually said: 'Did you ever come across a book called — er — I believe its title is — er — *Lady Chatterley's Lover*?'

This was well before the Penguin reprint and the sensational Allen Lane prosecution, you must understand.

'Yes,' I admitted, poker-faced. 'I've come across it. I've read it.'

'*Disgusting* book,' he informed me with some heat. 'Absolutely filthy! I cannot imagine how anyone could allow such a book to be printed!'

I probably nodded in agreement, but I made no comment. Yet I was aghast at the man's hypocrisy. Here before me was the very personification of outraged respectability. Was he trying to con me into thinking that the contents of that bottom cupboard were merely for sociological study, or something?

Rather strangely, I cannot recall that we ever saw the little Indian gentleman again. He must now be long gone.

His name, by the way, was not actually Mr. Poonawallah. I have just plucked this rather common Indian appellation for convenience. Although I have a clear recollection of most of our dealings together I have, quite honestly, forgotten his real name.

I can't remember exactly how much I made in cash, either. But I do recollect that it was something over eleven pounds but not quite twelve. By my own reckoning, probably wrong, that adds up to getting on for three thousand volumes.

I also recall that as I bounced home down the hill into Notting Vale that last evening I now possessed the wherewithal to purchase my ticket at Victoria Station to Gay Paree — train, cattle-truck crossing on the boat, and then train again — which came to something less than nine pounds! With the few quid I had already saved my young wife and I got a room in a tiny hotel behind the Galeries Lafayette for a week or so. We lived on *café au lait* and those elongated and substantial *sanwichs jambon* so beloved by the French. I even managed to buy a couple of books on the rue de Rivoli, in Galignani's. Ah, that was a wonderful holiday!

'Pornography and So On'

Having recounted at some length my dealings with one particular collector of the more out-of-the-way books and literature, it might be appropriate at this point to touch briefly upon the general aspects of this fascinating branch of the trade. I have encountered a great many men, and not so many women, who would have absolutely nothing at all to do with such dubious stuff — publicly. But I have also come across very few, of either sex, who were entirely averse to having a surreptitious glance at the illustrations, or of curling up for a read of the text if nobody was about to see the nature of the subject matter. I don't think it is a cause for condemnation. I think only relatively few people become addicts, once a natural curiosity has become assuaged. In any case, if you are treated to a surfeit of it the whole thing becomes a bit of a bore.

I suppose no bookselling business ever existed without a certain amount of pornography, erotica, or so-called curiosa coming its way, whether solicited or not. I would imagine that specialists in interests like irrigation, sewage, nuclear fission, and suchlike see the least. General booksellers in the Charing Cross Road area are offered rather more, I fancy. But outside of those dealers who make a point of confining their business deliberately to seeking out the stuff I would guess that the book auctioneers are confronted with more of it than anyone else.

Now, any bookseller who happens to buy a private library and discovers after he has sorted through it that he is in possession of certain items that he cannot easily put on show in his shop window or even list in his catalogue would be a fool, indeed, if he consigned that merchandise to the flames or put it aside in some corner as quite unsaleable. If sooner or later, he didn't have some furtive clergyman or dirty-raincoated collector approaching him with oblique requests he would certainly boast a unique clientele.

Before the permissive age, the auctioneer was in a different position. The wares he offered were for *public sale*, everything was listed in a catalogue that was distributed very widely, and the choicer and more rare and expensive items were advertised in the leading dailies and weeklies. Today, books like *Lady Chatterley's Lover* and *Fanny Hill* are printed and sold openly, and almost any new work of fiction which doesn't contain a few four-letter words or the detailed description of one copulation, at least, doesn't stand much chance of a good sale. But it only seems a few years

134

ago, to me, at any rate, when to sell or to advertise such books as those I have named was to invite the chance of a prosecution. Copies had to be smuggled into England by adventurous tourists. Even the now innocuous Havelock Ellis's *Studies in the Psychology of Sex* was placed in a bookcase under lock and key for fear of its being purloined from the open shelves. I even remember some misguided and over-zealous inspector of police organising a raid on a Tottenham Court Road bookshop and both seizing the stock and arresting the proprietor for having on sale a copy of Boccaccio's *Decameron*! That one caused a laugh in the book trade, I can assure you.

In the *old*, old days — long before my time — books of a suspect nature were returned to the vendor as unsuitable for sale. I have been told of one auctioneer, a pillar of rectitude, who was known to destroy such offerings without consulting anybody. But in the old days of my own time in the trade, the more dubious works of authors like Frank Harris, Norman Douglas, George Augustus Sala — and even Mark Twain — were held over but not catalogued. They were placed in the safe in the corner of the office, along with exquisitely-illustrated works in French by authors like the Marquis de Sade. Then, on viewing days, when certain dealers came into Hodgson's Rooms to work on an imminent sale, they were privately and individually invited into the sanctum to inspect the goods, always with some embarrassment on one side and sometimes on both. Confidential offers were invited: the highest one got the prize.

Over the years, specifically after 1960 and the big challenge to the 1959 Obscene Publications Act in the first important prosecution after its passing, things relaxed considerably. *Lady Chatterley, My Life and Loves, Fanny Hill*, and the various works of Henry Miller became openly sold in both hard covers and in paperback, and today there is little or nothing that could not be catalogued and sold at public auction. But the 'hard porn' still remains, and you have to watch it. That, and even any book which might bear an illustration which at one time was known as 'suppressed', still goes behind lock and key, simply for safety's sake. There are persons who would not be seen to *buy* such works, but they are not above dropping them into the voluminous pockets of their raincoats and walking off with them if they think they are not being observed.

Sidney Hodgson, who could hardly have been termed a broad-minded man, or even a man of the world, hated to deal with items of this inevitable facet of his business, and he preferred to let other members of his staff handle them. If was even acutely embarrassing to have to discuss such things with him. I recall one particular occasion which I think bears recounting. Alex Rogoyski was cataloguing a private library, and the literary contents of some of the books were both exotic *and* erotic. Most of the bindings were handsome and even sumptuous. Now Sidney was a busy man, and he had neither the time nor the inclination to look into everything in detail that was being catalogued, but he liked to give most things a glance and an over-all editing. He picked up one book: Alex had shown it to me earlier. How often, I wonder, does the average person look *very* closely at the intricate gilt designs round a fine binding? No inter-twined leaves or detailed filigrees here. Close observation revealed a minute repetition of the male genitalia. Alex had described it without being too specific. Sidney passed his hand across the binding lovingly.

'Oh,' he said, admiring the volume at arm's length, 'oh, how nice. But — Rogoyski — I don't think you've done it justice. Look at that work.' He drew it a little closer, and nodded. Alex wilted and waited. 'Yes, yes, now write this down: "Straight-grained full gilt morocco." Got that? *"Richly tooled."* '

The italics — need I add? — are mine.

A Note on Bad Taste

A regular attender at most of the London book auction sales in the early nineteen-fifties was an astute young business-man from the East End. He went by the name of Sam Goldman. I think he was quite prosperous — certainly prosperous enough to leave the running of his tailoring establishment in the care of some underling. Sam himself spent much of the working day in various bookshops and sale rooms.

I wouldn't say he did much reading, but he was certainly absorbed with books. While he didn't actually despise what they had to say he never showed a great deal of respect for their physical contents. And yet at the same time he was inordinately fond of their outer appearance. Good and unusual bindings of all sorts were his passion. And provided a volume wasn't *too* handsomely bound — for even philistine Sam had his limits — it contributed towards a thriving little sideline he conducted. He would delicately paste all the pages of a book together and then, with an extremely sharp tool, cut away practically all of the inside contents of the volume, making a neat and rectangular box-like hole. With the front cover closed you would never have guessed at the hollow interior. Sam sold the examples of his art to firms like Harrod's, Selfridge's, and anyone else who would take them, as novelty cigarette-cases or cigar-boxes.

I think they were the forerunners of the so-called 'coffee table books'. Many a bourgeois lounge sported one of Sam's elaborately-tooled bindings — even if there wasn't another book to be found in the house — and if one of the guests didn't sooner or later pick up the striking volume from beside his drink to admire his host's culture and quite unsuspected scholarship, you may be sure that the host would raise the book himself, flip open the front cover — or lid — and offer his guests a smoke from this most ingenious of receptacles.

Personally, I have always bracketed these books-cum-boxes with those gimmicky household ornaments like the statuettes of the Venus de Milo with small clocks where her bowels should be. As far as taste is concerned, I place them about one degree below the plaster ducks flying diagonally across the flowered wallpaper, or those intricately sand-blasted mirrors over the mantelpiece, in which you can't see your reflection for artistic patterns.

But Sam Goldman thought them a bit of all right, and he bought many a beautifully-bound book which eventually ended its days in solitary splendour housing fags on a glass-topped table.

He was very proud of his lovely young wife, and also of her accomplishments. She was, it seemed, something of an amateur artist. Sam told me that she did fore-edge paintings on some of his books, and I was most impressed by this information. I was impressed because I have always had a great interest in the better examples of this dubious art, which flourished in the early part of the nineteenth century. More than ninety-nine out of a hundred fore-edge paintings you ever see, of course, are modern examples executed with an intention to deceive — phonies, and rather poor ones at that, with the paint hardly dry upon them.

Briefly, and for the benefit of the uninitiated, an explanation: you can fan out the leaves of a gilt-edged book and discover a hidden painting, usually pastoral or topographical, presented. You close the book up again, and it has miraculously disappeared: you see nothing but the gilt edge. I have no doubt that the early ones were painted before the gilt was applied. That effectively hid any evidence that there was a painting beneath when the book was closed. A century later, when the cult caught on, many a suitable volume offered itself which some dealers thought *should* have a painting concealed. But how to put it on?

Quite an army of people have had a shot at it, but relatively few with very much success, in my opinion, although there are plenty of examples about. In my more impecunious days I applied myself to unravelling the mysteries of the art of the successful but phoney fore-edge painting — or should I term it the craft? Anyway, I discovered a method of producing excellent examples of these hidden pictures, which I am not about to reveal here. It is sufficient to say that as in most cases of apparent mystery — like a conjuring trick — it is not at all complicated or involved, but simplicity itself. But, like almost everything else in my life at which I have grown adept, it is not particularly remunerative. I had been a commercial artist and cartoonist before the war, so I was competent enough, at the very least. But the best price I ever obtained for a fore-edge painting in those far-off days was a couple of quid. Considering the time involved and the energy expended it was hardly worth the trouble.

I should like to say here that the accepted father of the true or 'contemporary' fore-edge was the famous binder, Edwards of Halifax. The most prolific perpetrator of the modern 'phoney' I ever knew was a certain unreliable souse from across the river who only seemed able to paint one scene. This had a tree and a house or two in the background. In the foreground, for the sake of composition, was a stretch of river, and upon it in a boat sat a little man, fishing. I hope you haven't just realised that *you* have one of these books on your shelves! This drunken artist knocked out innumerable examples of this scene for years, for any bookseller who supplied him with a suitable volume. He charged only a pound or two, but those gullible dealers unwise enough to advance him the money *with* the book never saw the man or the volume again, except by accident. (This chap had a second string to his bow, by the way. He made horn books!)

By far the best practitioner of the modern fore-edge painting was Clayton 'Kyd' Clark, the accomplished Dickens illustrator. I never knew the man, to my everlasting chagrin, although we must have 'overlapped' very slightly. But I have handled his work, and it was truly magnificent. Two of the best paintings of this genre I ever saw were authenticated for me as Kyd's work by dear old Fatty Warne, who used to run the firm of Walford Bros., in Southampton Row. This gentleman, by the way, also showed me the proper way to fan a fore edge and display it to its full advantage. I have seen very few people do it the right way.

The paintings I write of were detailed hunting scenes, after Henry Alken, on two small octavos of green straight-grained morocco. These two fore-edges, bought at auction for the then respectable sum of £14 by myself for Walter T. Spencer, would certainly realise several hundred pounds if they turned up today.

But the very *best* fore-edge painting I ever saw, a monochrome, and not at all in the style of Kyd, was bought at auction by Raymond Sawyer. Unfortunately, the stitching of the book had broken, and one gathering of the leaves was loose, and had 'lifted' slightly. You may imagine what this did to the effect of the painting when the volume was fanned. But I am sure that the purchaser knew quite well what he was about; within a week or two I'll bet that book was without a fault. Incidentally, and very appropriately, try to get hold of the excellent little booklet on Kyd produced by Richard Sawyer, son of Raymond, and the third generation representative of the famous firm of Chas. J. Sawyer. It also contains a hitherto unpublished essay on fore-edge painting by Clayton Clark himself.

To return to the point: when Sam Goldman eventually came into our premises and proudly showed me one of his wife's fore-edge paintings I was definitely *not* impressed. It was a rather poor daub, on a foxed surface, and it was not at all concealed when the book was closed. Now, Sam was something of a genius at the game of one-upmanship, and he had capped us all more than once. I felt determined to quash him this time, and to let him know just what *could* be done in this direction.

I searched for some time until I found a suitable volume. Even then, it was dated many years after the 'right' period. It was very late Victorian, in full vellum over boards, nicely-tooled and with a red label — hardly a suitable exterior to carry a painting on its fore edge. But it was beautifully gilded, and it fanned out nicely for my particular purpose. For any other, a white elephant, if ever I saw one. It wasn't worth more than a couple of bob, as it stood, for it was a volume of religious sermons. It had been privately produced and printed by some comfortably-off female lay preacher, obviously for presentation to a few admiring friends. This also suited my purpose, but for quite another reason. I wanted to show Sam Goldman what bad taste could *really* be. Upon its fore edge I painted my masterpiece: an extremely bawdy cartoon.

Sam was absolutely determined to have it — as I know now. But, alas, Joe Muggins didn't realise just how much he wanted it at the time. I had executed the thing really in order to show the man what a concealed fore-edge painting *could* be in comparison with his wife's efforts. I sold it to him for twenty-five shillings, and I was glad to get the money at the time. Sam bested me once again. Many years later he would come into our Sale Room and relate how he would often proffer this pretty but rather dull volume to one of his guests for approbation. While that bemused and nonplussed guest was frantically searching his mind for some quite insincere but complimentary words as he thumbed through those prosaic sermons, Sam would take the book from him, pause dramatically, and then fan it out. A good laugh would be had by all. This became Sam's party piece. My cartoon must have enlivened many a dead gathering.

Now, what I did must surely be in the very depth of bad taste. I am perfectly aware of this. If art I possess, I most certainly prostituted that art. And yet the only thing I am sorry about today is that I sold that job so cheaply then. Although I say it myself, I think that cartoon compared quite favourably with some of Aubrey Beardsley's illustrations for *Lysistrata*. My line might not have been quite so good, but I think I had a slight edge in my knowledge of anatomical proportions!

My previous paragraphs have castigated Sam Goldman somewhat for turning nicely-bound books into gimmicky cigar-boxes. Yet I turned a nicely-bound book into a bawdy fore-edge painting. I have no excuse, except perhaps to say that I didn't make an industry of it. Sam did, in his particular direction. If he could have found a sufficient number of well-bound and suitable books at the right price no respectable home in the country would have been complete without its full calf or morocco volume on the coffee table surreptitiously harbouring smokes.

I am not utterly unaware that there must be many of those reading these lines who have never before encountered these book-boxes, or even heard of them. I sincerely hope they never do again. And yet, if you are one of these and you are intrigued, and my former description is inadequate, visit the premises of one of the several bookselling firms who proudly shelve a set of the Nonesuch edition of the *Works of Charles Dickens*. Take down the last and twenty-fourth volume: you might be surprised. It isn't a book at all. It's a book-box, housing an original block or steel plate, in a downy nest. By the way, it was never a book to start with, so don't get the idea that I am having a go at Nonesuch for vandalism. I am not. Their idea was a brilliant one: each set has a different plate or block, and the edition is limited to the number that were available. The rest of the volumes form the most beautiful collection of Dickens' works I know of, as far as typography and printing are concerned. If you have the means, you should buy a set. After all, Sam Goldman might still be around, and ever on the prowl.

Sam wasn't a bad sort of chap, really. He and I got on famously together, for the most part. But he, being Jewish, had lived a life with many Gentile hands often against him. I sympathised, of course, but intolerance is a fact of life with all minorities in our very imperfect society. Sam, perhaps quite rightly, could never accept this. He was a very proud and sensitive man, and whenever he scored or pulled off a successful deal against the *goyim* he couldn't resist letting the opposition know all about it. Quite natural, I suppose. He must have scored many a time elsewhere, I expect, for he was a very astute chap, but we seldom heard a lot about those occasions. And yet, most certainly, we never failed to learn every detail whenever he managed to put one over on us in the auction room.

There was the time when he fancied some big bundles of books which were stacked under one of the tables. They were all nicely-bound, but they were 'oddments'. This is why there were so many books in the lot. For instance, one bundle might have in it only a single volume of a two-volume set. Perhaps another contained an obviously imperfect or defective book, or possibly works which were otherwise undesirable to the discerning buyer. I remember Sam buying one such lot very cheaply on the strength of three most beautifully-bound books in full blue morocco. The only snag was that the full set called for four, or five, so everyone else had shunned the lot. Some weeks later he came in to look over another sale, which contained more property belonging to the same vendor. Sam took a fancy to a similar bundle, and he bought it for practically nothing at all. Inevitably, that lot included the odd volumes, which made up his set and increased its value enormously. He didn't let us forget that in a hurry.

Now, something of this sort has been done many times, in both the auction rooms and in bookshops. Most people keep quiet about it, for obvious reasons. Not Sam Goldman. He had to come back and tell everybody about the way he had bested us.

But he wasn't always quite so successful. I recall when he latched on to a lot of various bindings, some of which had jewels, either real or imitation — I don't know which — set into the corners of the gilt tooling on their front covers. Sam took a great fancy to these books, and he dropped in several times to look at them during the viewing days. But on the morning of the sale, shortly before they were to be sold by auction, he came up to me very agitatedly with one volume in his hand.

'Here, one of these stones has fallen out of its setting. Have you seen it? Has anyone handed it in?'

I made enquiries, and we searched the floor, but the thing was nowhere to be seen. I asked him if he was sure that the stone had been there in the first place. He hesitated, but he seemed pretty certain. Our cataloguer couldn't remember either: he hadn't mentioned a missing stone in his description. Well, eventually Sam bought the lot, with a somewhat glum countenance, but he spent a long time looking about for that missing gem, and he kept coming back for days afterwards to ask if it had turned up. It never did, and I am afraid that this buy was one of Sam Goldman's few disappointments.

He had the last laugh, though. This was a triumph of his one-upmanship. It was a completely separate and much later occasion. Sam had come in to look over the items for sale, as usual, and he was much taken with some really hideous volumes which were located in the high, deep shelves under the clock by the door.

They were all large folios, heavy and unwieldly. Now, unless books of this size have names like Angas, Piranesi, and others equally illustrious attached to them, they are usually shunned by the average viewer. These books had no such names attached. In fact, they were hardly books at all. I suppose you *could* call them albums. Each leaf was about an eighth of an inch thick, and it mounted a large sepia photographic portrait. The bindings were of sumptuous but dusty plush or velvet, with rounded and bevelled edges — I hardly know how to describe them — and their colours were purple, maroon, and a near-magenta. They were certainly all very plummy-looking, with the dust on them giving the effect of a light down.

Further, much additional labour had been applied to these bindings. They were embellished with intricate scrolled and filigreed metal work: dull and tarnished shapes seemingly of brass or wrought iron. They were damned heavy, I know that. They looked to be the very acme of late nineteenth century bad taste. I remember that I had the job of putting them up on to the shelves initially. I *hated* the blasted things, for their weight, their appearance, and for everything else about them.

But they were still books, they were on view for sale, and I watched over them very carefully. Whenever someone tried to draw one out from those awkward shelves to have a closer look there was always the chance that they might be scored by the sharp metal on the adjacent volume.

Indeed, one or two had already been knocked about a bit in the past, and I didn't want to see them damaged further.

Our cataloguers had thought them no great shakes. The things had been lotted into twos and threes, and their brief descriptions, in all, occupied about a third of one page of the catalogue at the most. We knew that they had formerly been in the possession of the Emperor Franz Josef, and that the portraits were probably of minor royal personages, but this in itself had not seemed very important and was not stressed. It was felt that the things would have a very limited appeal.

When they came up for sale only two people were the slightest bit interested in bidding on them. One was Sam Goldman, of course. The other was old Van Dam, a very shrewd veteran dealer, whom many of my older readers in the trade will remember very well. A lot of people tended to laugh at him on the sly for the odd things he was inclined to buy at auction. In addition to a partiality for imperfect old books which were almost falling to pieces, which he matched up with other faulty copies to make up a complete volume, he was always intrigued by things like prayer wheels, zoëtropes, stereoscopes, magic lanterns, or Chinese scrolls, which occasionally turned up at the tail end of individual properties in the miscellaneous book sales. Other clients were also amused by the prices he was prepared to pay. But Van Dam knew quite well what he was up to, and he flourished for many years.

He went after those monstrosities strongly, and he gave Sam Goldman quite a time. He even managed to take one or two of the lots away from our man, during the bidding, but in the end Sam got the lion's share. He seemed very pleased with his acquisitions.

We were glad to see the back of them, and very soon they were quite forgotten as a new sale began to make its appearance on the shelves. Sam took the things home, and he smartened them up more than a little. Many months later he came back to see us. He was grinning widely, and he seemed very pleased with himself. Obviously, he had made a killing. And naturally, he couldn't resist letting us know all about it.

'Remember those terrible old monsters with the iron bindings I bought?' he asked. 'You all thought I was daft, didn't you, now — bidding against old Van Dam like that? Well, they polished up lovely. Your blokes catalogued them in two or three lines. I took them up to Sotheby's — and they described them in *two and a half pages*! They made a packet! Do you know what that mouldy old metal on the bindings really was? It was *solid gold*!'

Some Sale Room Eccentrics

I have known a great number of whimsical and eccentric booksellers, collectors, and mere dabblers. They were a motley crew, as might well be imagined. One or two of them I have heard referred to as being absolutely mad, and this was meant quite literally. Others were actually told to their faces: 'You know — you're crazy.' This was not meant to be taken quite literally, and it seldom was. The remark, more often than not, was accepted in the spirit in which it was made. With very few exceptions, such people were well aware of their idiosyncracies. They were extremely good-natured, and more than just one or two of them delighted in playing the part of the eccentric bookman.

Not that all of them were conscious of their oddities. One man I knew, who lived in a large house in the southern home counties, had as his library a very spacious room with a vast, bright red carpet covering the central part of the floor. The four walls were furnished with extremely elegant glazed bookcases, and for several years much of this gentleman's leisure was occupied in filling them with sumptuously-bound sets of the works of all the great masters of our literature. He didn't particularly care what he had to pay for them, but the bindings, preferably full morocco, *had* to be red. 'To match my carpet,' he explained.

I never saw that library when it was fully-stocked, and I have only been able to imagine it, but at the desk in the auction room I bought on his behalf many of the sets which eventually graced his shelves. He spent quite a lot on them. He would have spent a lot more, had it been necessary.

'How much is *this* set going to make?' he would ask me excitedly, with his eyes gleaming, on a viewing day.

As best I could, I might reckon the probable value of a single volume — taking into consideration the status of the author, the title of the book, and the quality of the binding and tooling. Then I would hastily count the number of the books in the set, do a rapid piece of mental multiplication, and finally add on a fiver or a tenner for good luck.

'Oh, fifty — sixty pounds, perhaps,' I would tell him.

This was well before the days of printed estimate lists, now included with every copy of the catalogue, but at that time prices were a lot more stable than they are today, and it was not nearly so difficult as it is at present to 'reckon' a lot.

'Are you sure I'll get it for that?'

A sale at Hodgson's
By Thomas Rowlandson. c. 1820.

Henry Hill Hodgson. 1837-1919.

Edmund Hodgson. 1793-1875.

Old Jim in his declining years, unloading a consignment of books in Chancery Lane. For once in his life he was being aided by someone tinier than himself. *(Photo: Wilfrid B. Hodgson).*

Firm's outing, to Stratford-on-Avon in 1907, in celebration of the centenary of Hodgson & Co. In the centre sit Henry Hill Hodgson and his wife, flanked by their sons John Edmund and Sidney, both still remembered as auctioneers. Old Jim, then a very much younger Jim, sits in the bottom right-hand corner.

Solomon Pottesman, photographed at the Europa Book
Fair, towards the end of his life. *(Photo: Keith
Fletcher)*.

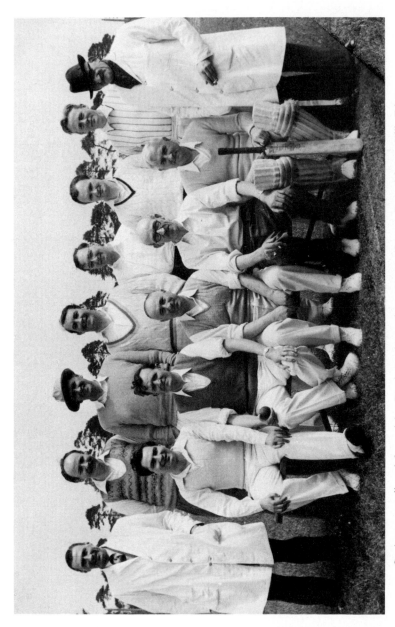

Guv'nors, standing, left to right: Frank Doel (umpire); Norman Storey; Peter Murray Hill; Edgar Chalmers Hallam; Walter Goldwater; Woodiwiss; Alec Clunes; Jack Joseph (umpire). Sitting, left to right: Frank Cass; Charles Traylen; Max Elte; Bill Fletcher; Bob Forster. *(Photo courtesy of Bernard Simpson).*

Bibliomites *versus* Guv'nors Annual Cricket Match, mid-nineteen-fifties. Bibs, standing, left to right: Frank Doel (Marks, umpire); Stan Wheeler (Harding's); Barton Day; Charles Harris (Edwards); Frank Westwood (Edwards); Reg Wheeler (Harding's); unidentified; Jack Joseph (umpire). Sitting, left to right: Raymond Kilgarriff (Howes); Fred Baker (Traylen's); Bernard Simpson (Joseph's); Don Berry (Edw. G. Allen's); John Simpson (Thorp's). *(Photo courtesy of Bernard Simpson).*

Helene Hanff, pictured beneath the commemorative plaque erected outside 84 Charing Cross Road during its redevelopment in 1981. *(Photo courtesy of Michael Redington, Tillymic Productions Ltd.).*

Below: Marks & Co.'s shop in the 'sixties. *(Photograph: Alec Bolton, reproduced by courtesy of Andre Deutsch).*

Printed and Published by W. J. Jacobs & Sons, Tracy Street, Plymouth

An early campaign picture of Isaac Foot when he stood
as a Parliamentary candidate at Plymouth for the
Liberals. *(Photo courtesy of Rt. Hon. Michael Foot, MP).*

Outside Hodgson's Rooms in 1967. From left to right: Alex Rogoyski, the author, Paul Grinke, Sidney Hodgson, and Wilfred B. Hodgson. *(Photo: W. B. Hodgson).*

Harry Mushlin viewing lots at auction shortly before he died. With him is William Lent, over fifty years with Maggs Bros., and still going strong.

Wilfrid B. Hodgson and the author at the rostrum in 1967, at the time Sotheby's took over the Chancery Lane premises. *(Photo: Jeff Vickers).*

and below

The last sale held at Hodgson's Rooms. Chancery Lane. Wilfrid B. Hodgson is at the rostrum. Next to him is the author, with Sarah Herbert-Jones assisting. Below the rostrum sit Wilfrid's wife and sister. Also to be identified, in back view, are Eddie Maggs and his mentor, Bill Lent, with Eric Blundell on the right. *(Photo by Joanna Smith).*

A sale at Sotheby's by Thomas Rowlandson.

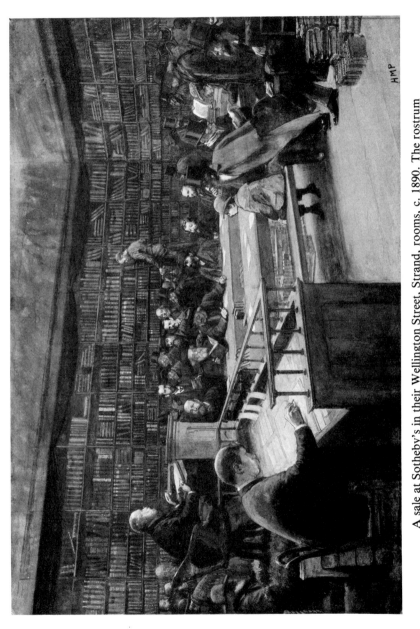

A sale at Sotheby's in their Wellington Street, Strand, rooms, c. 1890. The rostrum and the clerk's desk are still in use in the Grosvenor Room at Sotheby's Bloomfield Place premises.

Peter and Helen Kroger take their first drink together for nine years as they fly off to Warsaw after serving imprisonment for spying.

At the opening party of Sotheby's new Book Dept. in Bloomfield Place, Spring, 1981. Left to right: the author; Raymond Toole Stott, MBE, bibliographer of Somerset Maugham, the circus, and conjuring; David Temperley, Birmingham bookseller; Leslie Cole, Executive Librarian of the Magic Circle. *(Photo: Joanna Smith)*.

Anatomy of an Antiquarian Bookseller [175 x 60cm]

- Small dent in fore-edge
- t.e.g
- lacks headband
- Hinges weak
- One corner 'slightly 'bumped'
- Dogeared
- Slightly worn at head
- Spotted
- Dentelles nicely tooled
- Edges untrimmed
- One section loose
- New as issued
- Rebacked
- lovingly thumbed by former owner
- Contents very good
- Trifle soiled
- Back defective
- Spare label tipped in
- Slightly split
- Some creasing
- fore-edge shaken
- Corners rubbed
- Spine cracked
- Leather label
- Name on fly
- Stitching loose
- Original cloth slightly discoloured
- Some inkstains
- Blank at end
- Some foxing
- Rear hinges cracked
- signature detached
- Tear neatly repaired
- Joints badly worn
- Mottled calf
- Ronald Searle
- Lower margins frayed
- Worn at foot
- Running title

Ronald Searle's anatomical *jeu d'esprit,* which graced the rare
book catalogue commemorating John Grant's Centenary.
(Reproduced by kind permission of Ian Grant)

'Not at all sure,' was my fairly stock answer.

I had very early on learned that to make certain and most definite assessments was disastrous. You only need just one exuberant competitor in any sale room to send a price wild and sky-high. I would tell him this.

'All right, go up to a hundred. But don't lose it for a pound or two.'

He would then give the set another loving glance and move towards the door. He invariably had second thoughts and came back.

'Make that a hundred and fifty.'

And more often than not he rang me up from his office shortly before the sale commenced and changed his mind again.

'I like that set. I want it. I've measured up my shelves. It will just fit in nicely. I'll go to a couple of hundred!'

You know, I could have rooked that chap till he bled. But this has never been a practice of the major auction houses, and very seldom by those of their employees entrusted with commission bids. It doesn't pay in the long run — and you might easily get tumbled in the short one. I never failed to buy this client what he wanted, and always well under his top figure. Sometimes it might have passed my original estimate. Again, with an unusual and beautifully-bound set, I might have had to pay even a bit more for the man, but as a rule he got what he wanted for about a third or well less than half of what he was prepared to spend. He was always most generous to me for my help, and he very soon became my favourite client. But alas and goddamm — as H. L. Mencken used to put it — the time must have come when he had filled his bookcases with red sets to match his carpet. I saw him no more.

I knew another man, who had spent most of his working life in France. He had married there, to a French lady, and he happened to be the father of that incredibly beautiful actress, Yvonne Furneaux, who took her mother's maiden name when she went on the stage. He was a retired bank manager, and he might have remained abroad during his declining days had he not discovered quite accidentally that since he had been called to the Bar in his younger days, although I don't think he ever practised, he was eligible for available chambers in the Temple. So here he lived with his wife, when I knew him, in rooms which were filled with built-in shelves and recesses, installed by a former resident. But no shelf was more than three and a quarter inches high, and proportionately deep. I think they must have been built for a collector of either snuff-boxes or *netsuke*. But my man happened to like books. He almost haunted our Sale Room for a few years — just a short walk across Fleet Street from his chambers. But he would never buy any set, or a single volume — and not even bid on it, without first pulling out a tape-measure or borrowing my ruler, in order to make sure that it would fit his little shelves before he did so!

Samuel Pepys, it would appear, was so meticulous and fastidious a book-collector in that particular direction, that he liked to see all the volumes on his bookshelves standing at exactly the same height. If one or two were an inch or so shorter than the others he would have a wooden block made on which to stand them. I was told this, with some incredulity, by a person who had just visited Magdalene College Library, at Cambridge, to see the Pepys collection. But I could easily cap that one. I was aware of a book-collector who, if he bought a folio volume which wouldn't quite fit on to his lower shelf, *sawed* through the binding and the pages until it did. And if you think that this is nothing more than sheer vandalism, I ought to add that he didn't saw off the bottom. He sawed off the top! I am not making an attempt at sensational fiction; this happens to be quite true, incredible as it seems.

I should now like to tell you about Mr. Einstein. He was a strange and very lonely man of Jewish extraction. He had made his money, after fleeing Nazidom, in textiles. He collected — or rather amassed — an enormous accumulation of printed Hebraica and Judaica. He would always ask to look at an auction catalogue, but he would seldom buy one. They cost sixpence each in those days. When it was proffered, he would always snatch it. But if the catalogue happened to be composed largely, or to some extent, of his interests, he would invest his tanner in a copy. Mr. Einstein still snatched. And after perusing it he would never explore the shelves to find the lot he wanted. He would always ask a porter or myself to find it for him. Once it was offered there was still that rapid snatch. There is obviously some psychological explanation for this idiosyncracy. Simple as it might be, I have never figured it out completely.

Those Jewish dealer and collector friends of mine who knew Einstein have all told the same story about him, with very few variations. In earlier days, when he was continually bemoaning his solitary state, he had been urged to marry some nice Jewish girl. A wedding was eventually arranged. But he got cold feet after the ceremony, or else he became appalled at the momentousness of the occasion — much the same thing, perhaps. At any rate, he left his bride either on the wedding day or very soon after it. The lady went straight into a mental home. He never sought a divorce, or even made a will.

But the time arrived when Einstein began to think more about immediate cash in hand than his accumulation of books, although I don't think he was ever short of a bob or two.

'What's your selling commission?' he must have asked me at least a dozen times.

'Fifteen percent,' I would tell him, as it was in those days. 'But it's only twelve and a half to the trade.'

'*I'm* not a member of the trade. I'm a *private collector*.' Then would come a quick nod and a wink. 'But how about twelve and a half for me?'

'Why not?' I would say. 'Just prove that you have dealt in books and we can come to an arrangement.'

But no, this would never do for Einstein. He *must* retain his status as a collector and private buyer, and also have his name in the catalogue as the owner of the books, but he would only pay the trade commission. The spirit of the bazaar and the market place died very, very hard.

Having received no satisfaction from me, and perhaps from other menials in the various London auction houses, he eventually approached my immediate superior, Wilfrid B. Hodgson.

'Just walk up the Lane with me,' he suggested. 'Come and see my books. I think you'll like them.' His collection was housed deep in the vaults at the other end of Chancery Lane from ours.

Wilfrid went with him. The mass of volumes was truly impressive, and once it had been agreed that all the books were well worth selling, Einstein sat himself down comfortably on a pile of valuable folios and went through his well-worn ritual again.

But Wilfrid had been well-primed, and he was adamant. 'The terms are fifteen percent for the private collector and twelve and a half for the trade.'

Well, the man never did come to a final agreement — not with us, nor with any other firm of book auctioneers. He wanted to eat his cake and have it, too. In course of time he died, intestate. His next-of-kin, and apparently his only traceable relative, was his unfortunate wife. She, poor soul, although inheriting his entire estate, was in no mental condition to manage it. The whole thing was placed in the hands of the Official Solicitor, as is usual in such cases. He immediately came to Hodgson's, since we were literally just round the corner, and put the collection up for auction. There followed a magnificent sale of early-printed books of Hebraica and Judaica, with Einstein's name in the catalogue. The commission, naturally, was fifteen percent.

One of the nicest bookmen I ever knew in my life was, perhaps, something of an eccentric, and yet in the strictest sense of the term he could hardly be called a collector. He was a book-buyer, certainly, a bibliophile, yes, and a bibliomaniac, possibly. He was to some extent a magpie, an undisciplined accumulator who just couldn't keep away from the auction room. His name was Isaac Foot.

He was an elderly man when I first knew him, a widower with a trio of famous sons. One might have expected him, at this time of life, to be taking it rather easily and quietly in retirement during the evening of his days. But the man was still full of energy. He was the head of a family firm of solicitors, a former Lord Mayor of Plymouth, a Member of Parliament, a staunch pillar of the Liberal Party, a Privy Councillor, and he seemed to me to spend half his time driving backwards and forwards between London and his home at Callington, in distant Cornwall.

During the time I knew him he made a companionate marriage with his housekeeper, a lady I met on a couple of occasions — a long-suffering body if ever there was one. She knew it, and he knew it, too. There was no nonsense about Isaac. When he came and told me that he had acquired a new wife he also told me that he had quite frankly informed her of facts she must already have known about his house in Callington.

'First of all, this place is a library. Secondly, it's a dogs' home. Next, it's a stable. Fourth and last, it is now your home and mine.'

His grown children, by then widely-dispersed, had all been told this and had learned the lesson early in life. Grandchildren, too, had been influenced. Among the scions were Sir Hugh Foot, later Lord Caradon, the much-loved Governor of Jamaica, who was later a bigwig at the United Nations, and his son, the Honorable Paul, a left-wing journalist who very early in life developed a love for books. Then there was Dingle Foot, who made his name as a barrister and Member of Parliament for the Liberals, but who became disillusioned and turned to the Labour Party. And, of course, there was the young Michael Foot, at that time a black-haired and intrepid young journalist and sometime Labout back-bencher, a maverick forever getting into hot water with his party. He was both a staunch Bevanite and a rabid supporter of Plymouth Argyle, which for some reason struck me as odd. We knew him mainly as one of the group of youthful crusaders who, under the collective name of 'Cato', had written the book, *Guilty Men*, early in the war, and who to a considerable extent had been responsible for the resignation of Chamberlain and the emergence from the wilderness of Winston Churchill.

Altogether, with the other lesser-known members, it was a most prepossessing family. There had long been a somewhat obvious and inevitable joke, and it was rampant from the West Indies to Whitehall: big Isaac Foot and all the little Feet.

I have no idea at all how the old man got on with this most precocious and talented brood. There must have been many family gatherings over the years at Callington, and I would dearly have loved to have eavesdropped on one or two. Isaac himself was an extremely devout Protestant, something of a Puritan, and with the name of Oliver Cromwell never far from his lips. He was also explosive and dogmatic; Michael was a chip off the old block in many ways, but with a variety of opinions opposed to those of his father.

They thought a lot of Isaac down at Plymouth. He was probably the town's most famous and well-loved citizen. One day, he was striding along the main street thoughtfully, with his hands thrust deep into his coat pockets. One of the townspeople, out with his young son, crossed the road and accosted the old man.

'Mr Foot, I'm surprised at you!' he said. 'I've always taught my lad to look up to you — but you're not a very good example. Here you are walking along with your hands in your pockets.'

'You should be pleased,' retorted Isaac, quick as a flash. 'You'll usually find lawyers with their hands in other people's pockets!'

He loved old Bibles; the older and bigger the better, it always seemed to me. In his time he must have bought hundreds of them. On one occasion, in a mixed lot, he came across a single volume of an enormous seventeenth-century two-volume edition.

'Ha! I've got the companion to that!' he shouted to me in glee. 'I *must* have it. They've been together for so many years it would be a crime to keep them apart any longer!'

Another time he got into conversation with old Wally Harris, a mild and rather affable little man who had at that time been between forty and fifty years with the famous firm of Thorp's, then esconced in Albemarle Street. Isaac had seen him about for ages, in the various sale rooms, and obviously felt there was a chance he might have something of interest to himself.

'Do you get many old Bibles come into your place?' he inquired conversationally.

'Bibles?' said Wally laconically, and somewhat disparagingly. 'We don't stock that sort of junk.'

Isaac exploded. 'Junk? *Junk?* May God forgive you, man! You are taking the Lord's name in vain!'

Poor little Wally retired abashed. I think he was in fear of being *bashed*. The normally pink-faced Isaac Foot was now florid, and looked ready for physical assault.

The old chap was usually content to view a sale himself and then leave his bids with me, while he trotted off to Whitehall or the Liberal Club. He was a very busy man, particularly after King George VI died, the young Elizabeth had succeeded him, and preparations for the 1953 Coronation were in full swing. 'Can't stop — much as I'd like to. Privy Council meeting, you know. Got to see the girl off properly!'

But very occasionally he would spend an afternoon in our Sale Room, and bid on his own behalf throughout the auction. This was fatal: he was

as hooked as any drug addict. After the sale was over he would come up
to me at the desk and get the total of his bill.

'Ah,' he would sigh, every time. 'I didn't intend to spend so much . . .'

He wasn't exactly alone in this direction. There is an insidious disease,
and there's been a lot of it about for many, many years. It is known as
auction fever.

Isaac Foot had the devil of a job getting his books home. For years he
would leave Old Jim to pack numerous tea-chests and get him to forward
them by Carter Paterson, the forerunner of British Road Services and the
present Roadline. But it would mean a lapse of a week or so before he had
the chance of getting his hands on his acquisitions, and he grew too
impatient to wait. So his car would be stuffed with volumes, and off on the
drive to Cornwall he would go, and then sometimes come back again
during the ensuing days for a second or third journey to clear the whole of
his purchases. I once asked him where on earth he put them all, but it seems
that he retained only a relatively small percentage of the miscellaneous lots
he bought, after he had 'creamed' them. The rest he always presented to
Plymouth Public Library. I don't know what the staff there thought, or
what they did with them all. Some books were acceptable, quite naturally,
but I think the majority of them must have been pulped or otherwise
disposed of. Isaac Foot was a pretty big man in that district, and his gifts
were never refused.

He exhibited what might be termed loosely a catholic taste in literature
(although I think he himself would have employed an alternative adjective,
despite the lower case initial). It must have been just about the last time I
ever saw him that he came in one day, plonked himself down directly
opposite the auctioneer, and proceeded to buy heavily in a manner which
seemed totally out of character for the man. On this occasion he bid
recklessly on a particular kind of book in which I would have imagined he
had not the slightest interest. I really did think that here was a certain case
of bibliomania and advanced auction fever.

It was some years afterwards that I was chatting to a good friend and
young client of mine, one F. T. Copplestone. He was a book-collector in
his own right, but during the course of conversation it transpired that he
happened to be the nephew of Isaac Foot's latterly-acquired wife. She had
informed her husband of the young man's interest in books, and he had
immediately been invited down to stay for a weekend at Callington.
Inevitably, he had soon been shown into the library, and had spent much
of his stay there.

'Dear old Isaac,' I remarked to him, 'how he loved his books! The last
time I saw him he came in here when we had a sale mostly devoted to
Modern Firsts — a lot of it poetry. *Quite* out of his line, I'd have thought.

You know, he went through those lots like a dose of salts — bought almost everything!'

Copplestone laughed. 'Yes, I know. When he was showing me round the place he asked me what I thought of his collection. I was certainly impressed, but he'd asked me for my opinion. I gave it to him. "Excellent," I said, "but there's a gap."'

'Gap? How — where?' Isaac Foot had asked.

'Well,' he had been informed, with all the brashness and authority of youth, 'you've got no modern poets.'

'Modern poets? *Poets?* Who do you mean?'

A few were named. Some of them were Auden, Isherwood, Spender, MacNeice, Day Lewis, Dylan Thomas... But these, it appeared, were people who had passed the old chap by — or rather he had passed *them* by. Yet he had remedied the matter on the very next occasion that had presented itself, much to the dismay, I am sure, of hopeful regulars like Bertram Rota and Dusty Miller.

'I would never have dreamed,' said Copplestone, 'that I could have impressed or influenced Isaac Foot that much!'

When he died, in the late nineteen-fifties, and his books were disposed of, a large part of his diverse library was bought by the University of California at Santa Barbara, for £40,000. There it rests, for the delight and appreciation of all book-lovers. The late Raymond Toole Stott, MBE, quite recently paid a visit to California to see his own vast collection, which is also housed in the university library.

'I don't think old Foot would be very pleased with the company he's keeping,' he told me with a chuckle. 'My books are there — next to his. On the other side of him is the libarary of Dr. Marie C. Stopes!'

Death of a Bookshop

Marks and Co. was one of those good, old-fashioned, and dependable firms of antiquarian and second-hand booksellers which flourished in the 'twenties and 'thirties before the Second World War, during it, and for a fairly lengthy period afterwards. This type of bookshop seems to be dying out rapidly. That, of course, is primarily because the proprietors of such businesses have completed their full span of years and have died out too. But there are other things which have contributed to the decease of such institutions. One of them is the increasingly high rental demanded in central London and its West End. These booksellers go to the wall. To them, a 'five pound book' will always be worth five pounds. They can't bring themselves to pay more for it, and they would feel like criminals to mark it up at more than a reasonable profit.

The boss-man of the particular enterprise I write of here was an old chap called Benny Marks. I have heard a great deal about him, but I only ever saw him once. He was what is known in the trade as an 'inside' man. His partner, the 'and Co.' of Marks and Co., was — almost unbelievably — named Mark Cohen. I knew this man very well. He was the 'outside' man: that is, he viewed the auction sales, attended those sales, and made visits to private premises when the firm was called in to inspect a personal collection of books and to make an offer for its purchase.

In my youth I must have walked past the shop of Marks and Co. quite literally thousands of times, without giving it more than a cursory glance. It was in the northern part of Charing Cross Road, within spitting distance of Cambridge Circus, opposite and adjacent to those strange establishments whose window-displays extolled the virtues of surgical trusses, elastic bandages and arch supporters, but whose business mainly seemed to depend upon the sale of contraceptives and rejuvenating pills.

I was primarily interested in the new and glossy publications in those days, and when I passed Marks and Co., travelling northwards, my sights were usually set on shops like Foyle's. There I could find the latest Hemingway, Steinbeck, or Graham Greene. Departing from the best-selling fiction of the time, and inclining towards the writings of people like the then little-known George Orwell, and those authors published in the stereotyped format of Victor Gollancz, I went south instead of north, and usually finished up in Collet's.

Marks's window-display never attracted me then. In later years, when I

152

knew the firm a lot better, I must confess that it never attracted me very much more. I came to be acquainted with the titles it proclaimed in the 'fifties and 'sixties, of course, having handled them many times in the auction room. Familiarity does not breed contempt, if you spend your life dealing with books, but it takes something unusual to make you excited. In that window you could always rely upon seeing dull sets of Morris's *British Birds*, in its green cloth, Halkett and Laing in its fading red buckram, and any amount of editions of Gibbon's *Decline and Fall*, bound in varieties of calf or morocco.

The shop faced west. It caught the strong summer sun all afternoon and much of the evening. The open space of Cambridge Circus hard by did nothing to help, and although I'm sure Marks and Cohen kept their sun-blind down as much as possible, their wares always looked a bit tatty.

If I was not particularly interested in Marks and Co. as a shop, I was most certainly attracted to the people who ran it and who had worked in it, after I had entered the trade. First, there was old Mark Cohen. He was a swarthy, bald-headed and bespectacled gentleman of Jewish extraction. He had a perennial pipe in his mouth and a fund of reminiscence and bibliographical erudition forever on his lips. Inevitably, he became a bit of a bore to some of the youngsters on their way up, who thought they knew it all at the time. (Isn't it strange? Some of those very youngsters are now middle-aged and paunchy, already beginning to declaim boringly if knowledgeably upon the shortcomings of new and emerging youngsters in our occupation.) Marks and Cohen had been together for many years, having both started as assistants in 1904 with the famous firm of Sotheran's, a business which has probably produced more first-rate bookmen than any other shop in London. Mark Cohen seemed to know every tiny point and deviation in the incredibly complicated bibliography of Charles Dickens, and I never knew him to refer to a work of reference to check or prove his pronouncements.

Second, there were those employees of Marks's. One was John Watson. He was a man of much the same age as myself, a bookman who first served a good apprenticeship with this firm in Charing Cross Road, then went on to manage the house of Bernard Quaritch, and was eventually a director at Francis Edwards. He became one of my closest friends; he was a wonderful companion, and a 'guv'nor' whose success altered his attitude towards the humbler members of the book trade not one bit.

Then there was 'Pat', a packer and porter of books, who gave the impression of being forever put upon. Nobody outside of Marks's seemed to know him by any other name: he seemed to invite those quotation marks. He was 'butch' in the extreme in his appearance, but as fluffy and feminine in his actions as any girl. Every Monday morning after an auction sale, as regular as the proverbial clockwork, he would come tearing into the Chancery Lane rooms to pay for and to clear his firm's purchases. In powder-blue suit of tight and advanced cut he lumbered out sets and piles of dusty books with an exaggerated air of urgency. The more our porters kidded him for his effeminacy, the more he encouraged it and relished it. Hardworking cockney labourer as I knew him to be, I cannot but help remembering 'Pat' in my fancy with stilletto heels, short frilly apron, and feather duster. He was a wonderful character. But the greatest of all those Marks and Co. assistants was the famous Frank Doel.

Frank was a few years older than most of us, but he looked much younger. He was a very quiet and unassuming chap, somewhat reserved until you got to know him. He was with this same firm for practically the whole of his working life; perhaps some people may be forgiven for thinking of him as a rather dull and dry old stick. Certainly he gave that impression to many. Little did *I*, for one, dream that during the many years I knew him he was quite unwittingly building for himself a little monument in correspondence with a certain enterprising client of his.

I saw him most often in the auction room, when he came to view the lots, but I did visit him several times at the shop, and always for the same reason. A book which came up for sale fairly regularly was John Hodgson's *History of Aeronautics in Great Britain*. This had been published by the Oxford University Press in the early 'twenties at two guineas, as I have mentioned earlier. After a time it had been 'remaindered', and Frank informed me that Marks and Co. held the remaining stock. I felt a proprietory interest in this handsome book, since its author, old John Hodgson, was my boss and the senior auctioneer. Whenever a copy of the book came up for sale it would always make about the same price: five pounds or five guineas, depending upon condition. I would be sure to notice the identity of the under-bidder, and immediately after the sale I would ask him if he wanted a mint copy of the book at a fiver. The answer was always yes. I would then run round to Marks and Co. in my next lunch hour and buy a copy from Frank less 10% dealer's discount. (They retailed the book at the same figure it usually fetched at auction!) I thus made myself about five shillings. It seems laughable now, but it was a respectable profit in those days: it was getting on for half of my weekly rent money!

But the time came when somebody went mad in our Sale Room, and Hodgson's *Aeronautics* realised the unprecedented sum of eight guineas! I had a little laugh with Mark Cohen after that sale.

'If only they knew they can get a copy from you for less than a fiver!' I said.

'Not any longer,' he told me. 'I'm "upping" the price of that one as soon as I get back.' Today that book makes £200, and occasionally more.

Frank Doel died very suddenly, just before Christmas, in 1968. He arrived home one evening before the holiday, complaining of abdominal pains. He was whipped into hospital and a ruptured appendix was diagnosed. He actually underwent the operation, quite successfully, I believe, and was sitting up and taking nourishment when peritonitis set in.

He was only sixty when he died, and we could hardly believe it. I shall never forget his funeral at the crematorium on that grim and frozen New Year's Day. The whole of the antiquarian book trade turned out. He was the first of his generation to go: the first of that little band of assistants-cum-guv'nors who had all more or less grown up together between the two big wars and who had been close friends for many years.

It was not too long afterwards that his widow, Nora Doel, handed me a slim little book at a Bibliomites' Annual Dinner Party. It had just been published in the United States. It appeared that one Helene Hanff, a New York journalist and television script-writer, had been a client of Marks and Co. since 1949. Many books and much correspondence had passed across the Atlantic every month or so, largely between Frank and Helene.

Helene Hanff was a rabid Anglophile with a taste for British antiquarian books, but she seemed to lack both the courage and the means to take the big step and visit her beloved London and this bookshop and its inhabitants she had discovered. It was only after Frank's death that she sought permission to publish the letters they had written to each other. The book that followed has been sneered at by some people of my acquaintance, but it is a fascinating little volume. Entitled *84 Charing Cross Road*, it can be read through at a sitting, and not a terribly long sitting at that. It is a 'gimmicky' book, admittedly, but anyone reading these present lines who does not find it absolutely absorbing has my profound sympathy.

'What began as a straightforward mail-order became a personal two-way letter-writing saga, with his assistants joining in,' Elkan Allan informed us in *The Sunday Times*. 'She sent food parcels and was sent recipes. They learnt all about each other, but they never met. Miss Hanff kept putting off her proposed visit to London (her teeth cost too much to be capped; she had to move to a more expensive apartment), until suddenly Frank Doel was dead and the shop closed.'

I found this book fascinating, primarily, because of the two quite different personalities of the main correspondents, and their very different literary styles. On the one hand is Helene Hanff: brash, racy, quite informal and often insulting, and very enthusiastic. On the other hand is Frank Doel, the staid bookseller being approached by one of those eccentric Yankees, and a female one at that. He is reserved, polite, most businesslike and very formal at first. He did break down a lot later on.

Very early on in the exchange: 'A Britisher whose girl lives upstairs translated the £1/17/6 for me and says I owe you $5.30 for the two books. I hope he got it right,' says Helene. 'I enclose a $5 bill and a single... Will you please translate your prices hereafter? I don't add too well in plain American, I haven't a prayer of ever mastering bilingual arithmetic.' She adds a postscript to FPD's (Frank's) very formal mode of addressing her in his opening letter: 'I hope "madam" doesn't mean over there what it does here.'

Dear old Frank didn't comment on this, but I notice that his reply begins: 'Dear Miss Hanff,' and he then goes on to suggest that she should, in future, remit by postal money order, 'as this would be quite a bit safer for you than entrusting dollar bills to the mails.'

But Helene will have nothing of this. She slaps him down. 'I enclose $4 to cover the $3.88 due to you, buy yourself a cup of coffee with the 12c. There's no post office near here and I am not running down to Rockefeller Plaza to stand in line for a $3.88 money order. If I wait till I get down there for something else, I won't have the $3.88 any more. I have implicit faith in the U.S. Airmail and His Majesty's Postal Service.'

Her letters grow more outrageous as time passes, but she is by no means merely the shrew. She knows what she is talking about, book-wise, and what dealer hasn't his own fund of stories about knowledgeable but eccentric clients?

Often Helene is downright insulting, but it's all done tongue-in-cheek. And she tempers her remarks with unusual kindnesses. She has learned about the rationing in post-war Britain, and hears 'you are all rationed to 2 ounces of meat per family per week and one egg per person per month and I am simply appalled.' She sends a Christmas gift to Marks and Co.

After she has sent it comes one of her brief messages which make the volume so amusing. (At this time, by the way, she only knew Frank by the three initials he signed at the end of his business letters.)

FPD! CRISIS!

I sent that package off. The chief item in it was a 6-pound ham, so I figured you could take it to a butcher and get it sliced up so everybody would have some to take home.

But I noticed on your last invoice it says: 'B. Marks. M. Cohen.' Props.

ARE THEY KOSHER? I could rush a tongue over.

ADVISE PLEASE!

Am I being ungracious when I say that possibly Helene Hanff, with an eye to the main chance, already saw, even this early, that there was the germ of an idea for a book in this interchange? She was Jewish herself: could she have believed that Marks and Co. was anything else, right from the start when she answered the advertisement in *The Saturday Review of Literature?*

The Sunday Times again: 'As 1949 became 1969, the people in the shop married, had children, emigrated. English prime ministers and American presidents changed. The Beatles and Brooklyn Dodgers had varying fortunes.'

With all her persistent needling of Frank Doel, the quiet and patient bookseller's assistant who was trying to get her the books she asked for, Helene Hanff had a romantic and sentimental streak. In a letter to another assistant, Cecily Farr, she says:

> Poor Frank, I give him such a hard time. I'm always bawling him out for something. I'm only teasing, but I know he'll take me seriously. I keep trying to puncture that proper British reserve, if he gets ulcers I did it.
> Please write and tell me about London, I live for the day when I step off the boat-train and feel its dirty sidewalks under my feet. I want to walk up Berkeley Square and down Wimpole Street and stand in St. Paul's where John Donne preached and sit on the step where Elizabeth sat on when she refused to enter the tower, and like that. A newspaper man I know, who was stationed in London during the war, says tourists go to England with preconceived notions, so they always find exactly what they go looking for. I told him I'd go looking for the England of English literature and he said:
> 'Then it's there.'

Strangely, one of the most interesting letters in the whole book isn't written by Helene, Frank, or anyone working in the shop. An actress friend of Helene's was doing a stint on the stage in London, and was asked by her to pay a visit to 84 Charing Cross Road and give her impressions of the place.

> It is the loveliest old shop straight out of Dickens, you would go absolutely out of your mind over it.
> There are stalls outside and I stopped and leafed through a few things just to establish myself as a browser before wandering in. It's dim inside, you smell the shop before you see it, it's a lovely smell, I can't articulate it easily, but it combines must and dust and age, and walls of wood and floors of wood. Toward the back of the shop at the left there's a desk with a work-lamp on it, a man was sitting there, he was about fifty with a Hogarth nose, he looked up and said 'Good afternoon?' in a North Country accent and I said I just wanted to browse and he said please do.

The shelves go on forever. They go up to the ceiling and they're very old and kind of grey, like old oak that has absorbed so much dust over the years they no longer are their true color. There's a print section, or rather a long print table, with Cruikshank and Rackham and Spy and all those old wonderful English caricaturists and illustrators that I'm not smart enough to know a lot about, and there are some lovely old, old illustrated magazines.

I stayed about half an hour hoping your Frank or one of the girls would turn up, but it was one-ish when I went in, I gather they were all out to lunch and I couldn't stay any longer.

Helene replied to this as follows:

Maxine, bless your golden heart, what a peachy description, you write better than I do...

I don't like to sound bitter, but I would like to know what YOU ever did that the good Lord lets YOU browse around my bookshop while I'm stuck here writing the TV Adventures of Ellery Queen...

Write me about London — the tube, the Inns of Court, Mayfair, the corner where the Globe Theatre stood, anything, I'm not fussy...

As may be imagined, the book was a success in America when it first came out. On that evening when Nora Doel showed me a copy I remember that I remarked what a pity it was that staid British publishers wouldn't see its merits and would probably write it off as too gimmicky to issue over here. How wrong I was! In what seemed a remarkably short time André Deutsch published it in an almost identical format, and it was very well received.

Michael Foot gave the book a lengthy and excellent review in *The Evening Standard*, sadly revolving about the fact that the shop of Marks and Co. had had to close, and that the site of 84 Charing Cross Road was to be redeveloped.

Benny Marks was dead. Shortly afterwards came the sudden demise of Frank Doel. Finally, poor old Mark Cohen was obliged to vacate his premises. He was very shocked, and a sick man. He found it almost impossible to continue, and he had sent the whole of his remaining stock into us for sale at Chancery Lane. I remember speaking to him just a few days before his books came up for auction. I asked him if the publication of Helene's book had had much effect on his business, and he smiled bitterly. 'I get eighty letters a week. If things had happened differently I could have sold everything I've got twice over.'

His books formed a heavy two-day sale. The hammer had hardly come down on the last lot on the Friday afternoon before I had a telephone call from his son-in-law that Mark Cohen had just died. I think a broken heart was responsible as much as anything else.

The irony of it all is that, at the moment of writing, 84 Charing Cross Road still stands. As David Benedictus said: '. . . the result of an insane and uncompleted road-widening scheme. By looking through the letter-box you can see a bare room, and, if you're Helene Hanff, ghosts.'

The ultimate was a televised dramatic adaptation of the little book, by Hugh Whitemore, at peak time in BBC's *Play for Today*. Anne Jackson took the part of Helene Hanff; Frank Finlay played Frank Doel. This particular actor happens to be one of my favourites, and I enjoyed his actual performance. The only thing wrong is that he just wasn't Frank Doel, or anything like him.

I thought the adaptation, on the whole, was a good one. The re-creation of the interior of Marks and Co. was well enough done, and the characters came across nicely. I think the 'voice-over' readings of Helene, Frank, and the others could hardly have sustained the interest of the average television-watcher for the hour and a quarter the play lasted. You would have had to be a keen book-lover or a bookseller for that. But it was inter-cut with newsreel shots of people and events of the decades between 1949 and 1969, during which Marks and Co. sent off parcels of books and Helene Hanff fired off abusive missives. Rationing, austerity and Cripps, the Coronation, Churchill's return to power, Truman, Ike and the young Nixon, McCarthyism, the Kennedy assassination, the Beatles, the Twist, Mick Jagger and the Rolling Stones — it was all there.

Finally, a sad note. John Watson, of Francis Edwards, who had worked with Frank Doel back in the 'thirties in Charing Cross Road, and who had been one of his closest friends, was called in on the making of the play as a technical adviser, and to offer help in establishing authenticity. It was on a Wednesday that I learned that the BBC was going to show the play. John died in tragic circumstances the very next night. *84 Charing Cross Road* was transmitted the following Tuesday, so by that time all the senior male members who had worked at Marks and Co. were dead and gone. Even the girl employees who had scribbled notes on the bottom of Frank's letters seem to have vanished without trace.

POSTSCRIPT

A few weeks after the above piece appeared in periodical form I received a letter from the United States. It is the first and only occasion I have ever received so-called 'fan mail' from a celebrity. But that is not why I reproduce it here. I think it is so delicious that it would be a crime to deprive its writer's admirers of a missive that could, in part, almost have fitted into the pages of *84 Charing Cross Road*.

My dear Mr. Snelling:

A fan sent me the March issue of the *ABMR* with your marvellously evocative description of the people at Marks and Co. in it. (You're right, I ought to have recognized that 'Marks' was Jewish but I didn't. It wasn't till I saw the 'Cohen' that it hit me.) And I write to say Thank You for all the kind words about my book. It wasn't all that successful over here, you know; what happened is that over the years it became a 'cult book'. (I don't remember who first described it that way but it's true.) It turned out to be the miracle of my life because it opened up a new writing career for me at a time when I desperately needed it. I've written several books since, none of which, I suspect, would have been published if it hadn't been for the fact that '84' preceded them.

Say hello for me to your friends that sneered at it. They keep me from giving myself airs. To tell you the truth, I never thought all that highly of the book — which, while I was writing it, I thought was a magazine story that might just possibly be suitable for *The New Yorker*. I asked a film company story editor, for whom I was working as a reader, to read it for me and to suggest cuts; instead of which, she passed it on to a publisher who bought it as a book. Inside my head, I still don't really think it classifies as a book. But I'll be grateful all my life to the readers who do!

This letter was just supposed to say thank you and I apologize for running on and on.

Thank you.

Helene Hanff

P.S. How to Lose Money By Writing A Book:

There's a paperback edition of *84* which includes the sequel (*The Duchess of Bloomsbury Street*.) Everybody who buys it writes to me. And I write back: Thank-you-for-your-letter.

The thank-you note costs me 22c. My royalty on the paperback is 11c. So every time somebody buys the paperback I lose 11c on the deal. Go tell Milton Friedman to straighten THAT out.

P.S. 2 (goes with P.S. 1): And the man who sent me the March *ABMR* want it back — and the post office wants a dollar from me to mail it back to him.

I had said that the ultimate was the televised dramatic adaptation of the little book. Who, at that time, could have envisaged that James Roose-Evans would take this collection of letters, turn them into a stage play, and bring it triumphantly to the Ambassadors' Theatre, no more than a minute or two's walk from the now famous bookshop? And could Helene Hanff ever have dreamed that one day in 1981 she would come to London, stand outside the site of the shop she had made world-renowned, more than ten years after it was announced that the area was to be redeveloped, and unveil a plaque commemorating the firm, her book, and herself?

The Book Runners

There is a small race of booksellers, sparsely represented in the population of any town or community, but almost unique in their way of life. They are nearly always immediately recognisable, and with few exceptions they are 'loners'. They live alone, they work alone, and for all anyone knows much to the contrary, they play, or pass most of their leisure time alone. The majority of them have no place of business but the teeming streets, modest 'caffs', and other dealers' shops. They very rarely ask anyone home. Indeed, few of us know exactly where they live. They tend to guard their home lives jealously. In the United States they are usually called 'scouts'. In this country they are known as 'runners'.

These men are hard workers. Some eke out a precarious existence, and appear barely to keep body and soul together. Big Bill is a good example of this fringe group — I never knew him by any other name. His knowledge of books was limited, but he never stopped trying. He was an enormous chap: chokered, dark-jowled, and menacing in appearance, but he was always the gentlest of people. I think he could have made a very good living with a pick and shovel, but he had long opted for something more genteel and scholarly. He trudged the streets of Bloomsbury and the West End of London, usually with a book or two of very little value, the titles and authors of which he might vaguely have heard, but I never knew him to make a sale. Yet this he must have done, or he could never have continued. He possessed a rather appealing desire for knowledge, as well as a yearning to find the 'knack' of telling a winner from a loser. Alas, I think Big Bill picked far more of the latter.

Other runners do very well indeed, but I think few of them could tell you just how well, even if they were so inclined. A lot of them don't keep accounts or look at balance sheets, and they deal almost exclusively in cash. I doubt if many of the older ones used to pay much income tax, and I am certain that some kept no record of their earnings. They are an integral part of the book trade. I wish them all good luck.

These men will walk into a bookshop, look about until they find something that takes their fancy and which they think might be underpriced, and will buy it. If they are known to the proprietor, or if they are able to prove that they are in the business professionally, they can claim a ten-percent discount: they are 'trade'. They will then take their purchase

161

and shoot off to another bookseller, whom they know specialises in the particular sort of merchandise they have bought, and they will sell it at a profit. The lesser ones make a few bob; the greater ones a few pounds. I have known several geniuses of this particular race who have more than once hit the jackpot.

The most popular story about these runners is that they will frequently buy a book from one shop, perhaps in Cecil Court or Charing Cross Road, and will walk into the establishment immediately adjoining it and complete their transaction. I have heard — and who hasn't, many times? — of those who would go regularly into big shops like Foyle's in the old days, buy a book from one department upstairs, and then walk down a flight or two and resell it at a handsome profit in another department. Such things *have* been done, of course. I knew one chap in the 'forties who did it too often, got tumbled, and was barred from the particular emporium. But these things are not done as frequently as we hear, I am quite sure.

Generally speaking, the runners are seedy-looking people. Again, generally speaking, they wear shabby clothes: down-at-heel footwear, and dirty raincoats. Perhaps this is all part of their stock-in-trade? After all, less chance of their picking up a book on the cheap if they look smart, affluent, and knowing, surely? — should they step into a shop where they are strangers.

Freddie Bason was, for many years, one of the most eminent of the clan, although perhaps he is not a typical example. He was a shrewd little cockney sparrow from Walworth, and in his earliest days he ran from shop to shop and from stall to stall and made his few shillings. As a youth he began to collect autographs of the famous, approaching the most important people imaginable with his cheeky, never-take-no-for-an-answer manner. He became something of a mascot, or court jester, in the world of the arts. Freddie grew very well known as a gallery first-nighter in the West End during the nineteen-twenties, and then he started to write.

The lad was cunning enough to know that so long as he retained his cleverly-built-up image as the lonely little waif who 'couldn't speak proper', who had 'never had no real education', and who was always looking for someone to love him, he could do all right. He thrived handsomely for many years, but not necessarily from the books he bought and sold, I feel sure, although he was a runner till the end. He became a prolific broadcaster in the heyday of steam radio, and he seemed to haunt Broadcasting House. And his series of *Diaries*, prefaced by some of the most eminent theatrical and literary figures of the age, never failed to find a publisher, and were well worth reading, while Leonard Russell's annual *Saturday Book* would not have been what it was without his regular and unfailing contribution in its later pages. But right to the finish he retained that choker-and-cloth-cap image.

I recall him bouncing into Hodgson's Rooms in 1953, when we were selling Neville Weston's collection of boxing books and ephemera. 'Catalogue, please!' he demanded loudly, slapping his sixpenny-piece on to the table with a bang. 'Bason's the name,' he added, intimating that everyone present should be both honoured and humble that he had graced the place. Actually, he was not a regular *habitué* of the sale rooms, and he felt somewhat out of place. His act was sheer bravado, and when he began to view the books for sale he made no attempt to claim acquaintance with any of the several assistant-booksellers who were there doing the same thing. He obviously felt that he might be encroaching upon their territory: not at all an uncommon misapprehension among a lot of people. I watched the charade from my raised vantage-point, and awaited events. Another viewer of the books happened to be old Arthur Wontner, formerly a famous Shakespeare tragedian, later a film star portraying Sherlock Holmes in nineteen-thirties movies, but at that time a somewhat impoverished character actor augmenting his income by dealing in sporting books. Freddie, who claimed intimate friendship with everyone on the stage, had not noticed him. In due course — perhaps inevitably — they bumped bums while rising from bent positions at the folio shelf, and they turned to each other to apologise.

'Arthur!' said Freddie.

'Freddie!' said Arthur.

They then spent the next half hour reminiscing and talking about their recent vicissitudes, book-buys, and theatrical visits. Freddie Bason was redeemed, as far as I was concerned, as a mere name-dropper, which some in our trade had long suspected him of being.

A sort of rider to that particular reunion: on the sale day they sat side by side, in pride of place, each bolstered by the other's somewhat dubious reputation as a bookseller. But they were tiddlers among the whales. Wontner, I recall, bought just one mixed bundle of books; Freddie managed a cigarette-card album.

Most people only tended to sneer about Bason as a booksy charlatan or mountebank. Perhaps he was. Most certainly, his published effort at a bibliography of Somerset Maugham in 1931 was a disaster, betraying his lack of knowledge.

Freddie had a proprietory interest in Maugham, whose writings he had long esteemed, and who had deigned to answer his fan mail. The famous author took him up, possibly as a cockney character quite capable of supplying copy and local colour if ever Maugham should choose to depart from the polite drawing-rooms of his plays, short stories, and novels and revert to the mean transpontine streets of his earliest success. Somerset Maugham was a privileged guest down at that near-slum house at Walworth.

So, for that matter, was Eric Barton, mercurial proprietor of the famous Baldur Bookshop in Richmond, who was invited with his wife to tea, one day. They arrived, but nobody was at home. But eventually Freddie turned up, with a single kipper wrapped in newspaper, for his next day's dinner. Once inside, he asked Mrs. Barton if she would do the honours. She was perfectly willing, and asked him where the tea was. 'In the pot!' said Freddie. 'From breakfast. We don't waste stuff, you know, in this part of the world!'

Despite his long-standing insistence upon his humble origins and his way of life, which he claimed to the last — inverted snobbery? — and his equally long-standing acquaintance with the very famous, which he was never backward in telling you about — lion-hunting? — this little book-runner was much maligned. He wrote down things honestly as *he* saw them, and most entertainingly, too. Read his very early account of how the great Mr. Somerset Maugham, at the height of his glory, came down to take high tea at the little man's home in Walworth in the nineteen-twenties, and of how they corresponded and kept in touch over the years. Then read the disillusioned piece he wrote of his last meeting with the great man some thirty-five or more years later, when he ventured to approach the famous author, whom he had always thought of as a close friend, in the lobby of a West End hotel. Freddie Bason may have been an opportunist, he may have been a know-nothing little git running books from one dealer to another, but I don't believe he merited the vitriolic treatment he received that day from the strange and embittered genius of Cap Ferrat.

The runner I knew best was named Pike. I saw him on and off for many years. In the winter he sported a filthy, belted raincoat, but in the warmer months he discarded it and one discovered that he also owned a sort of pepper-and-salt jacket, and baggy flannel slacks. All the year round he wore a greasy old trilby hat. I never saw him take it off. More, I never knew anyone else who did so. To this day I don't know if Pike was bald or had a full head of hair.

He lived on the ground floor of a house somewhere in the wilds of South London. His wife lived on the floor above, with her paramour, who had once been their lodger. This situation prevailed for about thirty years, and husband and wife never communicated.

Few people ever penetrated Pike's hovel, but one adventurous and persistent colleague of mine eventually did so, and he told me the squalor was indescribable. For instance, there had been a tiny leak in the bathroom for years, in one of the pipes. Nothing had ever been done about it, and the fungus was almost crawling. Again, Pike's kitchen gas-stove was only ever used to boil water for tea: the spent matches were placed carefully on the corner of a nearby table, and had built up to a formidable but precarious pyramid over the years.

Such things didn't bother him a bit. He ate out, apparently, in 'caffs', and he spent his evenings alone in the cinema. To me, he was always a bit of an enigma. I was intrigued, but I never liked to ask questions. Yet he was a gregarious soul: in comfortable circumstances he grew loquacious. Something *was* learned of his past.

It seems that at one time Pike had been quite a normal, conventional, and respectable man: an aeronautics engineer of considerable standing. He had worked, with many others, on the design and construction of that ill-fated dirigible airship, the R 101. Indeed, he once told me that he had been at the next desk to that of one N. S. Norway, who much later became world-famous as the best-selling novelist, Neville Shute, author of such books as *No Highway, On the Beach,* and *A Town Like Alice.* He had also worked with the inventor, Sir Barnes Wallis, as well as with that collector of aeronautica, the then Sir Harold Roxbee-Cox, later Lord Kings Norton.

When the R 101 crashed into that hill in Northern France in 1930, with the loss of so many lives and so many hopes, it seems that Pike had gone funny — 'a bit radio rental', as one of our cockney porters deliciously describes the condition. I am inclined to think that he had taken the whole disaster personally. Quite certainly he had chucked up his job, which I now imagine must have coincided with his wife's entanglement with the lodger. Things became too much for him. For the remainder of his life he plugged on solitarily, running books, and specialising in those on aeronautics. This was a subject on which he had considerable knowledge.

Pike broke away from almost everybody he had known in the past, but he was still far from being a misanthrope during normal working hours, and he loved to talk. During the day he was always dropping into Hodgson's, in the hope that one or another of us would come out and have a cuppa with him in the nearby Lyons' tea-shop, but at night, as far as we knew, he was a solitary again — in the handiest dark cinema — and then back to his lonely abode.

In the early 'sixties I came across a very good crime thriller, in paperback. It was called *Blue Octavo,* by one John Blackburn, and had a bookselling background. The author, whom I later learned was a book-seller himself, certainly seemed to know quite a lot about our trade. And one of the central characters, and the victim of the murder, incidentally, was a seedy, raincoated, and trilby-hatted runner called Roach. He specialised in books on mountaineering. I was more than halfway through this absorbing book before I suddenly tumbled that the fictional Roach was the real life Pike!

His proudest possession, or so he told us, was a copy of a very rare and valuable book, Robert Boyle's *The Sceptical Chymist*. He had picked it up for practically nothing, and he could not be induced to part with it. But when he died, and my firm was called in to dispose of his literary property, there were a great many books on his shelves, few of them of any unusual worth, but no sign at all of that one. Who had it? Or — perhaps — had *he* ever had it?

I think the hardest physical worker among the older runners is still at it, although I haven't seen him for years. But dozens of times I used to come across him in various parts of London, shuffling along painfully in his long coat, and weighed down by sacks or stringed cartons of books he could barely keep off the ground. I have been told that he once had a bookshop of his own, before the war, but returning home after years in a prisoner-of-war camp, he had been obliged to give it up. He did not feel that he could go back to the confines of a small establishment. He had to be out and about.

He lived well out of town, with a large and growing family to support when I first knew him. For year after year, come rain or shine, he travelled up to London each working day and did his rounds of the bookshops. He was a very mild and unaggressive man, extremely sensitive and intelligent, and with none of the brashness possessed by a lot of the other thick-skinned runners. I almost always came across him in the street or in shops, but I used to lunch regularly in Hill's in Fleet Street thirty years ago, and sometimes he would be there, too, having a solid meal at an adjacent table to fortify himself for the afternoon's slog. I knew *him*, but he didn't know me. I think he knew my face, and from his furtive glances I think he must have thought I was tailing him.

The man kept well away from the auction rooms. I understand that he was — quite mistakenly — under the impression that he was *persona non grata* with auctioneers. The fact of the matter is that I doubt if the bosses of any one of these firms even knew of his existence. Most certainly mine didn't. I recall the occasion when he bumped into Mushlin one day outside Hodgson's Rooms, and sold that most singular dealer a volume he happened to have with him. Mushlin dragged him back within our precincts in order to write him out a cheque in payment. I tried to engage the man in conversation, in an attempt to put him at his ease. It was the only time I ever spoke to him. I think perhaps he remembered my face. I have never seen a man so nervous and anxious to get away.

He would have been more than welcome in any auction room. No firm would have cared a jot had he been able to buy reasonably and sell profitably, if he had the knowledge to best their 'experts' — and specialised knowledge he certainly had. After all, the booksellers with whom he dealt regularly did not resent his presence in their shops. Why should we have done?

This runner was one of the few I ever knew who lived with a wife and family. In lean times he must have been hard put to it on many an occasion to feed the mouths in his household. He had the bibliographical knowledge to command a pretty good and regular salary with any one of a dozen top booksellers. I know for a fact that a close friend of mine, then managing a leading London business, once offered him such a post. But the man turned the offer down. He just couldn't bear the idea of being tied to the same spot all day long. There was nothing he could do about it.

A much more convivial runner, another of the conventionally shabby ones, was a very likeable chap who at present is still at it, too. For years he used to run almost exclusively on behalf of one bookseller in North London, but later he widened his activities and offered his goods to anyone who would buy them. In earlier days he had made a living as a pianist aboard the trans-Atlantic liners, and it is my opinion that during these runs he was offered plenty of free drinks. When I knew him he spent much of his leisure time in the pubs. Now this is a social pastime I am particularly drawn to myself, which is perhaps why I always liked him so much. I never knew a chap with a wider taste in drinks. He would sip and sample anything, and he frequently did. I don't think he had much faith in the more conventional doctors' medicines prescribed in the surgery, but he had a sovereign remedy for anything at all that ailed you, and it was always liquid and alcoholic.

'What's *your* trouble? Tummy upset? Keep off *that* stuff you're drinking, then. Brandy, that's what you want.' And he would buy it for you, too. Again, you might have a cold in the head, or a touch of the 'flu. 'White wine,' he would tell you emphatically. 'Only thing in the world. It'll clear it up in no time.' Headache, toothache, backache, or bellyache — he always knew the right medicine for it, and the cure was always immediately available on the rack behind the bar in whichever pharmacy he happened to be.

He was very good company, and he had a fine feeling for books. I remember him besting me once on a deal when I was making a private sale on behalf of one of our clients. I was much younger then, and far more naive. He looked so surprised when I accepted an offer of forty pounds, and paid me so quickly and got away with the loot in such haste in case I changed my mind, that I knew almost immediately that I might have asked double. But our customer was well satisfied, and I think everyone else concerned was happy. I certainly was.

An entirely different type of runner was a ruddy-faced little Scouse-Italian, whom I will refer to here for a particular reason, and rather appropriately, as Verdi. Until he tried to sell you something you might never have dreamed that he knew anything at all about books. And once that had been established you might have sworn that he possessed no particular talents at all in any other direction. He definitely didn't talk about them. Perhaps he fostered this image of himself.

One day, at a small party at Peter Kroger's not-then-notorious bungalow in Ruislip, well before any of us even imagined that our genial host was a Russian spy, doomed to be caught and imprisoned, a battered old '78' gramophone record was placed on the turntable. 'Try and guess who this is singing,' Peter asked us. 'You all know him.'

We listened to two sides, both of which were Neapolitan songs — probably *Santa Lucia* and *Torna a Surriento*. They were sung in a pretty fair tenor, although it cracked just a little on the top notes. Everyone present, of course, failed entirely to guess that it was the voice of the little runner, Verdi. He was no Caruso, admittedly, but one had the feeling that he could have made a good living singing in opera had he submitted to training early in life.

Years ago I heard that Verdi had quit the London scene and had returned to his native Merseyside, whether to run books in the north or to take up some other employment I never heard. He certainly vanished from my ken. But then one day I ran across John Moss, who used to manage Oppenheim's second-hand department in South Kensington, and who, incidentally, had done his own share of running books in earlier days. He mentioned having seen Verdi not long before.

'In London?' I said. 'The last time I heard of him he'd gone back to Liverpool.'

'Never.' John Moss laughed. 'He's still about. He's been talking about going back home to Liverpool for the past twenty years.'

Yet I still think it strange that a man one had encountered by chance in the streets and on buses for year after year should suddenly seem to disappear entirely and yet still frequent his usual haunts. I suppose that our paths just never crossed.

I mentioned Peter Kroger. Not a lot of people recall that well before he set up his bookselling business privately at home he used to have a couple of rooms in the Strand. His place was down a long corridor behind a tobacconist's shop. It was only a few minutes' walk from my place of employment, and I used to drop in there frequently. One morning I had some business or other with him, and I also had a spot of hot news to impart. But when I arrived there was another person there, an elderly man who had the unmistakable look of the runner about him. I had never met this person before, and since he was obviously doing business with Peter I let them get on with it, and browsed round the shelves. Finally the visitor took his leave, and then Peter turned to me.

'Well,' he said, in his usual style, 'what's new?'

'For a start,' I told him, 'I've just heard that Peter Murray Hill is dead.'

'What!' He was out of that door like a shot, running down the long corridor and shouting: 'Eric! Eric!'

Kroger caught the man in time, before he had been absorbed into the crowd, and back they came. I was introduced, and once again I imparted my bad news. I now found that I was talking to Eric Bligh, the man who ran books almost exclusively for Peter Murray Hill, upon whom he had depended for his livelihood.

I don't think I have ever seen anyone so shattered. Admittedly, the bottom had dropped out of his life and career in one short moment, but it was Murray Hill's wife, the actress Phyllis Calvert, for whom he was concerned — not himself.

'Oh, poor, poor Phyllis,' he kept muttering, 'I must get round there immediately.' And soon, off he went.

I am pleased to say that after Peter Murray Hill's very sudden and most premature death, his firm did not cease to operate, as we had all supposed it might do. It not only continued, but it continued to prosper, under the management of Martin Hamlyn, the senior assistant. But I never met Eric Bligh again.

From what I saw of him, he was a shy, rather timid, and almost inarticulate man. He had a bad stammer. But if he was unable to talk very easily he could certainly write. He had had published a sort of nostalgic autobiography called *Tooting Corner*, some years before, which had been extremely successful when it first appeared. But although he wrote other books, apparently he had no great desire to make a regular living from writing. He preferred to run from shop to shop, ever on the lookout for interesting books of the seventeenth and eighteenth centuries.

The younger generation of London runners now operating are a far more sophisticated crew — or would appear to be — although one or two are just as tatty in their dress as the older crop. Quite a few of them I think I can call my friends. But it would be unwise and unkind to name them here. *They* know they are runners, and I know it, too. Yet there is, perhaps, a certain quite unjustified stigma attached to the term. 'Oh, *him*. He's nothing more than a runner ...'Also, while most of them make good money, and some are well able to write a four- or even five-figure cheque when the occasion calls for it during the course of their business, they are still 'displaced persons'. They have no shops, no premises. They tend to gravitate towards one particular emporium or public house, where they know they are usually welcome, but most of them don't intent to spend the rest of their days in this manner. I'm sure some would like to have their own bookshops; others might even now be working on their first catalogues.

This brings me, finally, to a former runner of an entirely different type from all the others I have mentioned, although he was much nearer to the youngsters I have just referred to than the ones of the old school. When I first knew him he was already rapidly progressing from the humble dealer of the London streets to the very successful dealer he eventually became, with premises in fashionable New Bond Street for a time.

His name was M. H. Mushlin. He was one of the very few runners who literally did run. The man was forever on the move, and usually with one, and sometimes two, huge portmanteaux. He would breeze into a sale room heartily, place his enormous cases on to a table before him, and then proceed to bid in a reckless manner in order to disconcert his rivals, sometimes jumping with increases of fifty pounds at a time when the bidding was going up steadily in ones and fives. He told me that he had learned this tip from reading Arnold Bennett, but if it scared off one or two of the more timid private buyers these methods never worried the veterans and experienced dealers who knew the sale rooms inside out. Mostly, they rather disliked the man and avoided him when possible, but despite his brashness I always felt drawn towards him, and I enjoyed his company.

He was a great chap on 'one-upmanship'. No matter what gem or prize another dealer had just acquired, Harry Mushlin had always recently bought something a little better, and usually of the same nature. We are all human, and other booksellers would quite naturally resent being topped in this manner, particularly since the boastful Mushlin could always prove that he was telling the truth, and would often produce the book or books from his suitcase for inspection. He was the Jelly Roll Morton of the book trade: arrogant in the extreme but always able to back up every word he uttered. Now, *I* had no cause for envy or jealousy. I wasn't a dealer, only a very interested bystander. I always enjoyed listening to his tales and his explanations of 'points', particularly since I never heard him talk without improving my knowledge. Most of what I know about Modern Firsts and

Private Press books today, albeit limited, is due to a large extent from bending my ear attentively to M. H. Mushlin.

I could never make out how he had accumulated his extensive specialist knowledge, and I once asked him if he had ever worked for another bookseller in his 'prentice days. No, he told me, he had never worked for anyone else in his life, as regards to books. He had done some other work before the war, but had not been happy. After demobilisation he had been determined never to go back to a humdrum job. He was convinced that he could make a living out of books. He told me about his first day on the London streets.

Off he went with his suitcase, but with little experience and even less capital. After an hour or two in the shops he rushed off to a public telephone box to ring his young wife.

'Darling,' he told her exuberantly, 'I made a pound!'

It was the first pound of many more. He grew quite prosperous, but Mushlin never had a great desire to expand his business to any extent. His clientele remained small and extremely select. I remember him saying that he had no more than about a dozen regular customers.

He always had hard-and-fast business principles. He had never opened a credit account with any of the auctioneers. If he didn't have the money in the bank to settle immediately he wouldn't buy. He missed the best sale of Modern First Editions I have ever known, simply because he couldn't write a cheque for the amount he might have incurred that day, although he could easily have done so a week or two later.

In early middle age, Mushlin suddenly changed. From having been sleek, dark, fast, brash, and confident he became grizzled, grey, painfully slow, subdued, and uncertain. He had Parkinson's Disease. The man who had once rushed about the streets of London now tottered feebly from place to place. He grew worse and worse. 'That man's dying,' somebody said to me.

He grew a beard. It didn't suit him, but he had not cultivated it for the sake of his appearance. 'It takes me half an hour to shave,' he admitted.

Viewing a sale, he was pathetic, and it was painful to watch. He could take a slim book from a slip-case, but he could not get it back. I had to follow him about the room and help him as unobtrusively as possible — as unobtrusively to *him* as to anyone else. He got to the point where he needed a stick to aid him in reaching our premises, but more than once he departed and left it hanging on a shelf or the end of a table.

Once, in his last years, he tottered to my desk to settle a bill during a sale. I took his cheque, receipted his invoice, and off he shuffled to the porter to pick up his purchases. Five minutes later he was back beside me, writing out another cheque in his quivering hand.

'What's this?' I asked. 'You've already paid me once.'

He wasn't surprised, merely resigned. 'You're probably right,' he admitted, as he put his cheque-book away.

Suddenly — *miraculously* — Mushlin changed again. The beard went, the stick was left at home, there was even a spring in his step that reminded one of the man of old. I could not fail to remark upon his improvement in health. A new 'wonder drug' had been found and his doctor had prescribed it. I know little of such things, but it certainly seemed to be working. He told me the drug's name. I am acutely conscious of the irony, if not of the correct spelling. 'It's called El Dopa!' he said.

Poor old Harry Mushlin is now dead, but he is far from forgotten in the book trade. My last recollection of the man involves a long and exuberant conversation he held in our Sale Room one day with the doyen of our business. This gentleman is still very much alive, so he shall be nameless here. I watched these strange bedfellows in earnest and friendly conversation: in the old days they had never had a good word to say of each other, or to each other. After Mushlin had left, the other man came up to me and grinned ruefully and somewhat shamefacedly.

'Funny how things change. Remember how I couldn't stand that bugger? He's not a bad chap, really.'

Bookmen I've Liked

Since they are all unique people, I suppose one could say that there are almost as many kinds of booksellers as there are different sorts of books. Yet it is still a fact that they seem to fall into a few various types, or classes.

First, there is the bookseller by inheritance, so to speak. His father sold books, and maybe his grandfather did as well — or perhaps it was an uncle. He learned the basics of the trade at a very early age. He 'lisp'd in numbers' at his mother's knee — probably edition dates from title-pages. As Leslie Gutteridge, that cricket specialist who used to be with the Epworth Press, once informed me: 'I was born with a folio in my mouth.' The Dobells, the Rotas, the Josephs, the Masseys — indeed, the Hodgsons on the auctioneering side — all fall into this category. They begin their working lives with a head start.

There is a second group. Those contemporaries of mine who fall into this slot were working-class lads who left school at about the age of fourteen in the 'twenties or the 'thirties, often when jobs were very scarce. They grabbed anything that was going in the Situations Vacant columns where it said: 'Boy Wanted'. For instance, in 1924 Sotheran's advertised for a lad to sweep the floors, run errands, and do various odd jobs. If he showed promise he would be taught the trade. It was a rough apprenticeship. The boy who applied and got that position was named Bernard Simpson. A few years later, Marks and Co. needed a similar sort of youth. The successful applicant here was called John Watson. These two men, who became great friends, incidentally, were also to become the most expert and knowledgeable booksellers of their era. In time they acquired a certain polish, but neither ever lost the common touch. Each scorned the idea of putting on airs, at a period when some others around them grew rather intoxicated by success and would deign only to converse with royalty, peers of the realm, doctors of philosophy, or those who rubbed shoulders with such people. There was an imp in John Watson which delighted in carrying him right the other way and in humbling himself as much as possible. When he had risen to the position of managing director of the house of Bernard Quaritch, one of the most important antiquarian book businesses in the world, and after he had supervised its removal from redeveloped Grafton Street to the most palatial of premises just off Golden Square, he was occasionally asked what he did for a living by people he had just met. 'Oh,' he would say, 'I work for a second-hand bookshop in

Soho.' (When I was a Hodgson's man we weren't quite so self-disparaging; if somebody brought up the name of Sotheby's, our illustrious rivals with the spacious premises in New Bond Street, we might say:'D'you mean that place over the newspaper-kiosk in a side street off Piccadilly?')

There is a third type of bookseller. Examples of this sort are frequently scions of well-to-do or comfortably-off families. Some of them have been educated at public schools. Many of them have gone on to a university — Cambridge sometimes, but more often Oxford. You will find an occasional sprinkling from London University, while places like St. Andrew's have not been entirely unrepresented. Their *alumni*, for the most part, seem to do very well.

It doesn't necessarily always follow that these particular youngsters start off well-heeled when they enter our trade. Frequently their parents have been able to put them through the university and provide them with an education, sometimes manage to let them have a little capital, and then they are on their own. Often the capital is not forthcoming: the fledglings arrive in town, settle into a bed-sitter somewhere not too far from the centre of things, and get themselves a job — frequently badly-paid — and start learning the business of bookselling. Some stay as trusted employees all their lives; others branch out on their own. Among the younger men of this group who eventually made good on their own account I would cite Paul Grinke and Tobias Rodgers. Of an older generation, David Low is a good representative.

I have known and admired quite a lot of dealers in books who have sprung from all three groups I have mentioned, and I propose to rattle on for a bit about a few of them. I should like to introduce the first with one of my long-winded yarns.

It was in about 1929, when I passed what might now be called my 'eleven plus', but which we just called 'the scholarship' in those days, that I graduated from an elementary school to a secondary one in North London, which was then called Edmonton Latymer. It seemed to me a vast concern, with pupils swarming about the place like so many ants, and with a staff of teachers to match.

One of these teachers was a young man of about thirty, a bespectacled figure of authority, amazingly tall and incredibly thin. He streaked through the corridors with books clutched under his arm, and with his gown flowing and fluttering behind him. He taught Latin, I believe, which is a subject I never took and a language I never attained, so I had little to do with him. My one clear remembrance of the man in those days was on a certain Field Day, when he had been delegated to referee a soccer match in which I participated. All teachers, male and female, had been recruited as arbiters of the many football and netball matches in progress, whether they knew anything about the games or not. They were adults, and they carried authority. They were given a whistle, and their decision was final.

I can see him now: it was a blustering day, and the wind got up his unbelievably long and narrow trouser-legs, whipping him into a wild and grotesque eccentric dance he was quite unaware he was performing for us. With the cruelty of young adolescence we all laughed our heads off. But our amusement turned to derision and contempt as he allowed goals against our side time after time. He obviously had absolutely no knowledge of the fundamental offside rule. We were outraged: this was a serious match, and the honour of our House was at stake. Why should this clown be delegated to officiate, merely because he was an adult and a teacher?

A few years later I went on to art school for three years, then to a job with brush and pen for three more, which were to be followed by some six years in uniform during the war. It must have been in 1947 or 1948 that I saw the tall, spare figure of this man again. I saw him often: it always seemed to be on the tube train, at my local Underground station, or from my bed-sit window hard by. He hadn't changed, or didn't appear to have done so. I was quite sure it was the same man, but I did not dare to approach him and ask. When I was young he had always seemed austere and aloof. Now that I was a grown man, I still felt like a schoolboy when I passed him.

It was in my very first week at Hodgson's that this person walked into the Sale Room! I could hardly believe my eyes. What on earth was this school teacher doing here?

'Who's that chap? D'you know his name?' I asked a colleague.

'Yes, he's Arnold Muirhead,' I was told. 'He's a partner of Peter Murray Hill.'

So it *was* the same man. I now introduced myself, but he had no recollection of me, of course. Why should he have had? Over the years, as a teacher, he had dealt with many thousands of brats. I suggested that he must have been a young man only just starting in that profession when I first knew him. He doffed his hat and showed me his grey head.

'I'm fifty now,' he said.

He had continued teaching for years, but his love was collecting books, and he had amassed quite an array of early volumes on the subject of education. Apparently his erudition had impressed at least one of the dealers from whom he bought, for Peter Murray Hill had eventually said to him: 'Why don't you come in with me?'

Anyone who knew both Arnold Muirhead and Peter Murray Hill

cannot, surely, imagine an odder pair to work together, but work together they did, and for a good number of years. Peter had been an actor, but to say that he was a 'ham' before the footlights or the cameras would be to flatter him. I saw the man in one or two second-rate British films before the war, and he was pretty terrible. But he was a magnificent-looking chap: tall and handsome. He also had a penchant for early-printed books, the buying and selling of which kept the wolf from the door between histrionic engagements.

Peter met, fell in love with, and married a beautiful young actress named Phyllis Calvert. She became a star in the enormous post-war boom of British films, mainly engendered by J. Arthur Rank. Together with James Mason, Stewart Granger, Margaret Lockwood, and Jean Kent, she shot to the top of the tree. Phyllis became a partner in the bookselling firm of Peter Murray Hill Ltd., which now flourished beyond all expectations. If her husband's panache and profile did not come across fully on the screen, they most certainly did now in his day to day dealings with important and influential American clients and dealers. While he couldn't act very well to a script he was marvellous without one.

Arnold Muirhead joined Peter in the heyday of the firm. While he was a scholar, and perhaps gave the impression of being something of a pedant — and could have been perfectly cast had anyone wanted to make a film embracing such a character — Peter Murray Hill was the perennial swashbuckler with the flair. He and the lovely Phyllis made a scintillating couple at any social gathering. The business thrived.

Muirhead, it transpired, lived in what was actually the very next building to the one in which I was residing at the time, which was why I had happened to see him so often. He was just round the corner and in the first house of a street which was appropriately called Limes Avenue. I got to know him very well, but I was never able to shake off, quite, that schoolboy-schoolmaster relationship. In due course he parted amicably with Peter and started to issue catalogues of his own. At intervals he produced his 'Limes Miscellany', named after the leafy street, and very well it did, too. His catalogues became quite famous in the narrow but discerning book world. The time came when he was able to move out of London and into his own house in St. Albans, and to which every serious antiquarian book-buyer of any consequence must have pilgrimaged.

I saw him very infrequently then. Indeed, I once remarked to him that we seldom ran across him in the competitive sale rooms, and he gave me a knowing grin and a wink.

'I can buy pretty well from other booksellers,' he told me. 'You know, a good education is not a bad thing.'

*   *   *

I have mentioned the name of David Low several times earlier in these pages. Here is another educated and erudite bookseller. He had started off as a fledgling cataloguer with the Hodgsons, as I have described, and had then gone on to great things of his own. For years he had his famous little place at 17 Cecil Court — and that court is a pedestrian strip which must have harboured more fine booksellers than any other comparable area in the world, by the way — and in middle age he graduated to the idyllic confines of Emmington, in the rusticity and rurality of Little Chinnor, not too far from Oxford. Here he pursued his business. But, as he once admitted to me, and as the years progressed, he felt more and more inclined to devote his hours to gardening and less and less to the cataloguing and selling of books.

I liked the man very much, but I saw him only infrequently. For one thing, in his Cecil Court days, he was a sufficiently knowledgeable bookseller who could eschew the cut and thrust of the auction room, except for the odd and very unusual item, and for another, in his Chinnor days he rarely came up to town. But there was a brief period in the early 'seventies when he sought me out. I was flattered. He was writing a book, and one of his chapters was to be entitled: 'The Most Widely Known Bookseller of Our Time'. He referred to Peter Kroger, that most notorious man about whom I shall write at length in the following pages. David came to me with a typescript about Peter for my approval, to make sure that he had 'got it all right'. This, more than ten years after Kroger's arrest was, in all honesty, the first real intimation I encountered that I was looked upon in the book trade as being some sort of expert as far as anything to do with Kroger was concerned. But I certainly had enough to do with the man and his affairs.

Prince of all the book runners — for this is what he was to begin with, and he would be the first to admit it — is that remarkable man Martin Orskey. He started dealing in books when he was still at school, he told me, buying any volumes or magazines that were offered by his classmates. 'Half a crown for a small book; five bob for a big one.' That is as far as his expertise went in those days. He's come on quite a bit in nearly half a century. I know less than a dozen booksellers who have turned over rarer and more valuable items than Martin.

He was an extraordinary young man who tried all sorts of things in his youth. He failed in them all. His father, a Polish *émigré*, settled in Sutton, Surrey, as a ladies' hairdresser, and tried to establish his son in the same business, but without success. For a time, early in the war, Martin trained to become an instrument maker at a centre based at the old Waddon Airport, but that didn't last very long. He then actually talked himself into managing a factory of some sort at Sutton. 'For two weeks it lasted,' he told me. 'I was useless, I admit.' He has also admitted, quite cheerfully, that he never held a job for more than a couple of months until his mid-twenties. He was even chucked out of the army towards the end of the war as 'ceasing to fulfil medical requirements'. As a sheer euphemism, that one takes some beating. He was guarding prisoners of war one day when he fell asleep and dropped his rifle. He was rudely jerked awake by an ingratiating Italian, who handed his fallen weapon to him. I think Martin was lucky that he wasn't guarding German prisoners. Had he been, I think we might possibly have lost one of the more interesting characters ever to grace the book trade.

I think the incident which made up the minds of the military establishment to dispense with his services was the occasion when he was detailed to escort a number of Japanese civilian internees from one camp to another. This entailed a long train journey, and they had to change at somewhere like Crewe. He allowed his charges to retire to the station buffet for a cup of tea, only to discover that the second train was ready and waiting on another platform, and about to pull out. He rushed to the buffet in haste, brandishing his rifle, and hastily rounded up every yellow face he could see. He herded the party of very scared Orientals along the platform and into the train, and it was only after they were chugging along serenely and he was about to congratulate himself on not missing the connection that it was brought to his attention that he had, in fact, forcibly kidnapped a visiting delegation of Chinese chicken-sexers! The Japanese internees, presumably, were still sipping their tea, quite unescorted, back at the station.

Post-war, Martin tried a wide variety of things. One of those he attempted was picture-dealing. He and the late Ron Brinkman bought a huge quantity of terrible oil paintings for £2 at Reeves' Auction Rooms in Croydon, and *schlepped* them all round the West End galleries. Alas, no takers. Later, he shared a used paperback bookstall outside the old Frascati's restaurant in New Oxford Street. His partner in this venture was Freddie Read, another man who went on to greater things in the book world. Then he took to book-running in earnest. Nothing gave him more satisfaction than buying an old volume from one shop and selling it at a profit in another. He got to know a few booksellers, and he began to accumulate a knowledge of dates, values, and saleable merchandise. But things weren't easy. At his first visit to Sotheby's he bought six huge architectural folios for £4; he managed to sell five of them around the trade. But the last one he was left with was so heavy that on his way home he left it in the gents' toilet at Leicester Square Station. It was Gibbs's *Architecture*. 'It may still be there,' says Martin. 'It's worth £100 or so now...'

He was browsing through the English literature in a shop in Little Russell Street one day in 1949, when that nicest and warmest of men, dear old George McLeish, drew his attention to a vacancy in *The Clique*, advertising for a book cataloguer at Hodgson's. Martin was doubtful, but George insisted that he would be very suitable. He urged him to try; Martin applied, and he got the job.

Martin Orskey had been at it for about two or three months when I joined the firm and met him. Although, as I say, he had failed in every job he had had until then, he stayed with Hodgson's for fifteen years.

I was at the same premises for over thirty. No two careers could have been more disparate. I was methodical, dependable, accurate, and efficient — but I made no money. He was completely unmethodical, undependable, hopelessly inaccurate, and inefficient, but he nevertheless sowed the seeds of the fortune he was to make.

For all his shortcomings, the Hodgsons recognised his value in cataloguing and lotting the books, and they turned a blind eye to the hours he kept. He took an extended lunch hour, and knocked off at least thirty minutes before his time each evening. He was then off to the bookshops while they were still open. In this way he made some marvellous purchases, and pulled off some wonderful deals.

With another young man, Paul Dinnage, he formed the Holland Press. Possessing limited capital, but with an endless fund of ideas, he was one of the first men to see the possibilities in reprinting high-priced books which had long been virtually unobtainable. The first of his publications was Vicaire's *Bibliographie Gastronomique*, which was not only out of print but also out of copyright. Many other titles followed in the ensuing years, but soon other and better-capitalised publishers saw the possibilities in the scheme. Before long we were in the middle of a gigantic reprint craze.

After he had left Chancery Lane, Martin and his wife opened a small shop in the King's Road. This prospered immediately, but he was never really happy there. He was not the type to sit in one spot all day and wait for buyers and sellers to come to him. He had to be forever out and about, wheeling and dealing. As an itinerant bookseller, he rapidly went from strength to strength. Where he had once commuted from the suburbs of London to its West End, he now almost commuted across the Atlantic as regularly, it seemed to me. During the last decade he has bought two country house libraries in Scotland, another library in America, and with Ben Weinreb he purchased the entire Garrison Library in Gibraltar.

A remarkable 'nose' for the right book or collection of books has been developed through sheer experience, but I don't think he would deny that amazing luck has also played its part in his career. I should not be a bit surprised if one day he comes to me with his familiar grin and says that somebody read this short piece about him and decided that he was the ideal man to make an offer for an old book that had been cluttering up the place. If it doesn't turn out to be a Shakespeare First Folio it might well be something almost as valuable.

Martin is a keen collector, too. He knows quite a bit about Indian Miniatures, English Naive Paintings, and even scientific instruments. But books are his first love. Today he is admired and envied as one of the shrewdest, most successful, and most knowledgeable booksellers in the world. Nobody laughs at him now, as they did in the days of his callow youth and ineptitude. But one of his old friends did give a chuckle at the irony of the name of the house Martin bought in Kent some years ago.

'Little Gains House indeed!' remarked that friend.

I now go back to the nineteen-fifties, after the afore-mentioned Martin Orskey had just catalogued an enormous collection of books for sale by auction at Hodgson's. Now, it is almost inevitable that after any large library has been sieved through, and perhaps sieved through again, there remains a certain amount of dross. I have intimated this in my story of the Little Doctor. Today, Sotheby's write off such piles of volumes and pamphlets with the initials NSV, which means that they are of 'no saleable value'. They are either RTO, 'returned to owner', or with his permission sold privately for the best bid received from a number of small dealers.

I forget what we used to call such stacks in the old Hodgson days if, indeed, we called them anything at all specifically, but they were there, nevertheless. George Jeffery, of the Farringdon Road stalls, would always be ready to offer a pound or two, and so would Pusey, an amiable tat-merchant who had a shop in Monmouth Street and several pitches in various street markets.

The particular stack with which I am now concerned was just a little bit different. I can see it now: it was piled three to four feet high in several rows, by the rostrum. Perhaps the titles were dull, and the contents of the books even duller, but the calf and gilt lettering gleamed. It was mostly French literature, of an obscure nature, and therefore not terribly attractive to either Jeffery or Pusey, although each had made a half-hearted offer.

'I think I know someone who might like it,' said Martin Orskey to Wilfrid Hodgson.

Now Martin, in his multifarious lunchtime sojourns, had encountered quite a number of similar sojourners and browsers, and he never let an opportunity pass to make their acquaintance and learn their particular interests. One such was a young man of twenty-seven named Alexander Rogoyski. He was shy and very uncertain. But he was a fine bookseller in embryo, and with a penchant for continental literature.

When Alex was induced to come in and make an offer for that odd lot one day, he literally had hardly two ha'pennies to rub together, as the expression goes. Further, his small dealings had been confined to taking a solitary volume from the shelves of some bookseller, buying it for a small sum and perhaps netting himself a few shillings profit by selling it for a marginally larger sum. Confronted with this stack of gleaming calf, piled in the large room of an alien auctioneer's premises, and invited to make an offer for it, he had not the slightest idea of what to do or say.

I clearly recall this transaction. I see a tall, blond youngster in a leather-elbowed check sports jacket, light twill trousers, and chukka boots. He gazes, open-mouthed, with his head on one side, in the direction of those books. *I* saw a knowledgeable young dealer summing things up. Alex later confided to me the exact situation.

'How much must I offer?' he asked Martin.

'Say three pounds,' he was told. 'That ought to do it.' Martin Orskey, himself, had no idea at this stage if anyone else had topped the bid, and was taking a random guess.

So three pounds it was, and Alex Rogoyski made his first bulk buy. It laid the foundations of a fine career. Not too long afterwards, a vacancy for a cataloguer fell at Hodgson's, after the mid-season defection of old Alfred Sims, and once again Martin suggested the same young man. Alex came, and he stayed for twelve years. Speaking for the pair of us, I think I would count him as my best friend. Speaking for myself alone, of course, I would say that he possesses all the qualities and virtues which I admire and which I am only too well aware that I lack.

He had been a lad of eleven or twelve, living with his family in Warsaw, when the Germans invaded Poland in 1939. His father was an eminent economist, and a man of some importance connected with Dr. Beck's government. He was obliged to flee the country with his wife and child as Hitler's hordes moved in, virtually with nothing more than what they all stood up in. By a circuitous route through various countries of Europe they eventually reached Paris. The ultimate intention was to get to England, but the Rogoyski family were obliged to kick their heels for some time.

Alex was sent to a boarding school, a considerable way south of Paris. The boy was ensconced here during the months of the 'phoney war', when nothing seemed to happen. Then came Germany's 1940 *blitzkrieg*, the circumnavigation of the 'impregnable' Maginot Line, the drive through Belgium and France, and the march towards Paris.

The child's parents immediately despatched a message for Alex to make his way to Paris and meet them, in order to make a hasty retreat west.

Their way to the north coast of France had been cut off. Hosts of refugee military and civilian east-Europeans, facing either death or the concentration camps, had only one way to go: inhospitable but neutral fascist Spain, and thence to Portugal. The exodus began.

It must be remembered that Alex was a mere boy of twelve, and quite inexperienced. He spoke only his own language with any fluency, and had the barest smattering of French. With just the vaguest of instructions he arrived in Paris — by a long taxi-ride, no less — desperately seeking the rendezvous of a small Polish community. Inevitably, he became lost. He roamed the streets, looking for his parents, while they frantically searched for him. He has told me that he eventually joined up with a gang of homeless waifs and gamins in a similar plight.

Came the time when the mother and father were finally forced to accept the inevitable. The vanguard of Hitler's forces were already uncomfortably close to Paris, and all the roads south and west were jammed with fleeing refugees. Distraught at the idea of leaving their son behind, but having explored every method of finding him, they were actually on their way to the car that was to take them out of the city when they turned a corner and bumped into him! This is an incredibly melodramatic anecdote, I know, but one which Alex assures me is quite true.

There was more to it. Just a jump ahead of the enemy, there was an occasion in one French town when the Rogoyski car drove out of the western side of the market square as the first German car entered at the eastern side.

Alex has also told me of his experiences when they reached the border, at Hendaye. Here, everyone was obliged to produce their passports for entry into the safety of the Spanish town of Irun. It was demanded that the Polish officers surrendered their arms before passing through, but many hundreds of them, fiercely patriotic, staunchly refused to do so. They simply placed their revolvers to their temples and blew their brains out. This sort of gesture may appear admirable and heroic to some; Alex himself rather subscribed to the idea that it was honourable. My own view is that it was quite daft. After all, 'he who fights and runs away, lives to fight another day.' While I have never had much time for the ridiculous belief that because a proverb or couplet rhymes nicely it must necessarily be true, I do go along with the sentiments expressed in this one.

When S. N. Behrman's famous play, *Jacobowski and the Colonel*, was filmed in Hollywood as a vehicle for Danny Kaye as the Jewish refugee, Jacobowski, and Curt Jurgens as the Polish officer, I confess that I could not, at first, understand Alex Rogoyski's wild enthusiasm for the piece. I did not, at that juncture, know the story of his flight. The fact is that, watching this film, he lived his twelve-year-old experience all over again.

From Warsaw to Hendaye he had gone through much of the same travail as Jacobowski and the Colonel.

Alex and family drove through Spain and Portugal, and eventually they reached Lisbon. There, in that European melting-pot, then chock-full of spies, refugees, and intrigue, they waited impatiently for a passage to England. Once here, and finally settled, the boy went to school and began to learn a new language and absorb a new culture. I know the man so well today that I can barely detect an accent, although those who do not know him so well, or who have just met him, inform me that they can just tell that English is not his native tongue.

As I say, he was twenty-seven when I first met him. He had had a number of jobs, all stop-gaps, before he took a considerable cut in income to work at Hodgson's and learn about the books he loved. A dozen years later he branched out on his own, and he now runs a flourishing antiquarian business from his home. Like myself, he will probably never be a very rich man, but he is my idea of a successful one.

I never knew Charlie Lahr very well; I don't suppose I ever met him more than two or three times. But he was one of those well-loved booksellers of whom the old-timers have nothing but good words to say. His heyday was the nineteen-twenties, an era when his particular brand of mild bohemianism marked him as a figure of suspicion among the more respectable and conventional. Today, I think nobody would give him a second glance, but he wore a goatee beard when almost everybody was clean-shaven, baggy corduroy slacks when others favoured neatly-pressed flannels, and sandals without socks when highly-polished black shoes were the norm. When I first knew Charlie he had an untidy bookshop in Red Lion Street, but after the war he was to be found in a pokey hole-in-the-wall behind Leicester Square Underground Station.

He was on friendly and familiar terms with almost everybody in the London literary world, and he knew most of them long before they ever became famous. But whereas almost all of them passed through an inevitable phase of leftism and nonconforming and later grew out of it, Charlie never did. He embraced a sort of half-baked romantic socialism and pacifism, and right to the end he spent much of his time eliciting subscriptions to ill-printed left-wing magazines and pamphlets. You would see him dashing about London on his old bike in all weathers, eagerly delivering his periodical literature to middle-aged friends who had long lost all interest in it, and who now only subscribed out of charity to Charlie and for old times' sake.

He had an odd sense of humour, and getting through the day with a laugh or two was of infinitely more importance to him than making money by selling books. Stories of the man abound, and most of his old cronies who are still alive are recounting them yet. But there is one that I remember in particular.

It seems that he was digging in his garden one day and he unearthed an old bronze representation of an erect phallus. One can only conjecture how it got buried in his garden: my impression is that years before some rather strait-laced lady, recently widowed, had come across the thing among her late husband's effects. Afraid just to shove it into the dustbin, feeling that those who cleared her rubbish might come across it accidentally and recall that it was in *her* bin that it had been dumped, she probably buried it at the bottom of her garden at dead of night. Charlie Lahr cleaned it up and took it to his bookshop. He stuck it on a shelf right in the middle of a set of Charles Dickens. For quite a while his customers would browse along this shelf, and pass the all-too-familiar titles: *Martin Chuzzlewit, David Copperfield, Great Expectations, American Notes*... and there among them all stood this bronze phallus, with a label underneath it: 'Master Humphrey's Cock'.

Jack and Sam Joseph were two perfect examples of the 'inheritors' among London booksellers. Their parents had been famous dealers before them, but I think nobody can deny that the two sons far surpassed their teachers.

They were completely dissimilar in temperament and appearance, but each complemented the other. They were very fortunate in the situation of their premises — still very efficiently run by Jack's grandson, David Brass, by the way, with the co-operation of Peter Kay. Emanuel Joseph, their father, took a corner shop at 48a Charing Cross Road, almost directly opposite Leicester Square Underground Station. It had a basement consisting of two fair-sized rooms and a 'box-room'. He was later able to add the next door shop in Great Newport Street. This gave the firm pretty spacious premises. In the mid-'thirties the brothers also leased a large basement under one of the Joe Lyons' teashops a few yards up Great Newport Street, by the Arts Theatre Club. This acquisition gave the necessary room for expansion. In the ensuing years it became filled with one of the finest and most valuable collections of volumes in the world.

Throughout the nineteen-thirties, then after the war was over in the late 'forties, and well into the 'fifties, this pair was fortified by the shrewdness of Bernard Simpson, who attended most of the auction sales on the firm's behalf. Further, they had Harry Green, the 'inside man', who could sell you almost anything, if he put his mind to it. This formidable quartet buccaneered their way across the high seas of the bookselling world. No-one could deny their incredible ability.

When I was a very young man I was an occasional buyer in that pleasant vicinity. But while I was a comfortable browser in places like Foyle's, just up the road, and in the many other bookshops which adjoined each other, I very rarely attempted to penetrate Joseph's.

In the dimly-lit recesses of the tightly-packed shelves stood a burly man. To my impressionable young eyes he looked like a gangster's bodyguard. If one were rash enough to ask him if he had such-and-such a book he would merely shake his head or mutter a surly 'No.' It was always the same. We youngsters wondered how they ever did any business at all, at the time. What we didn't know then, and what I came to understand only many years later, was that Joseph's was a quite different sort of business from that of most of the shops we usually frequented. Their clientele was formed largely by the discerning and often well-to-do collector looking for fine and costly books, or the visiting dealer from abroad after richly-bound sets. Twenty years later I got to know that bodyguard of the rare volume very well, and we became quite friendly before he died. He was dear old Harry Green, who was actually a very simple and engaging soul with no harm in him at all. But, as a youth, I had been terrified even to approach him.

But if Harry was the 'heavy' minion manning the book bastions, Sam Joseph, the younger of the two brothers, was the 'glamorous' one in those early days. He had the dark, Latin good looks of those current Hollywood screen stars like Ricardo Cortez or George Raft. His hair was immaculately-parted and slicked down. At that time he was married to Binnie Barnes, a beautiful young British film actress who had just had a great success as one of Charles Laughton's several wives in *The Private Life of Henry VIII*. This in itself gave the man an aura of glamour and ultra-sophistication to the young and impressionable. He used to stand at the curb, just outside the shop, watching the passing scene pensively. Perhaps he had something to be pensive about: at just around this time Binnie Barnes got a call to go to Hollywood, and she became quite famous in American movies. Sam's marriage eventually broke up.

I didn't meet Jack Joseph, his brother and the senior partner, until after the war. He had the familiar physical characteristics of Mr. Punch, but Jack's book-knowledge was phenomenal, and he was multi-lingual. He was also an excellent man of business, and he drove a hard bargain. I have been told, on the other hand, that he could be remarkably kind and helpful, as well as generous, to the young bookseller just starting up in the trade. I shall remember him, primarily, for his extensive knowledge and his barbed and cruel tongue. He took an extraordinary delight in that verbal activity generally known as 'mickey-taking', particularly with those booksellers and assistants not quite so quick-witted as himself, or with auctioners at the rostrum who were not exactly in a position to halt proceedings and give him as good as they got in the repartee.

The fourth member of this redoubtable quartet was, of course, Bernard Simpson. It depended entirely upon how well you knew the man, but I think I would go so far as to say that he was either the best-liked or the least-liked person in the trade.

Those who knew him hardly or not at all saw only a wry, cynical, and somewhat sardonic-looking character who appraised a book with an eagle eye while viewing at an auction sale, and who bid professionally and impassively, always from the same spot below the rostrum. Hard at work, and concentrating keenly, he was inclined to be taciturn and mono-syllabic, if approached. Perhaps the small dealers and amateurs who usually congregate at the back of the room, those who would never dare to move nearer and claim a place among the old pros at the Pound, may be forgiven for imagining him to be surly and unapproachable. But these saw and heard him only from a distance. They never really got to know him.

I knew the man very well. While I must admit that at the very start, when I first joined Hodgson's, my impression was much the same as that of those others, gradually, over the years, our acquaintance ripened, and my attitude grew different. I have never known a warmer, kindlier, more generous and more humorous man in my life. He was also a brilliant raconteur. Most of his stories were hilarious, and sometimes they took a bit of believing, but he was not given to lying. I often heard only very slightly different versions from other sources — frequently from eye-witnesses. Some of these tales were to his credit, and some to his detriment, but I think the former outweigh, by far, the latter. Beneath a polished veneer of harsh implacability was a very understanding and sentimental man. I enjoyed his company.

Bernard started his career, as so many other great booksellers have done, with the famous firm of Sotheran's. He was then about fourteen years old, and just out of school. Here he did every menial task requested of him, but he *learned*. A few years later, wishing to spread his wings, he answered an advertisement for an assistant in the Rare Book Department of a very famous firm. He was interviewed, and it seems he could have got the job he was after, but he felt that he knew his true worth. He asked for a wage he believed he was entitled to, which was reasonable enough, but it was too much for that firm, who had never been big payers. It was their loss. He moved a short journey away and applied to the brothers Joseph. It was their gain. He stayed with them for twenty-five years — saving the break from 1941-46, when he was in the army during the Second World War.

(Incidentally, Joseph's paid an allowance to his wife and two children each week for the five years he was away. The firm regularly paid a weekly sum to the widows of long-serving and valued assistants. Loyalty isn't always the prerogative of the employee.) Before Bernard Simpson left the firm of E. Joseph he was probably the highest-paid bookseller's assistant in the country. He was certainly the most valuable. From my observation alone he was the most knowledgeable.

'He knew nothing when he first came to me,' Jack Joseph informed me once. This was not quite true. 'Now he knows more than I do.' I don't think that was exactly true, either. But I fully appreciate the sentiment he was attempting to express.

Harry Green was nominally his senior when young Bernard first started at Charing Cross Road, and I believe he led the boy quite the devil of a life at the beginning, 'shaping him up'. But as Bernard grew older, felt his feet more, and grew wider in experience, their roles gradually changed. They became firm friends in the end, and admired one another very much.

Bernard specialised, for the most part, in badly-needed scholarly works that were out of print. He had a mind like a card-index system. He must have made thousands of pounds for the firm by lighting upon books which were not normally 'reckoned' by most other dealers, until the 'fifties, when the reprint craze began. Then even he could no longer keep track of the once-rare items which were fast being re-issued.

He also had a keen scent and an eye for the fine, really well-bound book, and he particularly liked handsome sets. He had little time for Modern First Editions, and he seldom made any attempt to compete for the more esoteric offerings of the *soi-disant* Private Press — although there were certain exceptions. He proclaimed a total ignorance of anything outside his particular field, but the time was to come when he would be buying and selling merchandise he had never even contemplated before.

His contemporaries like Charlie Traylen and Frank Hammond had struck out on their own right after the war, but Bernard sat tight for a long time. It was not until well into the 'fifties that he first hinted to me that he was on the lookout for premises of his own.

At that time I thought of him setting up somewhere in London, and I think that he did, too. But when the opportunity came, it was from an entirely unexpected quarter. For many years Ma Brown had run an old-established and very famous firm from 87 High Street, Eton. It was known as Brown's Antiquarian Bookshop. It was now a somewhat run-down enterprise, but it had the advantage of spacious living accommodation above it. Bernard stepped in and bought the business. He moved his house and family from Petts Wood to Eton and set about building up the whole thing again. In what seemed to me a remarkably short time the business had become far more prosperous than it had ever been.

Bernard Simpson now lives quietly in what might officially be called retirement. But I don't think you ever quite retire from books. He still takes all the auction catalogues, he still keeps abreast of all events, and you will very occasionally see him at that familiar spot below the rostrum. May you still see him for many years to come.

Book Thieves

The surprising thing to me about those people who steal books is that, when apprehended, they more often than not turn out to be quite respectable-looking persons.

If a scruffy, furtive type walks into a bookshop or an auction room, and starts to move about the shelves, it is natural that one's suspicions should be aroused. I think it only normal behaviour to keep an eye on him, but more than ninety percent of this sort prove to be quite honest.

It is my experience that when we in the book trade are able to catch a thief in the act he turns out to be a lawyer, civil servant, teacher, parson, or university professor — in fact, the very kind of man you would not ordinarily suspect. I believe the same thing often happens in big department stores, with some of their shop-lifters. The obvious remedy is to suspect everybody, and to watch the lot of them. This must be extremely difficult in bookshops, but recent years in the auction rooms have seen at least one, and sometimes two, uniformed security men on the *qui vive*. They act as a strong deterrent, and there has been a marked reduction in petty purloining since the potential thief became aware of their presence.

The remark has often been made that people who would never dream of robbing a bank or breaking into a house look upon books as fair game. Public libraries, I believe, suffer a high turnover in missing volumes. I think that many of the books are unofficially 'borrowed', and that the borrowers forget to take them back, find it too much trouble, or else get cold feet.

I suppose it is not surprising that octavos and items of a smaller nature are likely to go missing from the shelves of bookshops, libraries, and sale rooms. It is not too difficult to slip a book into a pocket or down the front of the trousers while a porter's or an assistant's back is momentarily turned or his attention is elsewhere. But one thing that has always puzzled me, and a great many others, is how frequently thieves used to be able to sneak off undetected with large folios! It happened, and sometimes they got away with it. In comparatively recent times I have known copies of Camden's *Britannia* to 'walk' from the shelves of Bonham's and from our own bookcase at Hodgson's during a viewing, an expensive copy of the Ackermann *Microcosm of London* to go missing from Sotheby's in New Bond Street immediately before a sale started and in a crowded room, and

an enormous volume of Blaeu's *Atlas* disappear from the display window
of a Bloomsbury bookshop. But I think that the most outrageous thefts of
this sort took place in a series of purloinings many years ago.

Major Grant was a scrupulously honest retired military man who made
a respectable living by purchasing books of some value and desirability
and then sending them up to London for sale by auction. He advertised
widely, and one of his mediums was the *Exchange and Mart*. He picked up
some pretty fair bargains in this way, and I think that perhaps the 'best'
deal he ever did unfortunately proved to be his very last. Somebody wrote
in to him offering a collection of really beautiful colour-plate books, all of
which were extremely big. Among them, I remember, was a copy of one
of the largest books of its kind ever published: Angas's *Kafirs*. It needs two
hands to carry it across a room to a table.

After Major Grant had bought the books he sent them to us for sale. But
after they had been sold, and distributed widely to various parts of the
country, one of the purchasers recognised the book he had bought as being
the property of perhaps the most famous library of its kind in the world, in
a certain university town. We immediately contacted the unfortunate
vendor, and he confirmed with some dismay what we had already
suspected. He had bought the whole lot from the same man. A call to the
library elicited the information, also given with dismay, that all the books
belonged to them.

Grant, an elderly man, was utterly shattered. Apart from having
suffered a very heavy financial loss, it preyed upon his mind that he had
purchased stolen goods. That they had come from a most prestigious
library worsened his feeling of guilt, although in my opinion he had
nothing to feel guilty about. We did everything in our power to recall the
volumes, and we did, I think, recover them all but one. They were
eventually returned to their rightful home, and I imagine that that
institution's security measures were tightened immediately. How any
man had been able to walk boldly past a guard in uniform — not once, but
several times — with these most conspicuous books is something quite
beyond my comprehension. And it had not even been noticed that they
were missing, until we informed the librarian!

The thief was quickly apprehended, since Grant knew the name and
address of the man from whom he had bought the books, but that was
small consolation to the major. He was now virtually bankrupted, and he
died only a few months later.

Perhaps the oddest case of theft that I ever encountered on our premises
took place in the early 'seventies. A set of the Nonesuch *Dickens* had come
up for sale. I have described the unique qualities of this publication in detail
elsewhere in these pages, so it is sufficient to say here that the last and

twenty-fourth volume is a book-box usually containing a weighty engraved steel plate.

The particular set under discussion was a fairly good one, without being fine. We did not expect it to realise the £800 or £900 that more desirable ones had been making, and so it proved. Joseph's bought it for £520.

A day or two after the sale, in came Peter Kay to pick up his purchases for his firm. When it came to clearing the set of the Nonesuch *Dickens*, chance could have led him to lift the books in piles of five or six at a time, noticing nothing amiss. He may have done so, for all I know. But chance also led him to pick up the book-cum-box on its own, and up it went like a feather! He immediately looked inside. Of course, the plate had gone.

Now this loss did not make the set absolutely worthless, but it cut its value by more than half, and Joseph's did not particularly want it as it stood, quite understandably. We were resigned to putting it aside, paying the vendor the full auction price, and suffering the considerable loss. Later on it would be recatalogued, 'minus the plate', and the firm would be very lucky to recoup a couple of hundred.

That happened on a Friday. Imagine everybody's surprise when on the Monday morning following, the first arrival of the staff at Joseph's in Charing Cross Road opened the front door, bent to pick up the post from the floor and found that the thief had slipped the stolen plate through the letter-box over the weekend!

What strange quirk had led this individual to purloin the steel plate moments before the sale, sit in the auction room and watch the set sold and knocked down audibly to Joseph's, take his prize away with him, and then experience a change of heart and quietly return the thing to its purchaser? Or was it just a very hazardous practical joke?

Booksellers are continually complaining of the justice meted out to thieves, after they have been caught and tried. I am not greatly familiar with the fate of crooks caught out in other trades, but certainly those who steal books usually get bound over or fined a quite nominal sum. I would not say that habitual book thieves are exactly discouraged from their activity.

I particularly remember one series of thefts. Small atlases, old books of road maps, and similar volumes were continually being stolen from the shelves of the major sale rooms. All the books were 'breakers': whoever was pinching them would be hard to trace, for the missing books never turned up anywhere. Their plates and pages were removed very quickly, no doubt sold to various dealers, and very soon coloured and sold again. But as it happened, most of the thefts took place in Sotheby's old book room, off St. George Street, and two vigilant and experienced porters were the dour Frank Girdler and the canny Jock Campbell. By putting two and two together they felt that they had a pretty good idea who was responsible. The same chap was always present whenever such volumes were missing, or had been a short while earlier. A trap was laid, the firm's security officer was on hand, and the suspected man played his expected part. As he walked through the doors to the street, it was noticed that a certain book had gone, Jock gave the nod to the security officer, and that gentleman was out like a shot to apprehend the culprit.

It was a classic case of a thief being caught red-handed. When the police accompanied him to his home in South London, thousands upon thousands of maps and plates were found, but no books at all that could be identified as having been stolen. The man was a fairly high-ranking civil servant, with a good income, but he had obviously been living beyond his means. He was a regular supplier of goods to the trade, and he was quite well known to us all. It didn't take long for the grape-vine to get to work, and I don't think many people purchased much from him while he awaited trial.

Had he been tried early in the week, it is almost inevitable that there would have been mention of it in the daily papers, news that would have been picked up by the local weeklies, and the thief would have received considerable bad publicity. But his case came up on a Friday afternoon, probably too late for the press to mention it on Saturday, and by Monday it was no longer news. He was fined a nominal £70, and I think it doubtful if his superiors or his colleagues in the civil service ever heard about it.

Years later I saw him in our Sale Room, viewing the books on the shelves.

'What are you doing here?' I asked him. 'You're barred.'

'Oh, that was a long time ago,' he said. 'It's all over now.'

'Is it?' Just by sheer coincidence, the security officer who had arrested him happened to be in our office, making a 'phone call. I took the man in to see him.

'Am I to be penalised forever for something that happened over five years ago?' asked the book thief.

'You're damned right you are,' he was told. 'Out! And don't come back.'

Petty criminals of this inclination, while cunning and clever in one way, are often quite stupid in another. Not all that many years ago, two young men walked into Hodgson's between sales, while several thousands of books were on the shelves but not officially on view to the public. Normally, the two would have been discouraged from browsing. But one of them had been a former porter at Sotheby's in New Bond Street, and was acquainted with one of our own assistants. While he stopped and chatted with his former colleague, the other wandered round looking at the books. Later in the day, after they had left, two rather chunky but very elaborately-bound volumes were found to be missing. There was a wide open gap where they should have been. It was quite obvious who had taken them, for nobody else had been in. We knew the culprit's name, and the Personnel Department at New Bond Street had his address, but it would have been hard to prove anything.

A couple of days later in came a lady assistant from a large West End bookshop. She asked to look at the two books. I knew her well enough to explain that they had not been 'withdrawn' from the sale — a euphemism that is often used — but that they had, in fact, been knocked off.

'*I've* got them — back at the shop,' she informed me. 'We bought them two days ago. I wanted to compare them with the ones described in your catalogue. They seemed so similar.'

A quick telephone call to her boss was made, and we learned that he had paid for the books by cheque, with an invoice, to a resident of King's Road, Brighton. The man must have gone from WC2 to W1 in a matter of minutes, and sold them immediately.

'How much did you give?' I asked.

'A hundred and fifty. He took it, but he said he had been told they were worth two hundred.'

To add insult to injury, he had used our printed estimate!

It wasn't difficult to catch him. Sotheby's security staff had rapidly gone to Personnel and obtained a copy of his original application form for employment there, and it was eventually passed to me. I checked the address: it was King's Road, Leytonstone, which had been his true address at the time. He had given a phoney address to the bookseller, when receiving that cheque, but he hadn't used much imagination. He hadn't even falsified his street number! He actually lived at that number, and in that street — but a few miles along the coast from Brighton, in Worthing.

Sotheby's

It was in 1967. Things had relaxed a little at 115 Chancery Lane. I recall that the more immediate important jobs had all been disposed of, and that I was now devoting myself to the annual regular and lengthy chore of typing out names and addresses on the printed Catalogue Subscription Renewal Reminders, which were sent out to all corners of the world at this time of the year.

There I sat, at about nine-thirty one morning, already hammering away at my machine, when in walked Wilfrid Hodgson, looking unusually grim and purposeful.

'I want you and Rogoyski to come out and have a cup of coffee with me in about ten minutes' time,' he said, and disappeared into his office.

This, to put it mildly, was what is known as a right turn up for the book. The bosses, while always affable towards their employees, very rarely socialised with any of us. Wilfrid, particularly, always lunched alone — exactly where I never knew — but certainly not in any local pub or restaurant the members of his staff might have frequented. If he took a tea-break it was always late in the afternoon, and well after we had returned from ours. He was respected for this. I imagine that he, as the guv'nor, felt that he might inhibit the conversation over a cup of tea or coffee, and almost certainly he might have done so over a meal. He had always maintained that distance necessary between 'officers and other ranks', so to speak, in order for the sake of discipline, however loose. In some eighteen years of working together I don't think he and I had drunk a cup of tea at the same table more than once or twice — and then only accidentally.

To be asked out suddenly, like this, boded no good at all. Alex and I were a couple of very worried men. We speculated to extremes: it could mean one of only two things. First, we were going to be invited in as partners, something which was extremely unlikely, since neither of us had any cash to invest, and second, we were very shortly to be out on our ears and were about to get advance warning of the impending boot. *This* was quite likely.

We were utterly wrong in our surmises. Once the three of us had settled at a table in a Fleet Stret coffee-house, Wilfrid gave us the news. Sotheby's, in the person of Lord John Kerr, Head of their Book Department, had quite simply made him an offer he couldn't refuse.

Wilfrid Hodgson did not use that term. Mario Puzo, author of *The*

194

Godfather, had already penned it, but his book was still to be published, and the phrase had yet to resound throughout the world and become a stock utterance in everyday conversation. But that, in effect, was what had occurred.

For the past twenty years Sotheby's had been growing bigger and bigger, just as Hodgson's, as I have intimated earlier, had been shrinking more and more. As far as books and literary properties alone are concerned, Sotheby's had reached the point where they simply had no space or time to handle the sale of any more. The 'waiting list' was already six months to a year before anything got sold, and sometimes longer. On the other hand, Hodgson's had reached that point where the firm was just marking time. At the close of each season, after the accountants had gone through the books, Wilfrid and Sidney would see that while the business was giving a moderate living to all those concerned, it was doing this and absolutely nothing more. The prospect was that things would grow worse, rather than better. Sotheby's approach came at the ideal time.

It was *not* a 'take-over bid' — in the generally-accepted understanding of that term, which was rife at the time. What actually happened was this: Hodgson's ceased to trade from 115 Chancery Lane, and all members of the staff ceased to be employed by them. Sotheby's leased the premises, and each of us was offered immediate employment in exactly the same capacity and at the same salary. Everything would continue as previously, more or less, except that the place would be known as Sotheby's (Hodgson's Rooms), with some of the backlog and overflow of properties from New Bond Street to be sold at Chancery Lane. Wilfrid would continue as the auctioneer, and Sidney would be retained in an advisory and consultancy capacity.

The whole thing was a bit of a god-send to most of us. Almost all of the cataloguers, the porters, the packer, and the part-time secretary were happy — shall we say? — with the new arrangement. Yes, *almost*. But just two did not go along with the idea. One was very happy and one was not.

The happy one was a certain porter. For quite a long time he had wanted to move on — on to the dole, I imagine. Several times he had asked Wilfrid to sack him, in order that he could claim unemployment benefit. When his boss refused to do this, since he had no reason to, the man declined to ask for his cards. Had he left voluntarily he could have claimed no dole money, so he trudged on discontentedly. But when Sotheby's stepped in, that was an entirely different matter. He decided immediately that this was a heaven-sent opportunity to get away and *still* draw his dole. We saw him no more.

Considerably less happy was a certain part-time cataloguer who came in a couple of days a week. He put in two or three more with another firm of auctioneers, I believe. That firm, none too strong just then, *has* come on quite a bit in more recent years. Now, when Wilfrid Hodgson informed the rest of the staff, later that momentous morning, of what would be happening, he stressed the fact that we should all keep the matter to ourselves for the time being and wait for Sotheby's to make an announcement in the press. But I noticed that the young gentleman under discussion went streaking off for a morning cup of tea immediately afterwards. Ten minutes later came a telephone call for Wilfrid from the chairman of that other firm of auctioneers. He had heard a rumour, he said, to the effect that Hodgson's would be merging with Sotheby's. His suggestion was that Hodgson's should merge with his firm, instead!

Perhaps it is quite unnecessary to say that the young part-time cataloguer did not continue to work with us under the Sotheby's aegis. He could hardly have done so, anyway. One of the tales he had told us in the past, in order to impress, no doubt, was that he had for some time worked in the Book Department of the famous New Bond Street firm. Here he was, hoist with his own petard! The man had never put in a day's work for Sotheby's in his life.

Lord John Kerr was a rather reticent but very likeable man. He was a younger son of the Marquess of Lothian, and he once told me of how he had originally entered the book business. After some years in the armed service he had, in the early nineteen-fifties, re-entered civilian life with the full intention of somehow getting into books. His first hope had been that of entering publishing, and he went the rounds. But he gained very little encouragement. Nobody wanted a fledgling, and everywhere he was advised to try to get some experience first. So he then tried bookselling. But once again, nobody seemed to want an untried assistant at that time. He had just about given up all hope of ever getting into the book trade when he happened to drop into that famous little shop of David Low's, at 17 Cecil Court.

'I hear that Goldschmidt's, in Bond Street, are looking for a young assistant,' David told him. 'Why not try there?'

The youthful Lord John did so, and he got the job. He was taken on by Jacques Vellekoop, who had formerly been an assistant of E. P. Goldschmidt himself, and who had continued the business after the old man had died. Here Lord John Kerr took his first faltering steps in the antiquarian book world. I remember him well when he used to come down to Hodgson's to view the books, and to buy for his firm. He was then a cherubic-looking youth with dark, wavy hair. In those days I feel sure that he looked upon auctions and auctioneers as somewhat necessary evils, and had no intention at all of ever attempting to enter this particular field himself. Indeed, after he had accumulated a considerable amount of book knowledge he bought the famous firm known as Sanders of Oxford, and settled down quite happily to run a quiet life as a bookseller in the High Street of a university town.

I think he might be there yet, had he not been induced by Peter Wilson to come to London and enter Sotheby's as a director, the eventual intention being for him to take over as Head of the Book Department. Both his title and his courteous and gentlemanly mien would be great assets to this ever-expanding branch of Sotheby's. It was in the mid-'sixties that he took charge, replacing Anthony Hobson, who had run the Book Department very efficiently and successfully for a number of years, and who was now going into semi-retirement.

It was at this period that Lord John Kerr began to grow grey, and first commenced to cultivate those enormous and distinctive Edwardian side-whiskers. It was at this time, too, that he started to develop his style as an auctioneer at the rostrum. He is, I think, perhaps the best man with a gavel at present working in London. I have officiated at many sales with him over the past fifteen years, and everything has always gone very smoothly and happily.

This was the gentleman who originally had the idea of acquiring the well-established but somewhat Dickensian Hodgson's building as an adjunct to the rather over-burdened Book Gallery at New Bond Street, which was never exactly an ideal sale room. When he first came down to Chancery Lane and interviewed us all, he made it quite plain that it was not his intention to change or to streamline the place to any extent. He wanted things to carry on very much in the same way that they always had done, and he wished us to use the same styles and methods of cataloguing, numbering, and administration which had become familiar to *habitués* of the premises and regular subscribers to the catalogues.

Inevitably, perhaps, considerable changes *were* made. The very first innovation was the installation of a New Bond Street man to take charge. It was unthinkable, apparently, that any incumbent was capable of running the place. I suppose this is understandable, looking at things quite dispassionately, but the staff didn't think so at the time.

The second change to be made was an invasion of painters, carpenters, plasterers, and electricians. The whole place was done over. This move, although it disrupted work considerably, was long overdue, and it could not be opposed on any grounds that bore common-sense. The shelves were painted, the floor was carpeted, central heating was installed, clients now had chairs to sit on instead of backless benches, and there was a lavatory for both ladies and gentlemen!

However, it was not for several years — until Michael Morton-Smith came in as manager, and later, Michael Heseltine, when we developed the reputation for specialisation in illustrated works, modern literature, and children's books — that things began to settle down and the Chancery Lane side of the Sotheby business eased into solvency.

It has been said by somebody that 'Christie's are gentlemen, trying to be auctioneers; Sotheby's are auctioneers, trying to be gentlemen.' It's a glib phrase. It trips off the tongue lightly and easily, and it always causes a laugh or a smile when heard for the first time. Perhaps for this reason alone it is widely accepted as being true. My opinion is that it is absolute rubbish. In my experience, there is little to choose between the two firms with regard to professionalism and expertise at sale by auction; as far as those of noble and gentle birth are concerned, it is my guess that there must be more at New Bond Street than there are at King Street!

Most certainly, Sotheby's Board of Directors, when they first took on the humble Hodgson premises, bore a formidable and impressive number of influential names, with earls, lords, knights, and heavily-decorated personages spattered freely through the list. The staff itself was already pretty large — several hundred at New Bond Street alone at that time — but the first impression one got was that there were more Chiefs than Indians. I very quickly discovered, however, who actually ran the show. Momentous and major policy decisions may have come from on high, but the business was kept ticking over by the hard graft of about half a dozen very capable and long-serving employees, much in the same way as the company commander in most military units signs his name to orders and documents and returns salutes, while the real work is done by a senior non-commissioned officer and his staff.

It is true that certain members of the aristocracy, and some of those Establishment figures of the clubland area on the south side of Piccadilly, would still never dream of selling a work of art with anyone else but Christie's. This held good after the phenomenal rise of Sotheby's in the 'sixties: they were *still* viewed as jumped-up Johnny-come-latelys.

Public relations and advertising, with the developing New Bond Street firm, were in the hands of a firm called Clark Nelson, to a large extent. It hadn't been very long before they quickly saw the possibilities in this particular account. They virtually gave up everything else in order to promote Sotheby's, and with a hundred percent success. Turnover increased enormously. With it came added staff, additional premises, and the most ambitious branching out. One of the first developments some time after we were added to the firm was Sotheby's Belgravia, to be devoted largely to the sale of Victoriana. Not too long afterwards came the acquisition of Parke-Bernet Inc., the foremost American auction house. Before long there were offices or sale rooms in about forty different foreign countries.

Inevitably, Sotheby's profits mounted. Also inevitably, perhaps, things began to get a little out of hand. More and more business meant even more and more staff, and at one time the already rabbit-warren-like premises at New Bond Street grew to resemble a veritable ant-hill. Possibly this is by no means unique; perhaps it occurs in every vast organisation. But I have worked for no other vast organisation, and I can't be sure. I certainly witnessed it here.

I think the firm's apotheosis came at the time of the famous Mentmore sale in 1977, and the Robert von Hirsch sale in 1978. The eighteen sessions of the first realised a grand total of £6,390,000; the considerably smaller number of sessions devoted to the second surpassed all expectations and fetched the staggering sum of £18,500,000!

Another prestigious high-spot — if one not quite so grandiose as those others — came in 1980, with the publication of Frank Herrmann's *Sotheby's*, sub-titled *Portrait of an Auction House*. This impressive work, on which the author had laboured for several years, was undertaken at the suggestion of John Carter, who did not live to see its completion.

However, more or less concurrently with these events, came a couple of others which did not cause quite so much rejoicing within and around the firm.

First was the introduction of the buyers' premium, which was announced in June, 1975. The fact that Christie's had also announced *their* intention to levy a premium only a few days previously led to the charge of collusion between the two famous houses. The second event to cause some glum faces, in course of time, was the decision in 1977 to 'go public'.

With regard to the much-discussed buyers' premium, I think that I should remark here that its levying had been a common practice in the auction rooms of continental Europe for as long as I could remember. One of the things that made buying under the hammer in British houses so attractive was that no such thing existed here. Hitherto, a commission of from ten percent to fifteen percent had been charged to *the consignor alone*, depending upon the nature of the goods for sale. (For books, and for other items which had always needed considerably more handling and detailed cataloguing it had always been fifteen percent.) It was now intended to reduce this vendors' commission to an even ten percent but to take an *extra* ten percent from the purchaser, over and above the figure knocked down under the hammer. The auctioneers would thus be gathering a cut from

both buyer and seller, *and* increasing their share to twenty percent! Their
argument seemed a valid enough one at first: telephone charges had
increased enormously, postal rates never seemed to stop going up, and
printing costs were becoming prohibitively expensive. At one time the
premium was often referred to as a 'service charge'. It was later denied that
it had ever been so — and by a Sotheby's spokesman. But I distinctly recall
Peter Wilson, Chairman of Sotheby's at the time, in a television interview
during a programme devoted to the buyers' premium at the time of its
inception. That it was a service charge was not denied then. 'What services
do you give to justify it?' asked the interviewer, or words to that effect.
'Well — er — there's the electricity,' offered Wilson.

For some years the possibility of an action hung precariously over the
heads of both Christie's and Sotheby's, brought by branches of the various
trades with the help of the British Office of Fair Trading. The auctioneers
were extremely confident about the outcome, but so far it has not come to
court. The matter was resolved, to some extent, in 1981, although I never
met any person in any trade who was very happy about it. As usual, the
lawyers seemed to be the only ones who came out of things better off. But
the auctioneers did agree to the consideration of a change in their rates.
These were announced at the end of the year.

I am indebted to my friend Barry Phelps, of Irene Editions, the foremost
P. G. Wodehouse specialist, for what I consider to be a most succinct
exposition of the matter as it stands just at present. In addition to being a
bookseller, he is also a financial journalist, and he had this to say, in part, in
an article entitled 'Sotheby's Hit Back', in *The Daily Mail* on 27 January,
1982.

> In December Christie's scored a publicity victory when they cut the
> buyers' premium they charged from 10% to 8%... Sotheby's had
> increased their commission on items sold for under £500 from 10%
> to 15%.
>
> But comparisons aren't that simple; commissions vary at differing
> price levels. Let's look at the charges from the point of view of the seller.
> What amount of the sale price (which the buyer actually pays) does the
> seller receive?
>
> Sotheby's director, Peter Spira, tells me: 'In the crucial band, £500
> to £1,000, our charges are cheaper; and our experience is second
> to none.'
>
> Christie's also believe their expertise is second to none and add,
> simply: 'Compare the rates.'

Barry Phelps, in a boxed table, under the heading of 'What the seller
keeps at auction as a percentage of the buyer's cost', gave us the following
information:

	Sotheby's	Christie's
Under £500	74.2%	78.4%
£500 to £1,000	79.4%	78.4%
Over £1,000	79.4%	81.0%

VAT exemption and Christie's handling charges can make minor differences to these figures.

The change caused some little ebullience among those auction clients who wished to *sell*, but gave little satisfaction to the habitual sale room customer who wanted to *buy*. The fine art trades have been unhappy about the premiums from the very start, and they will continue to be so until they are dropped.

Reverting now to the offering of Sotheby's shares on the open market, these cost 150p each when the firm first went public. They were rapidly over-subscribed. Within two or three years, in the wake of the Mentmore and von Hirsch sales, they were worth well over 500p each. In the spring of 1982, as I write, they are down again to under 300p each, and with no immediate indication of a big recovery. A lot of people of my acquaintance have now unloaded rapidly — but not quite rapidly enough, for some of them.

I have no doubt that in course of time the value of these shares will increase again. There have been heavy slumps before, and more will occur in the future, but in between them everything will be riding high and handsome for a while, and I don't expect very much time will elapse before a fortunate few will be rubbing their hands in satisfaction as the art market improves. Meanwhile there are wage cuts, wholesale redundancies, and several other drastic measures, all taken in an effort to reduce overheads.

From my standpoint the matter is largely academic, but I will confess to a sympathy for the unfortunate employees of the auction houses who have found their careers suddenly cut short. I can whip up little compassion for those well-heeled shareholders who held on a bit too long and got their fingers burned.

Also in 1981 an event occurred at Sotheby's which had long been a cause for speculation. The firm had, well before, acquired a property known as the Aeolian Hall, almost directly opposite the main building in New Bond Street. I think there were quite a few battles among the hierarchy as to which departments should eventually be ensconced within it. It was on-again and off-again several times as far as Lord John Kerr and the Book Department were concerned. But at long last the matter was resolved. Hodgson's Rooms in Chancery Lane would be closed, its staff would be incorporated with those at New Bond Street, and the whole Book Department would be housed under one roof in a newly-constructed Aeolian Hall. The date of removal was set for Spring, 1981.

It took quite some time to gut the old place and to rebuild it as a magnificent new auction house, with three large sale rooms, ample storage space, and cataloguing and administration facilities. I have heard the cost estimated at £3,500,000. I shouldn't be a bit surprised if that figure was somewhere near the truth.

Final sales were eventually held at both Chancery Lane and the old gallery off St. George Street, to the due accompaniment of requiems and considerable sentiment. Speaking for myself, I walked out of Hodgson's for the last time, after over thirty years, with hardly a wrench. I am not unsentimental, but I think we were all far too busy making the move to experience many emotions about the matter.

The new premises are convenient, spacious, and very comfortable. They cannot be faulted on any reasonable grounds. Yet there are still those conservative, more mature clients who bemoan the loss of the musty, old-fashioned, but welcoming atmosphere of the building in Chancery Lane. Gone is the old Sale Room Pound, around which sat the book-sellers of generations; gone are those stolid shelves, reduced eventually to the colour of the dust which fell lightly upon them for so many years; gone, even, is the coconut-matting floor-covering which Sotheby's installed, and which was thought to be a great improvement upon the worn, bare boards of yore. Now the visiting client steps past huge and heavy doors of thick glass; he treads silently over the deep pile of wall-to-wall carpets; he climbs stairs with balusters of shiny, chromium-plated steel; he ascends smoothly and silently in the lift to the Coin and Jewellery Departments.

All a bit daunting to some, no doubt, but who can deny an improvement? And one or two eternities do prevail, in tangible form. The main ground floor Sale Room, in which the more prestigious and valuable book properties are sold, has been dubbed the Grosvenor Room, and at the far end is the same rostrum and clerk's desk used not only for years at New Bond Street, but long before that, in Sotheby's old Wellington Street days. Presiding here is the figure of Jock Campbell, surely the most durable and knowledgeable porter of books in the world? Next door, and hardly less spacious, is the gallery where the rather less important lots of books are sold, but which attracts far more ferreting viewers, and is much more popular. Here, just a little incongruous in its plush surroundings, perhaps, but ready and sturdy enough to do the service it has done since 1863 until the year 2063, and well beyond, stands the old Chancery Lane rostrum, and my broad mahogany desk. To perpetuate the memory of that well-loved family of auctioneers, this book gallery has been christened the Hodgson Room.

Book-lovers are an adaptable crew, in my experience. In next to no time at all they will accept these palatial premises entirely. The colour scheme, perhaps, *might* have been a little less bilious: the combination of tints was described, very early on, as 'olde-Englishe vommitte and goose-turd green'.

My Three Spies

The somewhat lengthy narrative which follows has been left until towards the end for a particular reason. The book, so far, has followed a loose chronological pattern, and I have tried to begin at the beginning and bring things up to the present time as best as I have been able. It has not been easy, because some of the events and anecdotes I have dealt with are connected with characters I have known over a period of many years. Most of the people I have written about are dead, and I have told you about them because I do not wish them to be entirely lost and forgotten. As regards the people I am about to deal with now, I think there is little chance that they will be forgotten by anyone who knew them well. As far as I know, two of them are still alive. The third has been reported dead, but I have my doubts about that. Further, I first encountered them fairly early on in my career, I had quite a lot to do with them over the years, I corresponded with them well after I ever expected to meet them again, and I have not entirely given up hope that I shall ever hear from them again. I still write to the address I know so well, my own return address is on the back of all my envelopes, but no letter has yet come back marked 'Not Known'. The very occasional Christmas card sneaks through, rarely to myself now, but a little oftener to other friends in this country. I live in hope that the story is not over completely.

Some years ago, when I began to jot down my original detailed recollections of my dealings with these people, I first typed a sort of chapter heading to them, just as I have done here, and I used 'My Three Spies' at that time. I confess that I had rather liked this as a possible title for a book. More than once, back in the nineteen-sixties, the thought *had* crossed my mind of submitting both the title and the idea to a publisher. Several people suggested it, and certainly I was approached by influential members of the press. I am quite sure that I could have got both an advance payment and the go-ahead from two Sunday newspapers, for a start.

But I recalled that I had promised these people I am talking about that I would not write about them for publication and pecuniary gain while they were incarcerated, their case was still 'alive', and their eventual fate was in some doubt. Several of their so-called friends sold 'inside revelations' while they were still in jail. A short-term prisoner cashed in almost immediately after his release in a now-defunct weekly periodical with a series which had quite obviously been concocted by a staff journalist. One gentleman made a few paltry quid by passing over to a national newspaper an amateur ciné film he had shot at the Bibliomites' annual Guv'nors versus Assistants cricket match, in which one of this trio starred rather flamboyantly. As far as I know, that film was never shown publicly, and it probably lies forgotten in the vaults of that tabloid. On the other hand, the closest bookselling friend of two of these people flatly turned down a very substantial offer for his story from the most profitable daily paper of the day, before the case ever came to trial — for publication after it had done so. For this alone I shall forever respect him. He was a very unhappy and disillusioned man; he never communicated with his friends after it transpired that they were enemy agents, and yet he always asked after their welfare in the ensuing years. He could have capitalised on their subsequent misfortune, far more than most, but he never did.

It is now over twenty years ago that this sensational story of the Portland Spy Ring first broke, and I became embroiled in the affairs of three of the five protagonists. As I have said, one of those three has long been reported dead. It is so long now since I have had a letter from either of the other two that I *could* reckon them dead as well, but I know that they are not. The following pages can do them no harm. Indeed, what I have to say might do their memory a bit of good. A whole new generation has now sprung up: most of the youngsters in our harmless and delightful trade have heard garbled tales and somewhat sensational stories of the bookselling spies within our midst; outsiders and fringers vaguely remember and pass down yarns of the microdot implanted within the pages of a book, and they talk to enthralled listeners of the infamous Ruislip House of Secrets. (Poor old Ruislip! John Betjeman planted the kiss of death on Slough in one short poem, and 45 Cranley Drive and Leslie Thomas's later *Tropic* must have done as much harm to the pleasant little town of Ruislip and its residents, in a way, as Crippen did to Camden Town and Holloway, or Christie to Notting Hill.)

It was in the year 1955 that I answered a telephone call, in that old-fashioned booth that used to stand in the far corner of Hodgson's Sale Room. It had been installed for the benefit of clients who wished to take or send private messages. I recall the occasion clearly — and I should do. In those days we didn't run to the luxury of a telephone by my desk; if nobody answered a ring in the office I was forever up and down and to and from that confounded booth.

The voice I listened to was deep and polite, and it obviously originated from across the Atlantic.

'My name is Peter J. Kroger. I am a Canadian bookseller.'

I believe that I was one of the very first persons in the book trade that this notorious man happened to contact in this country. I certainly know that I was the last, after my final visit to him behind bars, before he and his wife, Helen, waved goodbye to England, the cameramen, and the many rubbernecks as the pair walked up the gang-plank of the aircraft which took them behind the Iron Curtain to Poland.

Peter conned me that very first time, just as he conned everybody else he met for the next five years or so. But today I bear him no ill will — which is more than I can say for a great many others.

During that first conversation I learned that he was a book-dealer from the wilds of Canada. (I never did figure out exactly where he was supposed to have come from, now that I think of it.) Apparently he had journeyed to Britain with his wife to set up in business here for the sake of his health. I never found out for sure, either, just what was supposed to be wrong with him, for Peter was a master at being unspecific when questions got too personal and dangerous. Nobody had any reason to suspect him at that time, of course. Other friends of his asked him the same thing, too, but they are pretty vague in their recollections. Still, I would be interested to know exactly what explanations some of them got. I do have a distinct memory, as he and I walked back to no. 115 after a drink or two in the old *Mitre*, just a few yards away in Chancery Lane, that among other physical misfortunes he suffered from boils on the backside! Just why he had to come to England in order to overcome an affliction of this sort it did not occur to me to ask at the time, and I must have accepted the explanation.

But to revert to that first telephone call. He asked me to send him a copy of our current catalogue, and gave an address in South London. A day or two before the sale he came into our Rooms to view the books, and introduced himself.

At that time Peter was in his late forties. He was a striking-looking man: aquiline, and with a sallow complexion. His longish hair was completely white, 'wrapped round his head like a bandage', as Rebecca West reported in her description of him after his trial. He was dressed in a double-breasted suit of pale blue. It was wide-lapelled and with a drape cut. His shirt was 'whiter-than-white' nylon with long points to the collar. The shoes were highly-polished brown, in a basket weave. If his object was to draw attention to himself as an obvious American, or more accurately, an apparent Canadian — and I believe that it was — he could have done no better.

He won me over almost immediately. Before we had known each other very long we were on first name terms. When the day of the sale arrived I felt rather sorry for him. He plonked himself down on a bench at the Pound, which was a position normally occupied only by the more established regulars of the business. Right until the last, many people studiously avoided ensconcing themselves anywhere near it, for fear of being thought usurpers.

Peter was blithely unaware that he was on hallowed ground. He bid away on lot after lot, and he ran up an impressive bill. But he was an utter stranger to all those hard-bitten campaigners round that table, and they didn't let him have a thing at a bargain price.

'*Jesus*,' he said to me ruefully, some years later, when he had become fully accepted by the members of the trade, 'the boys really took me for a ride that day, didn't they?'

Shortly afterwards, Peter took premises in the Strand, a little east of the Aldwych, by St. Clement Dane's. Here, in a spot which you reached from a long corridor running behind a tobacconist's shop, he set up his business. He stocked his couple of rooms in a manner so profligate as to suggest that money was shortly going out of fashion. (That remark, I am well aware, is a cliché. But it was current at the time, and I think it is apt.)

He would outbid all the big boys in the Rooms — men who had been established for many years and who had the cream of the clientele. He did this not only at our premises, but at Sotheby's and Christie's. If this man could pay more than the leading booksellers in the country, who on earth, we wondered, could he be selling to?

Some of the lads *did*, of course, take him for a ride, as he had intimated. His inexperience was very obvious to a few sharp dealers. One such was a seedy little runner, who somehow got a smell of this wonderful windfall. He introduced Peter to a basement he rented. It was full of old books. The gullible Peter saw a magnificent chance to stock his shelves. He asked the price: it was £300 — a sum which was worth a lot more then, naturally, than it is today. 'Of course,' said the runner, 'you'd have to take pot luck with them. I can't guarantee that they're *all* perfect.' Peter bought the lot, and transferred the books to his place in the Strand. It transpired that *every* item, in one way or another, was imperfect! He had no redress, for the seller had made it quite clear beforehand that the collection was nôt being sold on the understanding that every book was 'right'. Peter regretted this transaction, as may be imagined, but he bore no resentment. He wrote the whole thing off to experience, and laughed it off.as a good joke against himself.

Somewhere round about this time Peter and Helen Kroger bought their bungalow in Cranley Drive, East Ruislip. This desirable residence, later to become so famous, was situated very conveniently at the end of a *cul-de-sac*. It was certainly strategically placed, and had considerable advantages. You may be sure that the newspapers made the most of it all, when the time came. Whether Peter and Helen planned things so, I do not know. But I believe that if some other circumstance had made the place remarkable, then the papers would have taken *that* up. As things were, with the house the last one at a dead end, it was suggested that dubious visitors could easily ascertain whether they were being followed. The police or suspicious British agents certainly couldn't have put what is known as 'a front tail' on anybody without giving the game away. But what if there had happened to be a telephone kiosk opposite the place, or something of that sort? I am sure that we would have had pictures in the papers of this innocuous telephone box, with hints that from here Peter and Helen's sinister callers rang him to make sure that they were alone.

This is not mere fancy: the late Nora Doel, who was a friend of both the Krogers and myself, was unwise enough to wave and nod to the pair from the Public Gallery when they first came up for trial, and they waved back. As a result of her indiscretion Nora was followed from the court by reporters, and she was hounded until she lost them all on the Underground, somewhere near Finsbury Park. But the next morning a half-page photo appeared in one daily newspaper, and she earned a brief but unwelcome notoriety as the mysterious 'woman in blue'. The most sinister things were made of the fact that she had eluded her pursuers. Millions of readers, I feel sure, were convinced that she was a glamorous spy who was swallowed up into the purlieus of the big city, probably with the aid of the KGB. Actually, she was a hard-working suburban wife and mother whose political opinions were the extreme opposite of the two friends of hers whose fate she had come to the court to learn.

But for all that, 45 Cranley Drive is a house that will not be forgotten quickly or easily by those of us who knew and visited it. Here you received good food, good wine, and the most wonderful hospitality. If, as you ate and drank, you also wondered how a naive bookseller like Peter Kroger could maintain such an establishment, unless he had private means — well, you were entitled to. The man certainly knew books, and literature and history, too — far more than most of us — but the craft of bookselling needs much more than that.

Yet Peter progressed. He cultivated the acquaintance of everyone he could, and he and his wife were liked by all. He attended the Bibliomites' darts matches, and he drank pint for pint. He played for the Guv'nors versus the Bibs, in their annual cricket match, wielding his willow like a baseball bat, and trying to knock home runs, to everybody's amusement. Eventually, Peter applied for membership to the Antiquarian Booksellers' Association, and was elected — no mean feat. In due course, he gave up his place in the Strand, and concentrated on selling his books by catalogue, from his home in Ruislip.

The man's industry and enthusiasm were amazing. For instance, some of the smaller auctioneers were wont to list certain lots something as follows: 'Bloggs (Joe). My Early Life; *cloth (worn)*, 1908, and 35 other vols.' Now, a local bookseller sufficiently interested might make a short journey and peruse those other volumes on a viewing day, but one in New York or Sydney, let us say, had no way of knowing what they were unless he had someone to look them over on his behalf. One such dealer, who happened to be based in Utrecht, found Kroger to be a ready viewer for him, particularly for lots of pocket classics, which came up for sale regularly at Hodgson's. I see Peter now, sitting at the corner of a table, taking up bundle after bundle, and listing the authors, titles and dates of the un-named books in lot after lot. At five-thirty, when we closed, he would not nearly be finished. He would plead to be allowed to continue. Wilfrid Hodgson, who more often than not worked on until after seven when the rest of us had gone, would reluctantly consent. The doors were closed and Peter ploughed on after hours for his fortunate client. He might get a commission to buy, or he might not. And if he was successful in buying, what did he make? Ten per cent. Was it worth all the trouble? Apparently Peter thought so.

We all laughed at him, gently, on the sly. How could this kind, convivial, obliging and most naive soul make a living among the un-scrupulous sharks of commerce? How long could he last? How long would it be before his capital came to an end? Peter and Helen Kroger, of course, were laughing at all of *us*. I give them the credit of laughing just as gently as we did. I truly believe that they had come to like us all as much as we liked them.

It was Martin Orskey and Alex Rogoyski, my two colleagues at Hodgson's on the cataloguing side, who first smelt a rat, I am sure, although they had no more idea of the nature of the rodent than anyone else, at the time. But this needs some elucidation.

We had all recently been treated to an outrageous but fascinating best-selling book by one George Adamski, called *Flying Saucers Have Landed*, which proved to be one of the first and more successful of the many books about Unidentified Flying Objects, or UFOs. The author claimed that he was in contact with a man from Venus, and indeed hinted that this earth was already infiltrated by more than a few representatives from that planet. He further suggested that these beings were indistinguishable from earth-lings and that they were quietly integrating with the human race. The three of us, Martin, Alex and myself, would huddle over our morning cuppas in the local Lyons' tea-shop, and they gleefully elaborated on this theme. I think, with their fantasies, that they practically convinced themselves that what they said was actually true. Peter Kroger was a man from Venus: a delegate sent down in human guise to take over the British book trade, *his* particular mission in the eventual subjugation of our civilisation by Outer Space. Helen, who was an exuberant extrovert, a termagent one minute and all gushingly lovey-dovey the next, was his Venusian consort, with her own part to play among the housewives and matrons of suburbia.

Of course, Martin and Alex had been reading too much science fiction, for one thing, and they each had an off-beat sense of humour, for another. But how close they came to the real truth, back there in the late 'fifties! For Peter and Helen Kroger *were* out of this world — our predictable little world, at any rate.

The bubble burst early in January, 1961. I was shaving, shortly after eight o'clock one Monday morning, when the telephone rang. It was Martin Orskey.

'Have you seen the papers?' he asked.

'No,' I said, somewhat petulantly, for I had just come in from the bathroom, and had soap on my face. 'What is it?'

'Hold on to your hat!' he said. 'Real James Bond stuff. Peter and Helen Kroger have been arrested! Russian spies!'

Quite naturally, the whole of our trade talked about little else for many months. Whereas people like Burgess and MacLean and Klaus Fuchs had been only half-real characters we had read about in the newspapers, here were two true-life individuals whom we all knew intimately. We had thought of them as a genuine, if somewhat strange couple, the one a bookseller and the other a housewife, and suddenly, literally overnight, they had become spies and traitors.

The coup had taken place over the weekend. One Gordon Lonsdale, a businessman, had been picked up in the Waterloo Road, after having been observed to have accepted documents from two civil service employees, Harry Houghton and Bunty Gee. This had been on the Saturday afternoon. Lonsdale's subsequent activity would have been to have journeyed to Cranley Drive, Ruislip, there to hand over his acquisitions to Peter and Helen, for onward transmission by radio to Moscow, by means of a powerful set that had been installed in the attic. This pattern had been observed weekly by Secret Service agents from a house directly opposite the Krogers' bungalow, although it could not have been known beforehand exactly where the transmitter was situated. When Peter and Helen answered the ring at their door-bell that Saturday evening, they fully expected to greet Gordon Lonsdale. Instead, they were confronted by Superintendent 'Moonraker' Smith, of Scotland Yard. He was a somewhat unglamorous but extremely efficient senior policeman and spy-catcher. It seems that *he* went on the air to Russia instead of those expected, and blandly told the opposition that the game was up and that the birds were in the bag. A very nice touch, if it is true.

The rest of the story is now history. It became known as the Case of the Portland Spy Ring. Most of us learned for the first time of such things as microdots, which were tiny spots placed, perhaps, in the margin of a book or where a punctuation mark should have been. The book would then be sent abroad, apparently in the normal course of commerce. These dots, magnified hugely, proved to be photographs of highly confidential documents. Then there was that so-called 'secret' attic at the Krogers' house, which contained the very powerful radio transmitter. Actually, there was nothing secret about the attic itself at all; we all knew it was there. Peter and Helen used to take us up, and show us the apples from their garden which they were storing there for ripening. Of course, they didn't show us the radio. Should they have done? But according to the newspapers, this attic was a sinister secret in itself. Balderdash! A certain husband and wife team of booksellers were so taken by the patent folding ladder which the Krogers demonstrated to all of us that they had installed one in their own attic, long before their erstwhile hosts were arrested as spies.

I am also somewhat concerned about the blah the papers made of this so-called 'House of Secrets'. Two or three sensational journalists made capital later on with books about this apparently impregnable fortress, locked and barred as no other normal home in the neighbourhood. Utter rot! I must make this very plain. I was priviledged to be a guest at this house long before it was ever suspected as being the home of spies, and I saw then no evidence of ultra-normal protection. Much later, after the gaff was blown, I went back several times, primarily to remove some of the effects and to supervise the transit of Peter's books for sale by auction. The publicity that had accrued led me to inspect the locks and bolts more thoroughly. After all, I had read the papers, too. I found no more protection than would have been usual in any home in that position, in what was a semi-rural district. Are those writers, who never got near the house, much less inside it, but who wrote about it so sensationally, aware that it was actually burgled twice between the Krogers' arrest and their trial? The culprits could have been, at one extreme, mere sensation-seekers. At the other extreme they could have been Soviet agents anxious to pick up something of importance Scotland Yard had missed. I don't know; as far as I am aware the burglars were never brought to book. And how about the Yard's instructions to the Ruislip constabulary to keep an eye on the place?

Of course, I am not denying for a moment that the couple used the house to secrete certain items. A hole was found beneath the lino and the floor of the kitchen, and it contained much incriminating evidence. I walked across it, quite unsuspectingly, in the early days, when I had no reason to suspect its existence. Later on, when I knew it was there, I had the greatest difficulty in finding it. Further, I discovered one or two things which the police had missed. I particularly recall what appeared to be a small, cylindrical pocket flash-lamp, complete with bulb, outside thumb-switch, and even the Ever Ready trade-mark. But the inside was completely smooth and utterly phoney, with no connections at all. Obviously this had been designed to hold a roll of negative film, or a slip of paper. But the police *had* picked up plenty of other evidence. One item was a large table lighter, which had always stood centrally on the table in the Krogers' lounge. We had used it often to light our cigarettes. It was genuine enough, as far as that goes. But it also contained a secret compartment at the base, and was offered as an exhibit at the trial. It did its part in helping to put our friends away.

Later, much was made of a single advertisement which had appeared in the booksellers' trade journal, *The Clique*. In a boxed display, Peter had requested any books on locks, keys, and related items. He had laughingly informed us of how he had also been offered such things as chastity belts and thumb screws. When the press got hold of this information, the oblique suggestion was that he nursed a morbid interest in such things, and that his speciality as a bookseller was in instruments of torture and restraint. In actuality, he had just one client, a member of the famous Chubb family, who was keen on his job and who collected early-printed books on all branches of the business. The obliging Peter, always one to do the best he could for any customer, was branded a pervert as well as a spy.

My first reaction immediately after Peter and Helen were arrested was to write to them both, and to express my concern for their present plight. I am sure that a great many others in our trade felt exactly the same way, but most of the couple's closest friends were very well-known booksellers who had to tread warily. Already the bloodhounds of Fleet Street had sniffed the scent, and it did a man in business for himself no good at all to be thought even remotely connected with this scandalous pair.

In my own case it was different: I was an employee. I had nothing to lose at all, were it known that I was a close friend of the two. Further, I had nothing to hide — not that I am suggesting that anyone else *had*. But I knew that I was 'clean', and I didn't give a damn what certain people might thing of my continued association with known communist spies. Of course, I have often wondered to myself what my reaction might have been had I been running a flourishing business on my own. Would I have courted the publicity that was then sure to have accumulated? Would I have chanced being labelled a commie or a potential traitor, perhaps even suspected of being a spy myself? I honestly don't know. I wasn't in that position.

But at the time I remembered certain things. When I was taken ill suddenly, and convalesced gradually at home after a spell in hospital, only two people bothered to brave the dark and long, cold bus journeys of those bitter winter evenings and visit me: Peter and Helen Kroger. I also recalled how they had dropped into Chancery Lane late one afternoon in 1959, how they had asked after my wife, whom they had known, and how I had informed them that she had just left me for another man. My dejection and depression must have been very apparent: they immediately insisted upon my coming out to dinner with them. It cheered me up enormously, and for a time the gloom lightened. There was that holiday my wife and I had taken in Amsterdam, at a time when I was desperately trying to save my marriage. The Krogers were touring Europe that summer, too, and Holland was on their itinerary during the week or so we were to be there. Nothing would do but that we must all meet for a meal. I treasure the memory of that Indonesian dinner, not for its forty-odd different dishes, but for the warmth and *bonhomie* the Krogers radiated throughout the rendezvous. In retrospect, of course, I am fully aware that the two might well have come to meet us hot-foot from a sinister conclave with certain of their masters on the continent, but I was not aware of any such thing at the time. Again, there was that elderly bookseller who was dying of cancer. His friends visited him, of course, but soon the visits grew sparser, and eventually they all but dropped off completely. A lengthy dying is an embarrassment and an unpleasant business, and few people relish a death-watch. I know for a fact that for night after night Peter Kroger sat by this man's bed and gave him what cheer and comfort he could.

Don't try to tell me this was all a front, that this very pleasant pair really cared not one jot about any of us who had made them our friends. They deceived us all, I know, but I believe they truly loved their fellow men, far more than most of us. They proved it time and again in both tangible and intangible ways. They did good by stealth, but they never 'blushed to find it fame'.

I remembered some of these things when I penned that brief letter to Peter Kroger in his cell. I added the note: 'Let me know if there is anything I can do.' I meant this, mark you, but I got a lot more than I had bargained for. Peter took me at my word, and for the next few years I was up to my ears in the affairs of the couple.

Admittedly, the two were spies for Soviet Russia. Yes, Peter ran a book business primarily as a cover, and many of those books he handled may have been highly suspect, but it was a business nevertheless. At the time of his arrest it had developed into a going concern, and when he was obliged to cease operations very abruptly, dozens of other dealers and all of his private clients were left high and dry. Money was owed by him, and money was owed to him. Books were still coming in by every post, and books that had been ordered were due to be sent out. His solicitors, of course, could have been left with the whole bag of tricks, but what sort of fist would they have made of it, and how much would they have cared? Then, apart from anything else, there was the economics of the matter to consider. As Peter once said to me when I visited him in Brixton Prison, with regard to lawyers: 'If you ask them to bring you in a packet of Woodbines they put it on the bill.' But, after all, I suppose you can't blame them. They were in it for a living.

The upshot was that I undertook to wind up his business. This was for two main reasons. One was to tidy everything up: to execute all his uncompleted orders and the half-done ones, and to save other booksellers from bad debts they could ill afford to incur. The other was to gather in as much money as possible from his debtors in order to pay the lawyers for Peter and Helen's defence. It could be argued that had they not possessed a penny they would have received a first class team of solicitors and barristers to act on their behalf nevertheless.

I have no doubt of this. I do not know whose eventual decision it was to sell the bungalow, the car, and the large stock of books, but the decision was made, and most of the proceeds went to the lawyers for the defence. It was Peter's own decision and wish that his books should be transferred to Hodgson's for sale by auction. The fact that I was acting for him more than probably influenced him in this direction. I am under no illusions. But I put no pressure on him by hint or otherwise. Under different circumstances I think the books might well have gone to our more illustrious rivals, Sotheby's or Christie's.

After the police had gone through that bungalow with a fine-tooth comb, and had confiscated everything they thought necessary for evidence against the pair, his friends were allowed in. People I had never met before were in charge of the sale of the house and most of the household effects; Martin Orskey and I went in to look after the removal of the books and literary property.

On the first occasion we were all there at the same time: the others had the keys. While Martin and I naturally made a bee-line for Peter's workroom and library, the other pair looked after the living-room and the bedroom. I did not discover until much later that one of these people came across a phoney passport and several thousand dollars in cash! It was supposed that there had been a thorough search by the police.

Had I come across these items in the rooms I investigated, I cannot say, honestly, what I would have done with them. My sense of civic duty, if you can call it that, might have led me to offer them to the prosecution. On the other hand, my loyalty to Peter and Helen might have induced me to offer them to the defence. But I'm pretty sure I would not have done what this other chap did. He sent the considerable funds to the lawyers for the defence, thus adding material incentive to keep the couple free, and he handed the false passport to the prosecution solicitors, which gave them added evidence to put the pair away!

I suppose the poor chap did what he thought was fair. He wasn't a friend of the Krogers, after all. I don't think he had ever met them: his connection was with the other big man in the case, Gordon Lonsdale, with whom he had been connected in business. It was a rotten dilemna. I am sure that he spent a few sleepless nights. He got a pretty bad press while the trial was in progress: he was one of the witnesses, and it all came out. I had a lonely rendezvous with him, on a road some way outside of Ruislip, a day or so later, where he was to hand over the keys of no. 45 to me. He felt pretty bad about the whole thing.

'What else could I do?' he asked.

The more cynical and the unscrupulous might retort: 'Burn the bloody passport and stuff the dollars into your back pocket.'

I could have quite easily followed this advice had I been the one to come across the evidence. But I would have had to live with it, too, and that would have been a difficult matter. Considerable jewellery that was in that house was never properly accounted for: the Krogers themselves always blamed the police. Had those several thousands of dollars never come to light Peter and his wife might have believed that minor officials had pocketed the cash. The police force, in any country, has a bad enough image because of some rotten apples. Why worsen it?

Peter was in Brixton Prison, and Helen was in Holloway. I didn't see Helen at all at this time, since although I wrote to her I did not receive a reply, but I know that she had regular visits from many of her female friends in the trade and the wives of several male booksellers. I was told — not by Helen herself — that at this time all her correspondence was opened, held up against a wall, and was only allowed to be read from a non-touching distance. I was never able to confirm this. I saw a lot of her later, but usually with female screws in the immediate vicinity. You just don't discuss such subjects in these circumstances. If this tale was true, muttered to a visitor while a blue back was momentarily turned, what was its object? Helen couldn't send out microdots to any of us, but we might be sending them in to her, perhaps? Did she have a microscope stashed in her cell?

I did see Peter regularly, every Saturday, in fact, and sometimes in the middle of the week. Since, at that stage, he had not been convicted, or had even come to trial, I did not need a Visiting Order to get inside to see him, and I was allowed to bring in cigarettes, decent meals, and a bottle of wine or two.

I thought the whole set-up remarkably civilised until one Saturday I journeyed down to Brixton, only to find that they would not let me in. Apparently he had already had one visitor earlier in the day, and therefore couldn't have another one. In vain I protested that this wasn't a purely social visit, that I was working on Peter's behalf in co-operation with his lawyers, which I was. Rules were rules, and they went by the book. I could have come down and seen him six days a week, it seemed, if it had been possible — which it wasn't, since I had another job to do, too — but if nobody at all came on a weekday he still couldn't have two visits on a Saturday! After that, I made sure that I was always an early arrival. The next week Peter told me that it had been dear old Ernest Seligmann who had pipped me the previous time. I am pretty sure that other friends called later on in the day some Saturdays and were sent empty away. I am sorry about this, particularly with old Seligmann. He was a kind and gentle soul who ran a business dealing mainly with art books from 25 Cecil Court, just off Charing Cross Road. Everyone liked and respected him, and we were all terribly shocked — the Krogers included — when he died hideously and violently in a car smash some fifteen years later. (Why does it usually seem to happen to the nice ones?)

But Peter and I had a lot of business to get through in the short time allotted to us, for visiting time was limited, and I had to get in first every time.

We always met in something they called the Solicitors' Box, which was a very small room with space for a table and a couple of chairs or so and nothing else. Peter was still in civilian clothes, of course, but his tie and belt had been taken away from him. The prison authorities didn't fancy the idea of his possibly trying to hang himself, it seemed. Later on, after trial and sentence, a tie was part of the regulation dress for all convicted prisoners. This always struck me as rather daft. Surely, a man who knew he was definitely facing a long sentence was more likely to think of doing away with himself than one on remand who at least stood some chance of being acquitted? But they didn't see it that way. All they were interested in was delivering their charge to the Old Bailey alive and intact. What happened to him afterwards was none of their business.

A prison officer was always present at those initial meetings, and on each occasion I was given strict instructions not to discuss the case. The upshot was that Peter and I spent almost the whole of these visits earnestly engaged in business, he desperately instructing me with details and myself making voluminous notes. Anyone who still imagines that Peter Kroger merely used bookselling as a cover for his activities, and cared nothing at all about his clients, should have been present at some of those meetings. Faced with the prospect of going to prison for a very long period, one might have thought that a spy's last thought and worry would have been his very convenient customers. The fact is that Peter was extremely anxious that every dealer and collector he had undertaken to supply should have his order completed. Many of these people were his friends. In some measure, this all gives an idea of his thoroughness, meticulous attention to detail, *and* the warmth and consideration of his nature.

For instance, he had bought an enormously long run of the *Philosophical Transactions* from Quaritch, for several hundred pounds. The eventual recipient, to whom he had sold it, was a university professor in Chicago. But the books were now with a binder in Wembley, who was rebacking them all when Peter was arrested. The easiest thing would have been to forget the whole project. It would have meant a disappointed client on one side, an equally disappointed firm of booksellers on the other, who had not yet been paid, by the way, and a very unfortunate young binder in the middle, landed with a big set of books which were of no use at all to him, and who would never get any money for the considerable work he had already done on some of them. The whole job had to be seen through to the finish. In the end, it *was* seen through, and everyone concerned was happy. But it took a long, long time.

Each American client Peter had ever had was examined thoroughly by the Federal Bureau of Investigation — that poor professor among them, I recall — and those perfectly innocent citizens were all scared to death by having even a remote connection, by post, with a man who appeared to have communist sympathies. Remember, this was happening not *too* long after the era of McCarthyism and the somewhat hysterical Witch Hunt of the 'fifties. Not one of these people would pay his account or conclude dealings with me until he had been given a clean bill of health. Up until that time I had had some idea of the power wielded by J. Edgar Hoover and his Bureau. I had admired his success in cleaning up much of the gangster element in the United States during the 'thirties, and I had seen the emergence of the new twentieth-century hero, the G-man, exemplified and glorified in so many Hollywood film productions. But I had never fully realised the frightening hold Hoover's quiet agents now had upon the average American citizen, after the commie-under-the-bed scare, and the cases of Colonel Abel, the Rosenbergs, and Alger Hiss. One had read, in sensational fiction, of the sinister Russian KGB. Suddenly, as far as I was concerned, here was the equally sinister FBI.

Let there be no mistake. I abhor the régime of Soviet Russia, with its corps of secret police able to whisk an individual away in a moment, never to be heard of again. I abhor, just as much, a body in a country which boasts of being the greatest democratic and liberal nation on earth, and which can yet leave its citizens quaking in their shoes because of a remote, and more than probably mistaken suspicion, of their having advanced left wing sympathies. Perhaps it is a mere truism for me to reiterate that while power corrupts, absolute power corrupts absolutely. J. Edgar Hoover is now the late, and unlamented J. Edgar Hoover. Bit by bit, things have been coming out about him. In the not too distant future, the full story will be told. It will make interesting, if not very pretty reading.

It took between eighteen months and two years before I eventually cleared everything up: got all monies in, shipped all books that were due, and paid each bill that was owing.

But to revert to those visits in the so-called Solicitors' Box down at Brixton in the days before the trial. On only one occasion was I able to talk to Peter at all intimately. I had come down one Saturday to conduct the usual business, and I had a piece of news which I knew I could not impart openly. Larry Sackin, who was then one of our porters at Hodgson's, was an expatriate Canadian, who kept in touch with his homeland by copies of the Toronto *Star*, which were sent to him regularly by his family, and which was quite an important and influential publication. One day, he showed me a full-page article, complete with portrait photograph. Someone over there had been doing a lot of research about the Canadian Krogers. It seemed that Peter J. Kroger wasn't Peter J. Kroger at all. He wasn't a Canadian, either. He was Morris Cohen, a former school teacher from the Bronx, New York. His wife, Helen, was really one Lola Petka. Both had disappeared mysteriously and — for them — very conveniently, at just about the time when the Rosenbergs had been arrested, back in the very early 'fifties, when the authorities had been closing in on the spy ring responsible for passing atomic secrets to Russia. Such information could not be published in British newspapers *before* the Krogers' trial, of course, and I don't suppose that one man in a million in this country was aware of the couple's true identity. I only learned myself through the chance of working with a Canadian who happened to receive copies of the *Star*.

On that particular Saturday, the prison officer with us was suddenly called out over some altercation involving an irate detainee in the corridor, and I hastily mentioned to Peter the information I had read. His face fell.

'So — they're on to that, are they?' he said grimly. Until then, I believe he thought that he and Helen stood some chance of getting away with things. After that, he knew that his goose was cooked.

I could not attend the trial. The Hodgsons had been lenient enough in allowing me time off in the middle of the week for Brixton visits, particularly once they knew that Peter's books would be coming to them for sale, but there was a limit. I did not feel that I could take the liberty of absenting myself for several full days up at the Old Bailey.

Still, the book trade was well represented in the Public Gallery, while all we others who did not attend but who had known the couple so closely followed every word that was printed in the newspapers each day.

There were five people in the dock. The so-called 'master-spy', Gordon Lonsdale, was the star turn. The papers made the most of him. Handsome, brash, and charming, he filled the bill as the big brain of the Portland case. He claimed to be a Canadian from Cobalt, Ontario. He lived in opulent surroundings at the White House, in Marylebone, and he was involved in several lucrative businesses as a cover. One of these had been selling juke-boxes to small cafés, and he later claimed to be one of the first people to introduce these abominations to British bars and restaurants. (I can forgive him for much, but not for that.)

Peter and Helen jointly played second lead. They appeared to have been the paymasters and go-betweens, among other things.

Harry Houghton and Ethel 'Bunty' Gee made up the quintet. Houghton was a minor civil servant who was earning about £15 a week at that time, but who had a taste for rather higher living than he could afford. He lived in a cottage near Weymouth. Lonsdale had been told by his superiors that Houghton was a more than likely candidate to betray naval secrets, and after a somewhat circumspect approach, when he told the man that he was an assistant to the American Naval Attaché in London, and that the information Houghton first showed him would be of great interest to the US Navy, he had little trouble thereafter. The civil servant was more than willing to pass over any information for cash. It was Harry Houghton's heavy drinking, carelessness, and reckless spending in public places which first brought this particular spy ring under suspicion. He came out of the whole business very badly in court, particulary so since he had ratted on the others to save his own skin, and had seduced Bunty Gee, the one who had had direct access to the more important secrets, and purely for monetary gain.

Each of these five people, of course, had their own close friends and acquaintances who had never known that they wers spies, and who no doubt wished them well, paid them visits, and looked after their outside interests. As I have said, I met a couple of strangers quite outside the book trade when we were first allowed entry to the Ruislip bungalow. There must have been many more people just as absorbed in this matter as I was, but whose paths seldom or never happened to cross mine. Indeed, I once sat in the grim waiting-room at Brixton, and one path *nearly* crossed another. I was directly opposite a smartly-dressed and pretty woman, and we were the only two people in the room. We sat in silence, and I idly wondered what sort of unfortunate she had come down to this forbidding place to visit. I was surprised when an officer clanked in with his keys — they always clank — called 'Lonsdale!' briefly, and the lady got up and walked out of my life. If *I* had been called first, with the name of 'Kroger!' would this very attractive woman, I wonder, have thought to herself: 'Who was *that* attractive man?' I doubt it.

But we in the book trade were only really interested in the fate of the Krogers, and nobody could whip up very much interest in the others at the time. I remembered this, later on.

It was a sensational trial, and something of a *cause célèbre*. Much was made of the central characters in the case, and their multifarious activities, some true, I am sure, and some untrue, I am quite equally sure. The prosecuting counsel was named Manningham-Buller, and I think he did very well for himself. Some years later I read of him, in regard to this trial, referred to as Bullying-Manner. I can't believe that he earned it in one fell swoop in maturity. With a name like his own he had probably heard that tag twenty or thirty years earlier.

Inevitably, all five were found guilty. Lonsdale got twenty-five years, but he came out of the business rather well. You couldn't exactly call him a hero, under the circumstances, but he did try to take all the blame himself, and stated that the Krogers had been his mere dupes, and had known nothing of what was going on. (He still maintained this fiction in his memoirs, years later, when he was free but the Krogers were still in jail.) It was a good try, but it didn't work. At the time, he could have had no knowledge of how far the police and the gentlemen of the press had delved into his background and that of the others.

Once the trial was over the truth came out. Much of his own earlier life was revealed, although he never admitted this. He was identified as Konon Molody, a Pole, but he always insisted that he was Gordon Arnold Lonsdale, a Canadian.

Peter and Helen Kroger were identified as Morris Cohen and Lola Petka. They couldn't deny it. When they had been arrested, Helen had protested strongly against being finger-printed, insisting that she was no criminal. It had then been a matter of routine for the police to contact other countries, and it was only a matter of time before the US authorities came up with a matching set of prints. A great deal of their past was put on show, and it transpired that they had only *just* got out of the United States in the nick of time, back in 1951, during the aftermath of the Rosenberg affair, as the police were closing in on them. There was no doubt that they were professional secret agents and dedicated communists. I also learned that Peter had been granted a passport back in the middle 'thirties, when he was a young man, on condition that he did not use it to engage in the Spanish Civil War, an idealogical battle then raging at its height. But he promptly enlisted in the famous Lincoln Brigade, and he did his bit against fascism in Spain before the world-wide holocaust a few years later. In those days, of course, you were a somewhat sympathetic character and were admired if you took a leftish and active stand against the menace of the Hitlers, the Mussolinis, and the Francos. Similarly-inclined Britons joined the International Brigade. I am old enough to recall how *I* admired, too, as a very young man with an emerging social conscience, but felt no stronger about the business.

Peter and Helen were awarded twenty years apiece. Harry Houghton and Bunty Gee, the one an ageing mercenary and the other a love-sick puppet, received the lightest sentences. They got fifteen years each.

I have no particular interest in Houghton and Gee, apart from the purely academic one. I do believe that they had a 'happy ending', according to the newspapers and the television reports, but I don't know a lot of the details. In fact, I had small interest in Gordon Lonsdale, at first. I knew little about him, I had never met him, and had no prospect, intention, or desire to meet him. But then things changed.

After the trial, the three males were first of all incarcerated at Wormwood Scrubs. (Did any house of detention bear a more suitable name? By comparison, Dartmoor, Strangeways, and Pentonville sound almost romantic.)

Here they awaited the result of their inevitable appeal, but they were now subject to very different conditions. Having been convicted, they no longer wore their own civilian clothes, less belt and tie, but the regulation prison garb. Further, I could no longer bring in cigarettes or food for Peter, and I could only see him at strict times on receipt of an official Visiting Order.

The papers told us that they were all under very close scrutiny, and *incommunicado* within the walls. Maybe Harry Houghton was: he had 'grassed'. That was one of the few unforgivable activities among criminals, and nobody would talk to him anyway — or so we learned. We were also informed that Peter and Gordon Lonsdale never moved a yard without two armed guards at their shoulders. I read something of this sort on the very first day I visited Peter at the Scrubs.

You may imagine how surprised I was, on that initial meeting with Peter as a convicted criminal, to be greeted by him in a communal hall. No officer accompanied him. We sat on folding chairs at a sort of card table, and other visitors sat with the prisoners at similar tables. It looked something like a whist drive, without the cards. I was able to go over to a canteen and buy tea and biscuits, and we then sat and chatted closely and uninhibitedly for a long period, with no supervision at all.

For almost the first time, Peter was able to discuss the case with me. Also, for the very first time, I had an inkling of his politics from the man himself. I particularly remember one remark he made on that occasion. 'As you'll have gathered by now,' he said in the American vernacular, '*I'm* for the ordinary Joe.'

Suddenly, while we were talking, he looked up, and glanced over my shoulder.

'Here,' he said, 'someone I'd like you to meet.'

I looked round. Into the room, admittedly with a prison officer, but one who was unarmed, walked a dark, pleasant-looking, thick-set man, dressed nattily in the obligatory dark blue battle-dress uniform of the prisoner.

'Gordon Lonsdale,' said Peter in introduction, and we shook hands. Why? I don't know, except that when Peter Kroger introduced you to a friend of his he did it in a way which somehow made you want to know and like that friend.

Shortly afterwards, Lonsdale excused himself and strolled over to an officer's table. Having read in a newspaper, only an hour or two previously, of how this very man could move a muscle only under armed escort, I watched him walk freely about that room with no escort at all! The original officer who had come in with him had faded away. This was my first major experience of imaginative newspaper blarney. Coupled with all the bull I had read about the House of Secrets, it didn't take me very long to discount most of what the papers said about Peter and Helen from then on.

Yet I *was* taken in once more in this respect, a year or so later. I was travelling up to Winson Green Prison, in Birmingham, with Nora Doel and another lady, to visit Peter and Helen, and we had prepared ourselves for the journey with all the daily papers. We were disturbed to read in one of the sensational tabloids — I don't recall exactly which one — that Peter was pining away for love of Helen, who was only a matter of a few yards away from him in the women's section of the prison, but whom he only saw very occasionally. We fully expected to be greeted by a man in poor health and acute despondency. Actually, we met an unusually cheerful one, further bolstered by a visit, which always raised his spirits. He, too, had read the report in that day's paper, as had many of the other inmates. All morning he had been ribbed and joshed as 'love-sick Kroger'.

Throughout most of the nineteen-sixties I was in constant correspondence with Peter and Helen Kroger, and I paid them visits in a wide variety of jails. I haven't journeyed to every prison in the country, of course, not by a very long chalk, but my friends got chopped and changed about quite a lot during their incarceration, and I think I can claim that there are very few people in my position who have visited so many 'monasteries', as Peter always liked to call them, as I have. They vary widely in location, surroundings, and conditions. In some I have been completely left alone with those I visited, and I could have passed to them firearms, secret messages, or poison for self-destruction. (All I ever gave them were cigarettes.) In other jails I have had an officer chaperoning every word and move. At a rough count, I know Brixton, Wormwood Scrubs, Winson Green, Strangeways, Styal, Wakefield, Holloway, and Parkhurst. I may have left one or two out. They are eminently forgettable, as temples of enshrinement, and their anatomy and architecture merge one with another. I shall have more to say about this later on.

The previous paragraph, in itself a short section of my narrative, telescopes or roughly puts into précis about a decade of prison visits. A genius such as Samuel Pepys may record the day by day trivialities of his life and make them interesting. I have no intention of detailing all the various happenings during my many meeting with my two old friends up and down the country. Much of what was said and done was personal. It was all very interesting to us, of course, but it would be terribly boring to others. I would like to keep to salient points.

Most of the things that Helen wrote to me to get for her were little feminine requirements, which were either very difficult or quite impossible to obtain in any of the prisons. They boosted her morale: items like hair-curlers, in-soles for her slippers, and the slippers themselves. Also, during the time she was at Winson Green I arranged that fresh flowers should be sent into her regularly every week. There happened to be a very convenient florist's almost opposite the front gates of the jail.

Peter was not particularly bothered about creature comforts, and his morale didn't need boosting, anyway. He had a natural ebullience which did not desert him during his years under detention. He very quickly gave up smoking, once he knew that cigarettes would not be easily forthcoming, but his wife was never able to. Once she had smoked her ration she would suck or chew a piece of orange peel, whenever she could get it.

Peter's primary requirements and requests revolved about books. He read all the reviews in the newspapers religiously, and hardly a month passed without my sending him a parcel or two of the new publications which had taken his fancy. I'm afraid that his taste in reading didn't correspond with my own: he asked for some of the dullest and heaviest stuff going. He rarely read works of fiction, and he wasn't particularly interested in what might be loosely termed 'literature'. His preference seemed to be for somewhat weighty, two-volume histories, while any new work whose title bore words like — let us say — 'dialectical materialism', or 'metaphysical contradictions' drew him like a magnet. Dedicated and convinced communist as he was, he continually read anything that explained or defended his advanced socialism. It was certainly a case of the authors preaching to the converted, if ever I saw one. On the other hand, there were surprising gaps in his knowledge. He had never even heard of Robert Tressall's famous *The Ragged-Trousered Philanthropists*, for instance. This particular classic, together with famous novels like Steinbeck's *The Grapes of Wrath*, probably attracted more people to socialism than the vast collected works of Lenin, Stalin, Marx, and Engels all lumped together. He very quickly became known as 'The Professor' among the incarcerees, and his natural inclination towards teaching led him to expound at great length. I don't think many of the inmates ploughed through the sort of book he would have offered and recommended.

One day Peter wrote to me to ask if I could get hold of certain books that a friend of his in Winson Green had had difficulty in obtaining. I didn't ask who the friend was, although I guessed. I said that I would try, and I asked for a list. Shortly afterwards I received a letter from Gordon Lonsdale himself, and he explained that he had been doing a lot of translating during his leisure to keep himself occupied. He had rendered several English books into Russian, and one of these, I recall, was the famous *Popski's Private Army*. He now had the idea of writing a definitive history of SOE activities during the war. He was certainly well qualified. He had worked extensively behind enemy lines himself in the nineteen-forties, and I am sure that this work had been something of an apprenticeship, in war, to the sort of activity he was later to be recruited to do during so-called peace.

His only contact outside the prison, as far as obtaining books is concerned, was the local branch of W. H. Smith's, in Birmingham. This famous firm, at that time excellent in obtaining a *new* book for any customer, was, of course, totally inadequate when it came to procuring a second-hand one. They weren't all that interested, either; they weren't geared to that sort of thing. Lonsdale sent me a long list of books, some immediately obtainable, but most long out of print and a little harder to obtain.

19th MAY, 1969   PARKHURST
                      ILE OF WIGHT.

PAPERBACKS — (CONTINUED) (4)

*) MORRIS: THE WASHING OF THE SPEARS (SPHERE P.B.

63) MORAN: WINSTON CHURCHILL: THE
        STRUGGLE FOR SURVIVAL.   (SPHERE P.B.)

64) LICHTHEIM: THE ORIGINS OF (WEIDENFELD + NICOLSON)
        SOCIALISM   P.B.

65) STERNE: [A SENTIMENTAL JOURNEY] (DENT EVERYMAN)
        { THE JOURNEY TO ELIZA }   P.B.

HARD BACKS

66) HOBSBAWN: INDUSTRY AND EMPIRE, AN ECONOMIC
        HISTORY OF BRITAIN SINCE 1750 (WEIDENFELD + NICOLSON)

67) " "   AGE OF REVOLUTION   ? "

68) DOBB: WELFARE ECONOMICS AND THE {C.U.P}
69) ECONOMICS OF SOCIALISM
    WOODS: POLAND: EAGLE IN THE {DEUTSCH.
        WOODS

No. 243a (29128—19-5-65)

(over)

A few of the titles requested by Peter Kroger for his bedtime reading
before Lights Out during his incarceration at Parkhurst in 1969

As fast as I got hold of these volumes he wanted, and sent them off to him, another list came. For many months I sent him dozens of books, and I am rather proud of the fact that of all the many titles he sent to me, I was eventually able to obtain about ninety-five percent of them. Not that I should take a lot of credit, really. Most of the donkey work was done by the Hammersmith Bookshop, and I should like to take this opportunity of thanking that firm publicly.

Lonsdale sent me funds, naturally. One thing I should stress: the Krogers and he were never short of money for the particular things they needed in prison, as far as their immediate comfort and well-being were concerned. I was able to open a joint account. I am not talking about thousands of pounds, which were necessary for their defence, and for which house, car, and effects had been sold, but hundreds of pounds. Whenever the account grew depleted, I had only to telephone their solicitors, and it was replenished.

Over the months and years, Gordon Lonsdale grew increasingly friendly and communicative towards me. While I learned that all the books I was sending to him were arriving safely, and without complications, he was encountering certain frustrations. For instance, no prison rule prevented him from having an exercise-book for writing. Indeed, that was encouraged. But once the book was exhausted, and he required a fresh one, he could only have it upon the relinquishing of the previous book! This struck me as being extraordinarily daft on the part of the authorities. They bent over backwards to encourage creative work among the inmates, but insisted on keeping to the letter of the rules when it came to actual tools and implements. It was as mad as Catch 22. Anyone who has ever attempted a lengthy written work, no matter what its nature might be, must appreciate the absolute necessity of continually referring to earlier pages. Lonsdale translated one book in eighteen closely-written note-books. As each one was completed, it was taken away from him and he was not allowed access to it again, even for reference. In my opinion, this is bureaucracy gone stark, staring mad.

But how did I come to know of these facts, you might wonder, which were not flattering to the prison authorities? Prisoners were limited to a small double-leafed sheet of ruled buff stationery for their letters, which were restricted, and also censored. The writers had to be very careful in what they said. The fact is that Lonsdale's 'official' letters to me were on this meagre stationery, and were confined to lists of books he wanted and little else. But I also received unofficial letters from him, written on generous foolscap, and on which he allowed himself to spread. These, presumably, were smuggled out of the prison. Just how, I don't know for sure, but I imagine that for a consideration a friendly warder wasn't averse to pocketing a missive and having it posted outside. I noticed that all these letters were postmarked in London, by the way, and never Birmingham.

Apart from conveying his grievances in this manner, Gordon was also able to pass on letters for me to send to Lord Stonham, who was active in prison reform, and from whom I believe he got some satisfaction, and I was able to deliver messages to his Member of Parliament, a former television news-presenter named Geoffrey Johnson Smith. This gentleman, I recall, was both irked and embarrassed to receive continual importunings from the most notorious and infamous of his constituents.

It is not generally known that Gordon Lonsdale had a wife and family in Poland. He had seen little enough of them in recent years, and his youngest child he had never even seen at all! I don't know how often he heard from them, but they certainly heard quite a lot from him. Apart from his letters, which were sent direct, they also received most generous gifts from time to time, as well as Christmas and birthday presents. He was wily enough never to divulge his wife's name and address, even to me. Everything was sent via his mother-in-law, to an address in Warsaw. He would send me long lists of things to get, like shirts, blouses, cardigans, and shoes, complete with their English sizes, and he also requested puzzles, children's games, and a few long-playing records. I would pass on these shopping lists to an excellent firm known as Universal Aunts. For what seemed to me to be a very reasonable sum they procured everything asked for and then packed it and sent it all to the address in Poland that I gave them. Gordon's children certainly had no cause to think that they had been forgotten by their father during the years he was away.

Although we were in constant correspondence, I visited Gordon Lonsdale in prison on only one occasion. Five or six prisoners sat on one side of a long table, and the same number of visitors sat opposite them. At the head of the table was a somewhat bored prison officer. I assume he was there to keep a sort of order, which he did on this particular visit when one of the prisoners grew a little obstreporous with a relative who had erred in some way or another. He was definitely not the slightest bit interested in what we all talked about. On reflection, I think Winson Green was one of the 'easiest' of all prisons to visit. I went there a good number of times, usually to see Helen and Peter, and on several of these occasions there was no supervision at all.

Gordon Lonsdale did not appear to be bothered very much by the prospect of serving a quarter of a century behind bars — less remission if he behaved himself — if, indeed, he actually believed in that possibility. He seemed to have a sort of Micawberish cheerfulness and certainty that 'something would turn up', although he was no more explicit than that. Maybe he knew a thing or two.

He also took great glee in telling me about George Blake, that remarkable double agent whose arrest, conviction, and sentence had recently overshadowed Lonsdale's own. Blake had drawn forty-two years! He was also here in Winson Green. Gordon chuckled.

'You read in the papers that we're kept apart, and never allowed to communicate. Rubbish. Actually, we speak together in four languages, and nobody here knows what the hell we're talking about!'

All this, of course, was before any of the sensational escapes of the Great Train Robbers. Security had not really been put into effect yet.

I believe that the seeds of George Blake's eventual dramatic escape from Wormwood Scrubs were sown at Winson Green, during his talks with Lonsdale. I am not condoning what came to take place: I merely report what I heard. Who, at that time, could ever have believed that Blake would be spirited away from Wormwood Scrubs so mysteriously? Who, for that matter, would have believed that a man could have climbed over the wall of Winson Green, *from the outside, into* the prison, unlock a cell door with a key that had been made for the purpose, and effect the escape of one of the Great Train Robbers? It happened. Gordon Lonsdale, by the way, was in the very next cell at the time — or so he told me much later.

I was travelling up to work on the train one morning during the rush hour when I happened to catch a glimpse of the headline on a fellow-traveller's newspaper. 'Lonsdale Exchanged'! I hastily glanced at my own paper. Nothing. Obviously, my neighbour had a later edition; there was certainly nothing in my own issue.

It was in this fashion that I first learned that Gordon Lonsdale, master-spy and arch-conspirator, had suddenly been repatriated. He had been exchanged, with the absolute minimum of fuss and publicity, for one Greville Wynne, a middle-aged businessman, who had been caught behind the Iron Curtain indulging in much the same sort of activity that Lonsdale had been perpetrating in England.

Those who recall Greville Wynne from the reams written about him in the British newspapers will remember that he was largely portrayed as an innocent dupe, a man who had unwittingly acted as a courier, but who had been conveniently grabbed by the Russians, and who was used to bargain with the British authorities for an exchange. There was a big show trial, he got a very sympathetic press in this country, and the unfortunate chap was shoved away in the Moscow clink for a long term. But he was not allowed to be forgotten. He was in bad health, we learned, he was being ill-treated, he was being brain-washed — while people like Lonsdale and the Krogers were living in relative luxury and comfort over here.

I will not deny that I believe my friends — and everyone else, for that matter — had it a damned sight easier in British prisons than any criminal or political detainee ever had it in Russian ones. By simple comparison, I think out institutions are humane and cushy, for all their petty frustrations. I know little of the Russian penal system, apart from what I have gleaned from writers like Aleksandr Solzhenitsyn, who do not paint a pleasant picture, but I do know rather more than the average person about British prisons, and I think I am qualified to speak.

But just how innocent was Greville Wynne? Gordon, of course, was openly cynical about the whole matter. He thought Wynne was as guilty as hell, and he considered the Englishman very small fry beside himself: the big fish? It was natural vanity, I suppose. There had earlier been the much-publicised Russo-American exchange of the formidable Colonel Abel for Garry Powers, the U-2 pilot. I think Gordon would have preferred something like that, but it just wasn't available. He had to make do with a courier. He had a lot to say about it, later on, but I never found it particularly offensive. He had a very charming and disarming way about him, even when discussing matters of this sort, which you could not resent. This was all part of his stock-in-trade, of course.

Well, I thought to myself, after this exchange of prisoners had been effected, that's the last we'll ever hear of Gordon Lonsdale. Although he and I had been close for quite a long period, I was now resigned to the fact that he would be swallowed up somewhere in eastern Europe and I would never see him or hear from him again.

How wrong I was! In a matter of months, after he had recovered from an illness in Warsaw, he wrote to me again. His illness, by the way, I believe to be the natural reaction to his period of imprisonment and the tension of the sort of life he had been living for many years. It was experienced, to some degree, by each and every political prisoner, British or foreign, of whom I am aware.

It may be wondered why he made contact with me again. Well, for one thing, he was anxious for news of the welfare of Peter and Helen Kroger, neither of whom were in the best of health themselves at that time. Although I am not so simple as to believe that he was unable to get in touch with other secret agents in this country, I was his only 'square' contact who was able to give him direct knowledge of how they both were faring. For another, he still needed a lot of English books, and I was always able to supply the titles he wanted. For yet another, a certain medicament had been prescribed in Poland, which was obtainable only on *this* side of the

Iron Curtain. He said that it was for a friend of his, but putting two and two together I gathered that he was in pretty poor health himself, and that it was *he* who needed the stuff. It cost something over a hundred pounds a throw. Since he was able to supply the cash and a doctor's prescription — albeit a Polish one — I had no great difficulty in obtaining the tablets whenever he wanted them. Walking into a Chancery Lane chemist's and writing a cheque for three figures at a time when most customers wanted a packet of aspirins, a bottle of nail varnish, or a film for a camera rapidly made me the most popular client that shop had ever had, I believe. As I write, it must be getting on for fifteen years since I put in my last order for the expensive stuff. Right until Hodgson's Rooms closed down in 1981 and I ceased to frequent that district, I still got a nod and a smile from the manager of that chemist's shop whenever I passed him in Chancery Lane. I think he had probably forgotten just *why* he should remember me, but he was pretty sure that he should.

A long-winded but necessary digression is indicated at this point. Late in 1963 I had experienced an enormous stroke of luck. Recuperating in hospital from a stomach operation — an event which was not exactly lucky in itself — I happened to notice a sort of nation-wide hysteria over the reception of the second James Bond film, *From Russia, With Love*, which was based on perhaps the best of the widely-read Ian Fleming novels about his fantastic character. I had idly toyed, in the past, on a magazine article about Bond. I now got the idea of doing a sort of irreverent and tongue-in-cheek full analysis of the fictional James Bond, together with a résumé of his career, based on the internal evidence of the Fleming books. Sherlock Holmes had suffered such a probing, more than once. Characters like Bulldog Drummond had been subjected, too. I put up the idea to a friend of mine, a publisher named Neville Armstrong. He ran a thriving business on his own, Neville Spearman Ltd., as well as partnering another friend of mine, Martin Orskey, in the Holland Press, pioneer of the reprint companies. Neville liked the idea. I submitted the basis of several chapters, he liked the idea even more, and he gave me an advance and the go-ahead to do the job.

But, once started, I discovered that someone else had got the same idea: Kingsley Amis, no less! Now, I was under no illusions; as a writer he could knock me into a cocked hat. But I had started, and he had not. I knew that his book was projected, and he knew nothing about mine. A discreet call to his publishers elicited the blithe information that his book was not expected to be published until the spring of 1965, so Neville and I determined to publish mine in the autumn of 1964.

But the thing had to be written. Anyone who imagines that the production of a book merely consists in the putting down of words on to paper and then bunging them off to a printer should attempt the job himself.

Virtually, I was obliged to re-read the twelve published Bond books, and to work with them by my side. I did three separate drafts, all painstakingly typed by myself. I would come home after a day's work at Hodgson's, settle down to my machine at about seven o'clock, and work through until one or two in the morning. Weekends, I jobbed on — solid.

There was no idea of any great financial remuneration in mind. I anticipated perhaps two or three hundred pounds in royalties if the book was well-received and I got lucky. Such a sum was not exactly small change at that time, although books of that nature seldom retailed at more than fifteen or eighteen shillings and the ten percent royalty wasn't enormous. My main desire was to be the first man to publish a study of the most talked-about and most widely-read fiction character since Sherlock Holmes.

Inevitably, perhaps I produced a hasty and somewhat botched job. My very first review, brief, but in the *Sunday Times Review*, referred to my effort as 'superficial'. All right, possibly it was. But at least, it was the *first*, and that was acknowledged in the notice, which was all I had really wanted.

But then things began to happen. Ian Fleming, the author of the Bond books I had been writing about, died suddenly almost simultaneously with the publication of my own book. The resultant publicity did me no harm at all. I should add that my publisher had already informed Fleming that the book was in production, and the author had said that he 'was delighted'. Neville had then sent Fleming, who was in hospital with a heart attack, a set of the proofs of my book. Whether or not he ever had the chance to read them I do not know. But it was jocularly suggested that their receipt and a perusal of them might have been a contributory cause of his sudden demise!

Neville was an astute publisher. As soon as my book was out — or perhaps even earlier — he contacted Pan, the foremost paperback reprint house, who had the rights of all the Bond books, with the proposition that they should eventually take my effort. But they turned thumbs down; they were in cahoots with Jonathan Cape, the hardback publishers of all the Fleming books, and they had been doing handsomely with the reprints. They had wind of Kingsley Amis's book, too, and that seemed a much better bet. After all, who was O.F. Snelling?

So Neville Armstrong went to Pan's closest competitors, Panther Books. They were very interested, but they had also heard about the projected Amis book, and that Cape and Pan were to publish it simultaneously, in hardback and paperback respectively. Yes, they said eventually, they would be pleased to have my book, but they must win the race into print. My paperback must be published on 1 January, 1965.

So my poor little production virtually had a life in hard covers of just four months. I say virtually — actually it was still in print until comparatively recently, and occasionally a few copies were sold to booksellers who appeared to be quite unaware that it was ever issued in a cheaper reprint. It has even sold at about £5 in second-hand booksellers' catalogues at a time when the few remaining mint copies could still be had from its publisher at the decimal equivalent of eighteen shillings!

But it really hit the jackpot as a paperback. At that time, anything with the name James Bond or the magic numerals 007 on it sold like those oft-quoted hot cakes.

I started getting royalty cheques coming in from Panther, and I joined the affluent society. Suddenly, I was richer than I had ever been in my life. When *The James Bond Dossier*, Kingsley Amis's book, came out, I think that a lot of people bought mine under the delusion that they were buying *his*, and my effort went into a couple of new impressions. Then we sold the book to the New American Library, Fleming's paperback publishers in the States. This was when the money really started rolling in. I never even saw a single review from across the Atlantic if, indeed, there ever were any, but I certainly saw the evidence of the sales. Apart from money, I also started getting fan letters. One of them informed me that I had topped the best-seller lists for two or three weeks in some states, which was an item of information the publishers never bothered to let me know. Not that *I* bothered, either: the size of their cheques cushioned the effrontery of the oversight.

A glossy Paris magazine bought a sizeable chunk of the book and printed the extract in one issue. Then the book was translated into Dutch, Portuguese, Japanese, and Hebrew. I have copies of the Dutch and Portuguese translations, but I never did see the Japanese and Israeli ones. I would have liked to have done, even though I couldn't have understood a word of them.

All this is a very lengthy preamble to that which I set out to say. With this great success, I naturally grew closer to my publisher, Neville Armstrong, and one day, over dinner, I told him about my relationship with the Krogers and Lonsdale. He was immensely interested, and he wondered aloud if there was a book there. I told him that I had no intention of writing about these friends of mine, particularly the Krogers, who were still in prison. His reply was that he had been thinking more of a book by Gordon Lonsdale. This was an idea that had crossed my own mind more than once, but I had dismissed it. But now that a publisher was interested it was an entirely different matter. The next time I wrote to Gordon I asked him if he had ever thought about writing his memoirs, and somewhat to my surprise he replied that he had. He had seen the success in the west in the post-war years of books like that of the spy, 'Cicero', for instance, and he had also collected quite a little library of all those reminiscences of the people who worked behind enemy lines during hostilities. I had sent him dozens of them. Gordon was no mug. Communist or capitalist, he was not averse to accumulating a sizeable chunk of currency if his own reminiscences about the spying trade were published in the west. But he was hundreds of miles away, he was now *persona non grata* in the free world, and he had no contacts at all with British publishers. He was inclined to trust very few people. But he trusted me, and he had seen the success Neville Armstrong had made of my little book. Gordon Lonsdale appointed me his unofficial go-between: a sort of amateur literary agent.

He sent me over a few typed anecdotes of his life here in England before he had been arrested. I showed them to Neville. They were written in much the same style as his letters to me, and showed that here was a man who had been on a deadly serious mission, but who was not necessarily deadly serious himself all the time. He was light-hearted, and a fun-lover. He had got a great kick out of pulling the wool over all of our collective eyes. Also, he seemed to have thrived on danger, which is something I have never done. I particularly remember one anecdote in that first brief missive. It revolved about his actually being invited to tea on the terrace of the House of Commons by a Member of Parliament. This was his 'fellow' Canadian, Beverly Baxter. Gordon had revelled in the occasion. I should have quaked.

The snippets we received were enough to prove to Neville Armstrong, with his nose for a seller, that here *was* a book. But it had to be negotiated, and Lonsdale wasn't going to sell it for peanuts. The upshot was that one winter weekend we travelled to West Berlin, crossed the famous 'Checkpoint Charlie' through Churchill's so-called Iron Curtain, and met Gordon in an East Berlin hotel to sign contracts for the book.

It was a happy occasion for all concerned. Neville and I were accompanied by Lilli, his delightful secretary, a German-Jewish woman who was now coming back to Berlin, her home town, for the first time since before the war. She proved invaluable in enabling us to get through terrain in a town we did not know and with a language we did not speak.

This was the first time I had met Gordon outside a prison and without his wearing the prison uniform. We sat in a comfortable and well-furnished room, he dressed in an immaculate and well-cut suit. Over drinks, we discussed the book and terms, and finally he and Neville signed contracts. Gordon was now extremely forthcoming about his former activities, and Neville happened to ask if he had ever met the famous Colonel Abel.

Gordon laughed. 'I'm meeting him in half an hour. He was my boss. That's why I can't ask you to lunch.'

In due course, the manuscript was completed and delivered to London. With it came numerous highly-interesting snapshots illustrating various episodes of Lonsdale's wartime life behind the lines and his peacetime life in England, also 'behind the lines'. We were a bit worried about Gordon's position, at that time, with his Soviet masters. Would they allow the book to be published? He airily brushed this aside. Theoretically, it seems, there is no censorship in Russia. He assured us that his manuscript had been vetted by certain authorities to whom he felt it should be submitted, and no objection had been made. I am not really surprised. It was a book which told of his fooling the west for years, and he poked endless fun at our dignitaries and prison system. I suppose it was considered excellent propaganda. More recent years have produced Aleksandr Solzhenitsyn, of course. *His* stories of happenings in *Russian* prisons were not looked upon so kindly by the Kremlin.

There was one snag about 'our' book — potentially a lucrative one. It took the form of a particular individual. Of all the persistent and irritating newspaper reporters who had clung to Gordon Lonsdale from the moment of his arrest, the most persistent was one Ken Gardner, of the *Sunday People*. I must really take my hat off to this man.

First, let us go back to the day when Lonsdale 'went down'. For the benefit of any who have encountered this term and know what it means without knowing how it originated, its quite literal meaning is that he did not walk out of the Old Bailey a free man after having been found not guilty, but *went down* the famous steps from the dock to the cells beneath it, here to await transportation to prison. After the verdict, all the reporters but one rushed off the few hundred yards down Ludgate Hill to their Fleet Street offices with their stories. Not so Ken Gardner. He went down after Lonsdale! How he actually got down, I don't exactly know, but I wouldn't be at all surprised if a few pounds changed hands somewhere. At any rate, he was actually able to interview Gordon Lonsdale in his cell, and he more than hinted that his paper was prepared to pay a considerable sum, if and when the time came, for the full and exclusive story. Gordon didn't forget it.

Second, while never at any time during this famous Portland Spy Case, when I was in close contact with the Krogers from the start, and with Gordon Lonsdale later, did the police ever approach me — although I am quite sure they were aware of me — it was an entirely different matter with the newspapers. Looking back, I believe that the only London daily which didn't send a man in to speak to me at Hodgson's was the then *Daily Worker*, a newspaper which soft-pedalled on the whole affair. Happily, they all stopped there, at Chancery Lane, and never penetrated further — except for Ken Gardner. He was the only reporter who found my home address and tried to get his foot in the front door. This was no great achievement in itself, of course — I was in the telephone directory — but he must have wormed out of the Winson Green warders the names and addresses of the people to whom the Krogers were sending letters. Further, he got to know the address of Lonsdale's in-laws in Poland, which I had kept confidential, except to the firm with which I had been sending presents abroad on Gordon's behalf. Obviously, there had been some 'dropsy' in connection with the prison officers in charge of handling the mail between Lonsdale and myself. Later on, when I got to know Ken Gardner quite well, I tried to get him to tell me how he had acquired this information, but he would never say. He was a reporter first, last, and always. He was the most unscrupulous of people when in search of a story, but he lived by his code and would not divulge his sources. He would have gone to prison first, just as Brendan Mulholland and Reginald Foster did some time later.

I don't think Gordon Lonsdale particularly liked Ken Gardner. I don't think Ken Gardner liked Gordon very much, either. But they had established a *rapport*, of a kind. A promise was made below the courtrooms of the Old Bailey that Ken should get first refusal if ever the story came up for sale. Gordon had his share of faults, like the rest of us, but I never knew him to welsh on a promise. Yet even as I say this, I am still not so naive that I discount the possibility of an advance having been paid into some account or other by the *Sunday People* on Gordon's behalf.

Now, publishing Lonsdale's memoirs in book form, with a whopping great pre-payment on account of royalties, was one thing. Getting one's money back, with a good profit, was quite another. Serialisation, in a sensational Sunday newspaper, a few weeks before the book came out, was absolutely essential. Neville and I both knew that Ken Gardner and the *Sunday People* were interested, but how much could be asked? Eventually, he decided on £10,000, and one evening he and I went along to the newspaper's offices in Long Acre to discuss the matter. On the way there, Neville told me that he was going to try for £15,000. I am a poor businessman myself, and I could only gasp in awe at the cheek of the man. Imagine my surprise, when we got into the office, and he asked for £20,000! They didn't even try to beat him down, which he had obviously expected. Finally, with syndication rights, the matter was settled for £23,000.

I learned a lot at that meeting. They were more concerned about the

elaborate conditions and clauses Gordon had insisted upon in the contract
— he had been a lawyer of sorts, among other things — than the figure that
was asked. Just how much a Sunday paper pays for its sensational stories is
not particularly important to it. 'We might sell a few extra copies because
of this series,' the business manager admitted, somewhat cynically, 'but
that makes no difference.' Their main revenue came from advertising, and
this depended entirely upon a constant supply of probes, scandals,
revelations, reminiscences, and confessions. If the time ever comes when
these dry up, which is unlikely, the sensational Sunday papers will dry up,
too.

But do not imagine that the *Sunday People* was just giving this money
away, without seeing the manuscript. They wanted facts, and sensational
facts. It was arranged that we should travel again to East Berlin, on this
occasion with Ken Gardner and a staff photographer, to meet Gordon
Lonsdale, get some pictures, and to iron out a few problems.

I didn't have a lot to do with these negotiations. I crossed from West
Berlin to East Berlin once only, this time, taking Gardner to the hotel
which had been agreed as the rendezvous. We went by hired car. Neville
and the photographer travelled separately from us, by train, as Gardner
didn't think it wise for four obvious Englishmen to go together through
Checkpoint Charlie. I think he was inclined to dramatise the whole thing.
He was looking for plain-clothes police on every street corner, and he
seemed convinced we were being followed. After that meeting, back in
West Berlin, I was suddenly taken ill with an old and recurring stomach
complaint, and I spent the rest of the jaunt in bed in my room in a
Kurfurstendamm hotel. Eventually, I was whisked to the airport, dumped
on to a 'plane, feeling more dead than alive, and in due course received the
dubious honour of being pushed through the halls of Heathrow in a
wheelchair without having to pass through Customs! I finally arrived
home to go to bed for a week or two.

I thus missed the exchanges, almost entirely, that went on in that East
Berlin hotel day after day between two very determined and forceful
personalities. I was present the first day, of course, and that was quite a
battle. There were several others during the ensuing days, but I am unable
to report upon them, except to say that Lonsdale wanted things his way,
and Gardner, paying the piper, naturally wished to call the tune.

What transpired is that the serialisation which eventually appeared in the
Sunday People differed somewhat from Gordon's own book. It was edited
and rewritten to conform with the paper's desires. My personal opinion is
that the whole battle was really much ado about nothing, and need never
have occurred, because while Gordon professed to be insisting on the
absolute truth, and Gardner was inclined towards embellishment, I know

for a fact that quite a lot of what was said in the original manuscript was blatant untruth, particularly with regard to the Krogers. Still, I was in his corner, so to speak, and I was rooting for my man to win.

There was quite a bit of blah on the front page of the issue of the *Sunday People* printing the first instalment. It was written by Ken Gardner, and it was certainly dramatic. It was all about the way in which he had tracked down this sinister spy to his hotel in communist Berlin, presumably in order to talk him into writing his story for the waiting millions of *People* readers. I had a cynical chuckle over this boxed appetiser, since the book had long since been written, and far from tracking Lonsdale down, Ken Gardner quite literally had to be led by myself to the master-spy's lair: a perfectly innocuous and comfortable hotel just off the main street in the busiest part of East Berlin.

The Sunday serialisation did very well, although its author was annoyed by the changes which had been made, as I have said. He was more satisfied with the book, when that was published, although he had wanted a dignified title something like 'The Memoirs of Gordon Lonsdale', which was only the sub-title, and Neville insisted upon the more eye-catching prefix of *Spy*. There is no doubt at all that that is what the man had been, but he never liked the term, and he was a bit sensitive on the subject. He wasn't all that keen on being called a secret agent, either. I remember asking him, in his Berlin Hotel, just *what* he would like to be called. 'Nowadays,' he informed me, and I must say that he said it with a rather shamefaced grin, 'there is a trend in America now to refer to us all as "intelligencers".' What a word!

His book did even better than the serialisation. It was sold to publishers in many countries, and it was translated into several languages. Copies of most of them came my way, via Neville Armstrong, but some of the more out-of-the-way ones didn't. It was from Gordon himself, three years later, that I one day received a large octavo paperback, entitled *Lonsdale, O Espiao de Moscou*. It originated from Brazil, and it bore a nice inscription, to me from Gordon. 'I'm sorry you can't read this, but neither can I. Sept. '68.' He was a great linguist, but Portuguese was not one of his accomplishments. I do not believe that Neville Armstrong ever sold the rights of the book to any East European countries, or even attempted to, but Gordon seemed to manage quite well on his own account. Eventually I received another paperback, this time squat and small, and evidently published in Warsaw. I couldn't read this one, either, although Gordon himself could, having written it, but I was able to see that it differed very considerably from the English version. It was entitled *Najwyzsza stawka*, which I'm sure just slays 'em in Poland. No doubt the sub-title, *Wspomnienia pracownika wywiadu*, helped to sell the book enormously. For my part, the inscription on my copy is sufficient: 'To Fred, with sincere appreciation of your part in my first steps in the literary world. Oct. 9, 1968. Gordon Lonsdale.'

Roughly at about the time of the publication of Gordon's book in Britain, the Kim Philby 'third man' story broke. Hitherto, hardly anyone in this country had ever heard of Philby, who, it transpired, had been the effective mover in the rather more sensational adventures of those two Foreign Office defectors, Burgess and MacLean, a number of years before.

That eminent journalist, David Leitch, had a bee in his bonnet, and he was quite convinced that Philby, who was a journalist like himself, and who had now defected to Russia as well, *must* have written Lonsdale's book for him. He interviewed me in a pub off Fleet Street, and suggested this. I said not: after all, I knew Lonsdale personally, I had talked with him, and had received dozens of letters from him. I knew the man's literacy, his fluency with language, and I was familiar with his style. Leitch, on the other hand, had never met Lonsdale, or even been in written contact with him. He knew of Gordon only as a more than probable East European who, for years, had posed as a Canadian, and it seemed quite beyond him to believe that such a man could be literate enough in what was, after all, a foreign language, actually to produce a book without 'ghosted' help. Journalist's natural and pardonable vanity, I suppose. I can't do *his* job; how can he possibly do mine?

Although I did my best to change his mind, David Leitch remained unconvinced. In fact, reviewing *Spy* for his paper, he said something like: 'It shouts Kim Philby from the rooftops.' As far as I am concerned, the book shouted Gordon Lonsdale from the rooftops.

Apart from the business of journalistic fluency, I must make the following point. Not possessing a gift for languages myself, I never ceased to be amazed at Lonsdale's command of some others than his native one. He spoke a colloquial English with only the merest trace of accent. It was hard to pinpoint it. You couldn't say American, certainly, but you *could* say Canadian. Like so many Canadians, there was a trace or two of the European, if you listened carefully. Well, French-Canadians have this. I have no doubt at all that this had been gone into thoroughly by his masters, long before he was ever given his new name and identity. His grammar and vocabulary, as far as English is concerned, were comparable with those of anybody native-born. And I wonder how many people are aware that Lonsdale actually produced a text-book on Chinese grammar, long, long before the slip-ups of Harry Houghton betrayed him as a spy for Soviet Russia?

I stayed in touch with him for a considerable time, by post, after his book was published. But we never met again. I should add that there was one long hiatus in our correspondence which coincided with George Blake going over the wall of Wormwood Scrubs and apparently disappearing into thin air. I was aware that Gordon Lonsdale and George Blake had got to know each other well at Winson Green: as I have said, I was told as much at the time. I believe that Lonsdale was the one employed to welcome Blake at the Iron Curtain and whisk him away into hiding after the dramatic escape in London. When the whole thing was over I started getting letters again.

Gordon was extremely concerned about the welfare and comfort of his two friends, Peter and Helen, for things changed rather suddenly. Readers will no doubt recall the extremely daring series of escapes from English prisons of some of the Great Train Robbers, all serving long terms, which culminated in the audacious absenteeism of the aforementioned Blake. These coups finally resulted in an extremely belated clamp-down on the part of the British authorities. All prisoners who were serving extended sentences became, overnight, 'security cases'.

Helen Kroger had, for a year or two, been transferred from the midlands to a so-called Open Prison at Styal, in Cheshire. It was situated right out in the country, and from my vantage-point, at least, it seemed a rather pleasant spot. Approaching it, the place looked more like a cottage hospital than anything else, the visiting rooms were easy and comfortable, tea and biscuits were served to my wife and myself when we met Helen, and I found the lady prison officers kindly, obliging, and understanding. They were more like welfare officers or nurses than female screws. Exactly what the prisoners' living quarters were like, of course, I never knew. I didn't penetrate that far. But I do believe that Helen was happier and more comfortable here than in the other institutions in which she had languished, despite the fact that she was wracked with a rheumatic or arthritic complaint at the time, and had suffered a broken finger, permanently malformed now, 'defending her honour' against an amorous Lesbian inmate.

Peter had been less lucky, although I believe he was always a model prisoner. He never reached an Open Prison. During his period of detention he had drawn Brixton, the Scrubs, Winson Green, Strangeways in Manchester, the Scrubs again, and now Wakefield. He had been sent south to London the second time for a particular reason. He had developed Dupruyten's Contraction in both hands, an awkward complaint in which the tendons of the palms shorten and the fingers are drawn into a permanent loose fist. He underwent two operations at Wormwood Scrubs, with each hand and arm in a sling for about six months: first one and then the other. He was fortunate enough to work in the prison library at this time, and it was a job for which he was extremely suitable. But once his hands had healed and he could use them properly again he was shifted back up north and to less congenial labour.

All the prisons I journeyed to in various parts of England during the 'sixties are much of a muchness as far as their architecture is concerned. I should like to say something about our penal institutions at this point.

Almost all of them appear to have been built on similar lines, and roughly at about the same time in the nineteenth century. You go in through the front, arched gateway, usually by a small door let into a much larger double door, if you are entering on foot. Once inside, you are shown to a waiting-room, for some reason always on the left. The room at the right seems to be the perpetual province of the authorities. Ensconced in the waiting-room, you sit and wait for your call. Ashtrays are provided on a central table, always in the form of empty boot-blacking tins. Once, I suppose, real ashtrays were provided, and were perpetually pinched. Who wants to knock off an old Cherry Blossom tin? Round the walls are an ample number of hard chairs. Invariably they are occupied by blowsy peroxide blondes with squawling brats. Periodically, during the waiting, the blondes and the brats will retire to a water-closet at the back of the room. My remembrances of numerous prison visits always conjure up the recollection of perpetually-filling cisterns.

Sooner or later, whether you are visiting a man or a woman, a surname gets called. It is always the name of the person you have come to see, and never your own. In the early days I was embarrassed by this: those names were much in the news, and I felt like an inmate myself as I got up in response to the call of 'Kroger', and slunk out with all eyes upon me. Gawd, I imagined those blondes saying to each other, d'you reckon 'e's a bleedin' spy, too?

The British authorities have long been famous for locking up the stable well after the horse has gone, and little was done about security in prisons, despite a number of daring escapes, until the star prisoner, Blake, made fools of everybody concerned. Because of the length of their sentences, Helen and Peter Kroger, as 'star' prisoners, were almost immediately transferred to what were now known as maximum security institutions. Nobody wanted to chance the possibility of either of these two doing a bunk. Helen, who wasn't in a fit condition to climb over a three-foot fence, much less a prison wall, was whisked from the rural Styal back to the urban Holloway, where she had commenced her imprisonment some years previously. Peter, who had always been a model prisoner, and who would never have agreed to any escape plan if it meant leaving his wife behind, got shunted off to Parkhurst, which is right in the middle of the Isle of Wight.

Once inside Parkhurst, anyone coming to see a maximum security prisoner, as Peter was now, had a long walk ahead of him. We by-passed the prison proper absolutely. In fact, I never even glimpsed another detainee in all the time I was going to Parkhurst.

We walked from the front entrance literally almost to the far end of the prison, and it is a big place. We were then confronted by a high brick wall, with a single door. The warder's ring would first elicit a peep through a spy-hole, to be followed by the unlocking of the door, once the peeper was satisfied. We then walked across a path through a small but nicely-kept flower garden to yet another locked door. The same process was repeated. Within this door we found ourselves in a tiny ante-room. Through a window one could glimpse an official. He communicated with another one on our side of the door by walkie-talkie, no less! Only after he was fully satisfied that we were *bona fide* visitors, and had not come to effect an escape, were we allowed through to meet our man. Throughout the whole time we sat and chatted with Peter there were at least three, and sometimes four uniformed officials present, as well as a civilian-clothed individual who always sat alone in a corner. I never quite figured out who he was, and could hardly ask, in that goldfish-bowl atmosphere. He was probably some sort of probation or welfare type. These lads were taking no chances at all.

The set-up at Parkhurst at that time has been termed in the press as a prison within a prison. I would go further than that. My impression is that the maximum security wing there was a prison within a prison within a prison. The place is also situated in the middle of an island several miles from the mainland. As far as I know, there have been no escapes from this petty fortress since the embarrassing Blake coup at the Scrubs, and I do not think there will be any. The rock of Alcatraz may have been a more unpleasant spot at which to reside, with its harsh regulations and un-bending restrictions, but I do not think it could have been a more difficult place to escape from.

Visiting Helen at Holloway, the first few times after the clamp-down, caused no bother at all. We went in, retired to the dingy waiting-room on the left, and awaited our call. There then followed a short walk across the prison yard, the crossing of an unlocked threshold, with much clanking and rattling of keys and chains, and we were inside the prison proper. Up a big curved staircase, round to the left, through a couple more narrow doors, each unlocked and then locked again, and then a short wait. Appurtenances like brief-case and handbag had to be left in a locker, and an apology was always given, together with the key. This was a nice touch, and I appreciated it. Then we were in.

During the visit, I could supply Helen with as many cigarettes as she cared to smoke. But once the visit was up she had to stub out. On one occasion, I remember, I had just offered her a fresh one when our time was called. She actually had it in her fingers, waiting for a light. We all stood up, and she naturally tried to pocket it, for future reference. But no — the officer had seen, she demanded its confiscation, and Helen, in quite natural annoyance and frustration, twisted and broke it into fragments before throwing it into the Cherry Blossom lid.

On the very last occasion I visited Holloway, one 'proud man, drest in a little brief authority', had decreed, it seems, that we could not pass! We did not possess authorised photographs of identity, which now, we were told, were obligatory for all visitors to maximum security prisoners. This, mark you, after those who commanded the very same authority had issued a Visiting Order, without mentioning the necessity of such refinements as identifying photographs.

On this one and only time in all the occasions I visited so many of Her Majesty's Prisons, I created one hell of a stink and an argument. This was not for my sake. I had come on only a very short journey, and had been inconvenienced hardly in the slightest — although *they* weren't to know that. But imagine if someone had spent a day travelling down from the north to see a loved one, and then that someone had blithely been told that the prisoner could not be seen, because of the lack of a photograph nobody had been told about!

The uniformed officers who barred us — both male and female — were helpful and polite, but adamant. They were doing their duty, they said, and following orders. I think I might have got nowhere, had not a certain lady come in through the main gate at just that time, as we were arguing in the courtyard. I employ the term of lady to denote her gender. She was, it seemed, some sort of deputy — or assistant-governor of the place. The screws were only too ready to pass the problem over to her for clarification. But she, possessing considerable say-so and influence, simply would not use it — either way. She just didn't want to know. Maybe because it was Saturday afternoon, it was her half day off, she had just come in from a good lunch and wanted to get her feet up, she couldn't be bothered. When I persisted she tried the old 'bullying manner'. This might have worked on previous occasions with some of those unfortunate blowsy blondes I have mentioned earlier, but it did not do so with me. I persisted, and when she saw that she could not intimidate me she turned her back and just brushed me off and left, with the situation still unresolved.

This put me into a terrible rage. Above all things, I loathe petty bureaucracy. My anger, which was real enough, was fortified by able and restrained histrionics, which I am not normally able to muster. It's amazing what you can do when you feel you're in the right. Anyway, I know that I put the fear of Christ up those screws. This is no mean achievement in itself. It sent them scuffling off to telephone the Governor, and eventually we got a clean bill of health to go through.

That evening I wrote an incensed letter to the lady in charge of Holloway Prison. I explained my case, and I said one or two rather uncomplimentary things about her second-in-charge. I received a very apologetic reply, but no reference was made to the lady who had dodged the issue. But I hope she got a jawing and a good ticking-off. Today, she may have attained the status of Governor herself, in some unhappy women's prison elsewhere in England. If she has, I pity the poor inmates. I think of her now as *Simone* Legree. She might live and work 'within these walls', but for the information of television viewers, she wasn't a bit like Googie Withers.

Peter and Helen Kroger did not serve their full sentences of twenty years each, of course, or anything like them. I think they did about nine years of the terms they had been awarded. Over this period, I did my best to keep their case alive. Periodically, somebody from the press would descend upon me for an interview, and from time to time I was able to do my bit in letting the public know how they were faring, and that they were still with us. Maybe they deserved everything they got. I would not attempt to dispute the actual justice of the case. But they were still my friends, they were two of the kindest and most considerate people I have ever met, and it seemed to me at the time that there were precious few people on the outside working actively to reduce their sentences or to get them exchanged. I did what little I could.

One thing that springs to mind is an abortive effort to prevent the making of a film called *Ring of Spies*. Just because they had been convicted, were safely tucked away, and were hardly in a position to defend themselves or insist upon their rights, there was hardly sufficient justification to portray them fictionally, with a necessarily somewhat sensational script. It occurred to me that there was the matter of libel to consider, if nothing else. But I was frustrated at all turns. Although the protagonists had contacted a local firm of solicitors, these people were quite uninterested. They did not even approach the film company! In the end, the film was made. I do not think it was very successful. The only triumph it enjoyed was a triumph of miscasting. David Kossoff, of all people, was chosen to play Peter, presumably because they both had white hair! Bernard Lee, a big and prepossessing actor, played Harry Houghton, who was small and most unprepossessing. I forget who was chosen as Helen. That excellent actress, Margaret Tyzack, seemed to me to be a little more true to type as Bunty Gee, from the very little I happen to know of that lady. Gordon Lonsdale, in the end, laughed the whole thing off and forgot it. The only thing that irked *him*, he said, was that they picked William Sylvester to portray him. That actor had an American accent, so he was considered suitable to play a quasi-Canadian.

All in all, I don't think my efforts on behalf of my friends, in any direction at all, were effective in influencing the powers that be. I see now that someone in Whitehall or its purlieus had the case well in hand. The Krogers were an embarrassment and a burden, and I think the British Government would have liked to have been well rid of them much earlier. But it must not be forgotten that they were American citizens, and they were on the 'wanted' list in the States from 'way back. They couldn't just be kicked out across the Iron Curtain. Washington would demand a say in *that* matter.

It is difficult to conjecture just what would have happened but for Gerald Brooke. This rather foolish young gentleman took it into his head to start spreading anti-Soviet propaganda within Russian territory. He was a sitting duck, if ever there was one. The naive 'courier', Greville Wynne, eventually effective in releasing Lonsdale, had been brilliant by comparison. Moscow just picked Brooke up, without the slightest trouble, gave him a massive show trial which was reported in detail everywhere, and put him inside.

I have not the slightest doubt that Gerald Brooke found things a lot tougher in a Russian prison than Peter and Helen did in Britain. Indeed, I believe that he was deliberately given a rough time in order to soften up the opposition and build bargaining power for an exchange. Western journalists were freely given the opportunity of seeing how he fared, and we all read rather startling reports. Some sort of compromise must have been reached with Washington, in due course, and Whitehall no doubt encouraged the trend of public opinion.

The result was that instead of a quiet and unheralded repatriation on both sides, as had happened with Lonsdale and Wynne, when none of us knew anything about it until it was all over, the public was given notice of the very day on which the exchange of Brooke with the Krogers would be effected. Brooke was to fly back to London; Peter and Helen were to go to Warsaw.

Then television roped me in on a *This Week* programme, which was entirely devoted to my friends and a review of the whole case, and Fleet Street descended upon me again, after a considerable let-up. Every time I answered the telephone there was a fifty-fifty chance that it was going to be about this business.

With regard to telephone calls, I really cannot pass mention of what I consider the most amusing thing that happened at this period. One evening, at home, I received a call from a stranger. He identified himself, although I have now quite forgotten his name. He was a former petty criminal, who had been in prison with Peter for some time. He had also appeared on the television *This Week* programme, in which I had featured, and had given his impression of his former fellow-inmate while within the walls. He gave me some garbled story of how a certain newspaper owed him thousands for his story, had welshed on the deal, and how he was determined to get the money from them. He seemed very anxious to make a name for himself and somehow to capitalise on his earlier proximity to a man in the news.

It was all rather mystifying to me. I was puzzled why he should be ringing me from a town in the north of England with this late-night farrago. We had little in common, except that we had both known Peter. But then it came. Just by chance, he said, he happened to be travelling down to Southampton on the very day that the two spies were to be repatriated. He was breaking his journey in London. Could we meet and have a drink together? I confess that I didn't want to know him particularly, but as it happened it wouldn't be putting me out. I told him the name of the pub I normally frequented in Chancery Lane at lunchtime, and stated the hour that he could find me there.

He did not turn up. I happened to mention this to a reporter acquaintance of mine a short while later, and he informed me that our man had put in an appearance at the airport and had travelled to Warsaw on the same 'plane as the Krogers. This was obviously in the mistaken hope that all the newspaper representatives and television men who also accompanied them on their flight would take him up and pay highly for his story. He had seen me as a possible rival when watching *This Week*, and had made the phoney appointment with me in Chancery Lane to make sure that I would be well out of the way. He went to a great deal of unnecessary trouble: I had not the slightest intention of going to Heathrow that day. My final farewells to both Helen and Peter had been made at Holloway and Parkhurst respectively, the two previous weekends.

He spent a lot of money, and he got no satisfaction. Fleet Street knew the day the Krogers were going, but they did not know on which flight, so they booked for them all, and were covered for the right one. I presume that this gentleman was obliged to do the same thing. It must have worked out rather expensive. The reporters avoided him, having much bigger fish to fry, and he got nowhere near Helen and Peter, either. The journey was fully covered by the *BBC* and *ITV News* cameras, and I watched it all that same evening on the box. There were so many competing newspapermen jostling for a word or two from the departing couple that even the camera-operators had their work cut out.

*   *   *

After the two were eventually exchanged successfully, and my long period of looking after their affairs and interests in this country came to an end, I heard from them again after they had settled in eastern Europe. I had a standing invitation to visit them, but I do not fancy that party of the world, particularly.

During my visits to Holloway, Helen often joked about the open date she had arranged to keep with Gordon Lonsdale, some day in the distant future, in Red Square, Moscow. She had told me that this was one of her priorities. Yet when she got to Warsaw, and later — as I know — to Moscow, she never mentioned in any letter that she had ever met Gordon again. Peter didn't, either, and I did not pursue the matter.

One day the papers here in Britain informed us that Gordon Lonsdale had met a sudden death, apparently from a heart attack while picking mushrooms early one morning in the Polish countryside. Neither Peter nor Helen ever referred to him or his demise in any of their letters, and he had been one of their closest friends.

It may seem fanciful, but I think it more than possible that the man is not dead. Certainly the false identity of Gordon Lonsdale, the Canadian businessman and fun-loving playboy is dead. I think there is just a chance that Konon Molody, or whatever his true name was, is still active somewhere, doing his utmost to promote world unity and an even balance of power according to his own lights. Of course, he could never again be used as an agent in some western state: his appearance remains too well known. But he would be a very handy man as a back-room boy. If I am right, and he is still alive, he would now be in middle age, and far too valuable and experienced to be wasted in premature retirement.

Of Peter and Helen Kroger I know nothing at the present time. We corresponded for a period, but then the letters began to drop off on both sides for want of something new to say. They had both been meticulous about sending Christmas cards, before their arrest, during all their years in prison, and after their release. Then these stopped, too. My last letters, usually giving news of the deaths of particular people in the book trade they had known, remain unanswered. They were always posted with my own return address on the backs of the envelopes, and I usually registered them, but they have never come back, so they must have been delivered to somebody. I know that Helen had a cousin in Warsaw, with whom they were probably living, but as far as I know that cousin did not read English.

All three may still be alive — in the flesh. But for the time being, and until they are heard from again, I fear they must be looked upon as dead.

These three people I knew were, I am quite sure, good and decent souls, and with the very highest of ideals. I liked each of them, and I believed, very broadly, in the ultimate end they were trying to achieve. But I did not like, or believe in, their means. I most definitely did not like or believe in the oppressive and repressive régime which fostered them.

It would be quite idle of me to speak of the present-day United States of America, with its many faults, and to draw favourable comparisons with its early hopes and intentions: the Declaration of Independence and the Spirit of 1776. *There* was a revolution betrayed, in far less than the two hundred years or so of its existence. I think it would be equally idle to compare the Russia of today with all its brave dreams and ideals of less than seventy years ago. Another revolution betrayed. Men like Karl Marx and Frederick Engels, Tom Paine and George Washington — if their entities endure — must watch aghast, to both east and west.

My three spies all lived in Great Britain and America for many years. They saw the good points of the west and its bad ones, too. I know for a fact that they all enjoyed the life they spent in England, until the pounce. They have now had a full opportunity to see the other side of the coin. Perhaps it is not *too* much to hope that one day I may be fortunate enough to be granted their honest opinions, and a comparison?

L'envoi

It was in the year 1981 that the house of Sotheby's, in its infinite wisdom, decided to dispense with my services. I was approaching the age of sixty-five and it was deemed, apparently, that the usefulness of those of us who had reached this accepted retirement age was now over. And so at Christmas of that year I was put out to pasture.

I am very well aware that in this world a great many unfortunate souls slog on through their days in a virtual lifetime of drudgery and monotony, and can hardly wait until that magic hour arrives, that official little buff envelope plops through the letter-box, and they are shot of it all for good. Louis MacNeice expressed it rather colourfully on behalf of civil-servant types in a famous pre-war poem: 'Sit on your arse for fifty years and hang your hat on a pension.'

In my case things were rather different. It is not at all a pleasant feeling to discover, when you are still vigorous, and in full possession of all your mental faculties and most of your physical ones, that you are virtually due for the scrap-heap. Also, when a person has devoted most of his time to looking after the interests of a never-ending parade of delightful people, a large majority of whom have grown to become personal friends, it is not easy to have to give it all up very suddenly.

But many millions discovered long before I did that all good things come to a finish. The cliché serves its purpose. I could continue: life must go on; we must grin and bear it; the world hasn't come to an end...

There was considerable satisfaction to be derived in discovering that almost the whole of the antiquarian book world, when its members heard of my impending departure, was somewhat aghast at the news. Those of their number who had relied on me to sort out and solve petty queries, see to it that their purchases were properly packed and despatched, act as a sort of liaison officer and to effect useful introductions — most of all, to bid on their behalf at auction — seemed quite bereft. At my farewell party, a glorious binge which took place a day or two before Christmas, and which started at about noon and went on until late evening while a snowstorm raged outside, I was very touched by the numerous gifts and tributes from so many of my old friends. David Drummond, of Cecil Court, had dug into his many 'Pleasures of Past Times'. He came up with a photograph of an ample and scantily-clad lady of the Edwardian era, gazing into the distance with a distraught look upon her face. A bubble, emerging from her mouth, had been appended: 'ALAS — SOTHEBY'S IS FRED-BARE!'

A considerable number of my friends wondered if I would still be available to act for them *in absentia*, and I was happy to inform them that I would. So, from the other side of the rostrum, I now devote much of my time to haunting the various London sale rooms, bidding on behalf of dealers and collectors of books who have neither the time nor the inclination to spend half a day in sitting about waiting for a few lots to come up. The 'glamour and romance of the auction room' soon wear off. Some of those lots they might acquire, but many of them are going to realise higher prices than they are prepared to pay, and will leave them with a feeling of frustration and of time wasted.

It is a pleasant enough occupation. I 'lose' far more bids than I 'win', but that's to be expected. Only recently, a certain young dealer was interested in acquiring *every single lot* in a particular sale held in the Hodgson Room at Sotheby's one morning — but at a reasonable price. Unfortunately, there were a lot more books he wanted in a similar sale to be held that afternoon just up the road at Phillips', and he hadn't yet had a chance to view them. He couldn't be in two places at once: would I look after him? Well, it took the best part of half an hour for him to price every lot in the sale and for me to jot down his figures in my catalogue, and in the end — as can be imagined — I bought him only about ten percent of the three hundred and seventy lots which came up for auction. But even this is pretty good going. He was very happy with the result, and so was I.

I don't make a lot of money these days, but I do keep in touch. I haven't got a lot to show, in any material way, after half a century of pottering around among books. But I certainly have a host of pleasant memories, and they come tumbling out of the dark recesses of the mind at the oddest of times. They embrace all facets of this remarkable and absorbing game.

For instance, I recall that exuberant young publisher, who collected books on art. I used to bid for him often, sometimes successfully and sometimes not. One day he spotted a certain book on the shelves: it was one of the rare auction catalogues produced by the Nazis in the late 'thirties when they were getting rid of what they considered undesirable pictures from some of their national museums. He was very excited.

'Go up to a hundred for me if you have to,' he said. 'It shouldn't make anything like that, but don't lose it just for the odd extra pound or two, either. I want it.'

After the sale he rang me up. 'Did you get it?' he asked urgently.

'Yes,' I told him.

'How much?' He was pretty anxious.

'Well,' I said, 'I opened the bidding at a pound, but nobody else bid against me. It's yours for a quid!'

He was delighted. That was one of my more spectacular successes. I had quite forgotten the occasion until my client reminded me of it a couple of years ago. He is Frank Herrmann, author of the history of Sotheby's.

Then there was that somewhat enterprising dealer who inveigled himself into the London flat and the good graces of the poet, T. S. Eliot, with words of flattery and a pile of the first editions of all that author's works. Would the master just deign to sign them, in order that they might be presented to the library of a certain university in the United States of America? Here they would be treasured, and would repose for hundreds of years to come...

Eliot was profoundly moved. He signed his name to each volume, and the dealer backed out in obeisance. He then shot round the corner as fast as he could to the leading shop specialising in Modern Firsts and sold the lot at a handsome profit. But rather unfortunately, T. S. Eliot got to hear what had happened, and thereafter he had the greatest reluctance to sign any of his books at all.

A friend of mine, thinking that this story might be merely apocryphal, wrote to Eliot and asked him if it were true.

'Yes,' replied the poet, and the memory still rankled after many years, 'it is quite true. He told me he wanted the books for his Alma Mater. He didn't even have an Alma *Pater!*'

Again, there is that expatriate English book-collector and client of mine, basking on the shores of sunny Mallorca. Every Christmas, with unfailing regularity, I get a nice long and chatty letter from him, telling me of all his doings. From his most recent: 'Soon, the quiet period arrives with its empty beaches and the resort towns becoming boarded up ghost towns. My wife and I have recently bought a metal detector and have already in a few weeks found 1,500 pesetas, a silver pendant, a diamond ring, a silver ring, and a gold ear-ring on the local beach! Always fancied myself as a beachcomber!'

And how shall I ever forget the rotund and walrus-like figure of John Gawsworth, King of Redonda? Penurious, oftener drunk than sober, he was both poet and bibliographer. 'He reached his peak at the age of eighteen,' his old friend Alan Thomas said to me, 'and from that time went steadily down!' I knew the man only in his later years, when he was doing some part-time job of research at the Public Records Office for about eight pounds a week, and used to drop into Hodgson's across the road, to browse and to chat. We would drink Guinness together in the nearby *Mitre*. 'This has kept me alive for years,' he said, raising his glass. Once, when we were discussing religion, I remember him saying: 'I have no particular beliefs. *My* religion is lyricism.' Not at all a bad sort of deism, perhaps?

The novelist, M.P.Shiel, had inherited from his father the tiny, un-inhabited island of Redonda, in the Caribbean, the kingdom of which he duly conferred upon Gawsworth. Although the penniless poet was never in a position to visit his domain, he took the matter seriously. He bestowed dukedoms upon Richard Aldington, Lawrence Durrell, and Henry Miller, among others, but nobody was as impressed as was His Majesty himself.

He reminded me, in a way, of that delightful character in Chaplin's *City Lights*, the drunken millionaire who, in his cups, threw his arms round the little tramp and welcomed him as a bosom pal, but who, the following morning in the cold and sober light of day, had no recollection of the tattered vagrant who claimed his acquaintance. John Gawsworth was like that with me. Primed with beer, wine, or spirits, he treated me like a long-lost friend, with whom he delighted to reminisce and to expound. But, still hung over, and his first drink of the day as yet untaken, he looked at me askance, and wondered who the hell I was, and why on earth I spoke to him so familiarly!

One last anecdote, and then I am done. It concerns that now long-gone Sotheby's employee, bleakly sorting through the massive pile of books and papers, the property of a deceased collector, and which now had to be put into some sort of order and then all written down. One large book fell open, and from it rolled a long cigar. Ah, cataloguer's perks! It was a bit dry, but otherwise in excellent condition. Feeling a little more contented about things, the man lit up. Halfway through his smoke, and in an aromatic cloud, he transferred his attention to the loose papers also inside the book. He picked up one of them and read: 'In appreciation of services rendered, during the Battle of Britain, this cigar was presented to me by the Rt. Hon. Winston S. Churchill...'

I could go on indefinitely, but this book must stop somewhere. Here is as good a place as any. I hope that it has amused you. I further hope that you bought the copy you are reading. If you did, no doubt you will be pleased to learn that all royalties which accrue will be going to charity. It is a very deserving cause: I am thinking of calling it the O.F. Snelling Old Age and Retirement Benefit Fund.

Index